Food, Nutrition, Diet and Health

FOOD, NUTRITION, DIET AND HEALTH

Dr. Hema Thapar

Pacific Books International

Food, Nutrition, Diet and Health

First Published : 2011

ISBN 978-93-80472-18-8

Published by :
PACIFIC BOOKS INTERNATIONAL
179, Kalyan Vihar,
Ground Floor, Delhi - 110 009
Mob. : 9212555570, 9212526400
e-mail : pacificbooks@rediffmail.com

Laser Typesetting by :
Rishu Computers
Delhi - 110092

Printed at :
Roshan Offset Printers
Delhi

PREFACE

Nutrition is the process in which you consume food or nourishing liquids, digest and absorb them and use them for health and growth. Upon digestion, food that we eat is broken into smaller molecules like glucose, amino acids, fats and vitamins. These molecules and nutrients are the elements that provide us energy. Between the extremes of optimal health and death from starvation or malnutrition, there is an array of disease states that can be caused or alleviated by changes in diet. Deficiencies, excesses and imbalances in diet can produce negative impacts on health, which may lead to diseases such as scurvy, obesity or osteoporosis, as well as psychological and behavioral problems.

Dietary habits and choices play a significant role in health and mortality, and can also define cultures and play a role in religion. Although humans are omnivores, each culture holds some food preferences and some food taboos. Individual dietary choices may be more or less healthy. Proper nutrition requires the proper ingestion and equally important, the absorption of vitamins, minerals, and fuel in the form of carbohydrates, proteins, and fats.

The present book elabortes how and why specific dietary aspects influence health. It will be an indispensable resource for food scientists and anyone involved in the study and research of food science and technology.

Dr. Hema Thapar

Contents

Contents

1

Food and Nutrition in India

The Indian economy has recently grown at historically unprecedented rates and is now one of the fastest-growing economies in the world. Real GDP per head grew at 3.95 percent a year from 1980 to 2005, and at 5.4 percent a year from 2000 to 2005. Measured at international prices, real per capita income in India, which was two-thirds of Kenya's in 1950, and about the same as Nigeria's, is now two and a half times as large as per capita income in both countries. Real per capita consumption has also grown rapidly, at 2.2 percent a year in the 1980s, at 2.5 percent a year in the 1990s, and at 3.9 percent a year from 2000 to 2005.

A related concern is that anthropometric indicators of nutrition in India, for both adults and children, are among the worst in the world. Furthermore, the improvement of these measures of nutrition appears to be slow relative to what might be expected in the light of international experience and of India's recent high rates of economic growth. Indeed, according to the National Family Health Survey, the proportion of underweight children remained virtually unchanged between 1998-99 and 2005-06 (from 47 to 46 percent for the age group of 0-3 years). Undernutrition levels in India remain higher even than for most countries of sub-Saharan Africa, even though those countries are currently much poorer than

India, have grown much more slowly, and have much higher levels of infant and child mortality.

Calorie Consumption And Nutrition Indicators

Food, Calories and Cereal Calories

In rural India, household per capita calorie consumption was 2,240 calories in 1983, 2,233 in 1987–88, and had fallen to 2,047 calories per head in 2004–05, a decline of 8.6 percent from 1983; urban per capita calorie consumption was only 49 calories (2.4 percent) lower than in 1983. Over the same period, rural (urban) per capita protein consumption fell by 12.1 percent (4.6 percent). Only per capita fat consumption, in the last two columns, moves in the same direction as household expenditures, growing at 1.2 percent and 1.1 percent a year in rural and urban India respectively.

The fraction of children (ages 0 to 14) in a rural household fell from an average of 0.36 in 1983 to 0.31 in 2004–05, a decline of 14 percent, with a larger decline, from 0.31 to 0.24, in urban India. In consequence, if we were to compute a measure of equivalent adults, in which children counted as less than one, we would find that the number of equivalents has been growing faster than the number of people, so that the decline in calorie per equivalent would be even larger than the decline in calorie per person. Against this, we should note that the reduction in fertility means that a shorter span of women's lives is spent in pregnancy or lactation, during which there is a sharp increase in recommended calorie needs. But it is not clear that most women in India obtain these extra calories, and we suspect that the saving from this source is small. In what follows, we mostly stick with the per capita measures recognizing that they almost certainly provide conservative estimates of a more appropriate measure of the fall in calories.

Table 1: Calories from cereal

Year	Rural	Urban	All India
1983	1,681	1,303	1,597
1987-8	1,648	1,296	1,569
1993-4	1,533	1,231	1,458
1999-0	1,455	1,200	1,392
2000-1	1,422	1,161	1,357
2001-2	1,391	1,130	1,330
2002(2)	1,381	1,137	1,318
2003	1,412	1,142	1,345
2004(1)	1,419	1,165	1,357
2004-5	1,386	1,147	1,326

Calorie deficiencies and self-reported hunger

When an increase in per capita expenditure is accompanied by a decrease in per calorie consumption, there will be a divergence between poverty measures that are based on real expenditures and those that are based on a calorie cutoff. Indian poverty lines were originally justified by reference to calorie norms, and at the time that the original lines were drawn, average per capita calorie consumption of rural households at the rural poverty line was 2,400 calories, and average per capita calorie consumption of urban households at the urban poverty line was 2,100 calories. But all subsequent official poverty calculations have held the lines fixed in real terms, so that the official poverty ratios have declined as the distribution of per capita expenditure has moved upwards. As has been suggested by several authors, including Palmer–Jones and Sen and Ray and Lancaster, we could take the calorie basis of the original lines more seriously and compute the fraction of the population living in households whose per capita calorie consumption falls beneath 2,400 calories in the rural sector and beneath 2,100 calories in the urban sector.

Because the distribution of per capita calories is moving to the left over time, these numbers show *rising* poverty rates, from two thirds of the rural population in 1983 to four-fifths in 2004–05, and from 65 percent to more than 75 percent in India as a whole. Without understanding why per capita calories are falling despite rising per capita expenditures, it is difficult to adjudicate between these "calorie" poverty rates and the conventional "expenditure" poverty rates.

In 1983 and 1993–94, respondents were asked whether everyone in the household got "two square meals a day", while in 1999–2000 and 2004–05 the question was whether everyone in the household got "enough food every day". There are several reasons to treat these numbers as suggestive rather than definitive: the phrasing of the question is not identical in different years, there may be translation issues, and the changes from 1983 to 1993–94 are suspiciously large in several states such as Bihar and Madhya Pradesh. In so far as they are reliable, these figures show that the fraction of rural persons going hungry has fallen from 17.3 percent in 1983 to 2.5 percent in 2004–05. In the latest survey, only West Bengal, Orissa, Assam, and Bihar are above the national average, with Chhattisgarh and Kerala at the average. The relatively high prevalence of self-reported hunger in Kerala is somewhat puzzling and raises further questions about the interpretation of these figures. What is potentially interesting is that the four states with high levels of hunger are all located in the "rice belt" of eastern India.

It is also worth noting that self-reported food adequacy is uncorrelated with calorie shortfall (i.e. whether or not a household is below the calorie norms). The correlation across rural households in 2004–05 is 0.02, and across NSS regions and states, it is actually *negative*, –0.17 for regions, and –0.09 for states. This lack of correlation might be taken as casting further doubt on the validity of the hunger questions, or on the relevance of the calorie norms, or even both. However, it should be noted that hunger and calorie shortfall are not the same thing, if only because the latter, as measured here, ignores differences in calorie needs, for example those associated with variations in activity levels

On calorie Engel curves

That calorie consumption should fall over time alongside an increase in total expenditure is in sharp contrast to what happens when we look across households at a moment of time, where there is a strong positive correlation between the two.

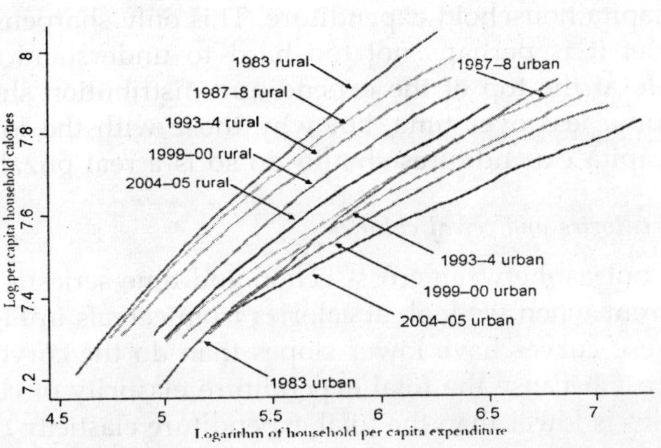

Figure 1: Calorie Engel curves, rural and urban India, 1983 to 2004–05

This conflict comes from the fact that, over time, there is a downward drift of the "calorie Engel curve" that plots calorie consumption against per capita household expenditure: calorie consumption at a given level of per-capita expenditure has steadily declined over the last 20 years. For each of the large rounds from 1983 to 2004–05, Figure 1 plots per capita calories against per capita total household expenditure (both in log terms). The top five curves are for rural India, and are moving down over time.

Because the NSS has changed its questionnaires over this period, the graphs in Figure 1 are subject to numerous qualifications, but we do not believe they are seriously misleading. They show that in both urban and rural sectors better-off households (at least measured by per capita expenditure) consistently consume more calories than worse-off households, at least on average. For the moment, note that because the calorie Engel curves do not cross (except for the 1983 urban curve), per capita consumption of calories has fallen at *all* levels of per capita household expenditure. This only sharpens the puzzle; it is perhaps not too hard to understand why people at the top of the expenditure distribution should consume less over time, but why those with the lowest per capita expenditures should do so is a real puzzle.

Total calories and cereal calories

The contrast between cross-section and time-series is also apparent when we look at calories from cereals in Figure 2. These curves have lower slopes than do the curves in Figure 1 because the total expenditure elasticity of cereal calories is lower than the total expenditure elasticity of all calories; at the margin, a higher fraction of each rupee is spent on non-cereal calories than on cereal calories. As was the case for total calories, the curves are falling through time within both rural and urban sectors (again with a partial exception for the 1983 urban curve), and as they fall they become flatter, so that the elasticity of cereal calories diminishes over time. In the lowest curve, for the urban sector in 2004–05, the elasticity is negative except at the very bottom of the per capita expenditure distribution. As is the case for total calories, the most recent rural curves are similar in position and in shape to the earliest urban curves; in other words, rural India today looks much like urban India 20 years ago as far as cereal consumption patterns are concerned.

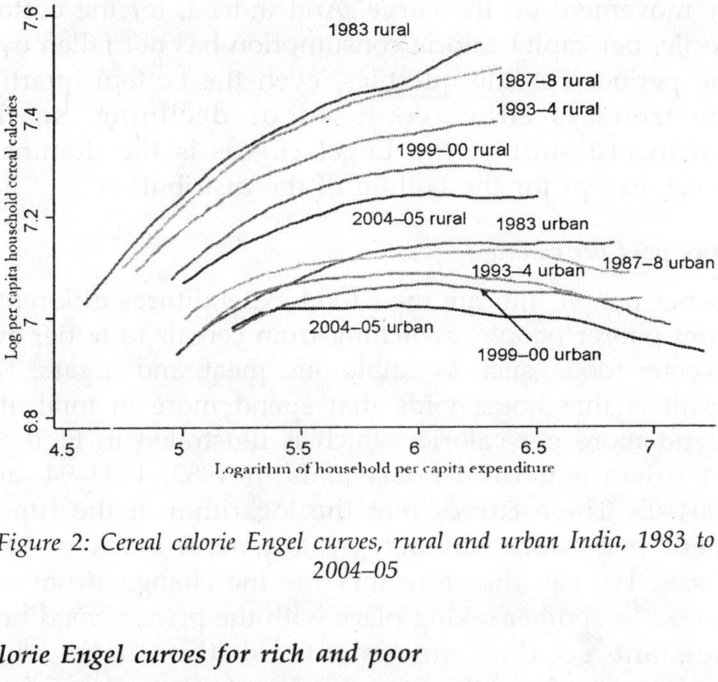

Figure 2: Cereal calorie Engel curves, rural and urban India, 1983 to 2004–05

Calorie Engel curves for rich and poor

Although all of the curves in Figures 1 and 2 are moving down over time, there are differences in the size of the shift at different points in the per capita expenditure distribution, as well as between cereal calories and all calories. In rural India, the total calorie curves shift down in a roughly parallel way, so that the percentage decline in total calories is more or less the same for the rich as for the poor. For cereal calories, the decline is much sharper among the better-off. These comparisons hold per capita household expenditure fixed, so we are defining "better-off" and "poor" in terms of fixed levels of real per capita expenditure. But it is also useful to arrange rich and poor, not by expenditure, but according to their position in the distribution. Because there is an increase in per capita expenditure over time, people in each decile or quartile have rising real expenditure levels, so that the downward movement of the Engel curves in Figures 1 and 2 is offset by movement up the curve. And indeed, for the bottom decile, per capita calorie consumption has not fallen over the period. For the quartiles, even the bottom quartile, the trend is either confused or declining, so the downward shift of the Engel curves is the dominant effect, except for the bottom of the distribution.

Price paid per calorie

Richer people allocate their food expenditures differently from poorer people, switching from cereals to fattier and sweeter foods, such as edible oils, meat, and sugars. The result is that households that spend more in total also spend more per calorie, which is illustrated in Figure 3 for urban and rural households in 1983, 1993–94, and 2004–05. These curves plot the logarithm of the rupees spent per calorie divided by a general index of food prices. We can therefore imagine the changes from one period to another taking place with the price of food held constant so that movements of the curves, like movements along the curves, come from switches from cheaper to more expensive calories, or vice versa, not from changes in the price of food. Given that the calories-from-cereal Engel curves in Figure 2 are moving down over time more rapidly than the total-calories Engel curves in Figure 1, we can expect the curves in Figure 3 to move up over time because, at any given level of total expenditure, households are reducing the relatively cheap cereal calories as a share of total calories. This is exactly what happens for rural households in Figure 3.

Surprisingly, the opposite happens for urban households, in spite of the fact that urban households are also cutting down on cereal calories (Figure 2).

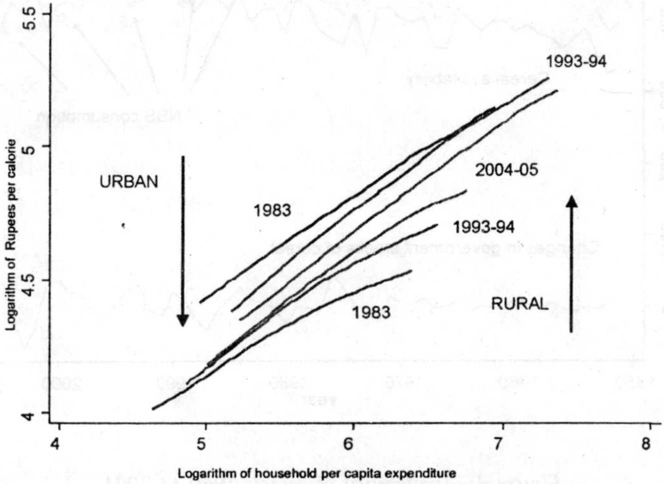

Figure 3: Cost per 1000 calories at constant prices, urban and rural India

Indeed the urban curves appear to be converging downwards towards the rural curves, though it should be noted that the overall food price indexes only account for differential inflation over time, and not for any original difference in the *levels* of urban and rural prices.

It is puzzling that a country as poor and malnourished as India should react to growing prosperity without increasing real food consumption and by actually cutting back on its calorie consumption, so it is important to check that the facts are indeed correct. Another cross-check, at least for cereal intake, comes from aggregate availability figures compiled from production data with the addition of net imports and the subtraction of addition to stocks—in practice mostly government stocks. Figure 4 shows the data from the 2006–7 Economic Survey, for cereals as well as for cereals plus pulses.

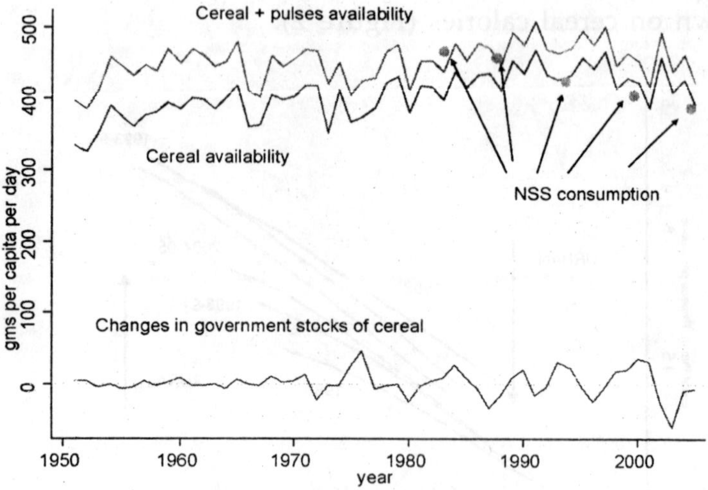

Figure 4: Availability of cereal, 1950 to 2004

The figure shows that there has been little net change in aggregate cereal (or cereal plus pulses) availability in India since independence and that there has been a clear downward trend since the early 1990s, up to fluctuations that are largely attributable to the build up and release of government stocks. Figure 4 also shows the estimates of aggregate cereal consumption from the large rounds of the NSS and, as has typically been found in the literature, at least since Minhas, there is reasonably close agreement between the NSS estimates and the data on availability, something that is in sharp contrast to the discrepancies between the NSS and National Accounts data on total consumer expenditure. These aggregate data are therefore consistent with the per capita calorie decline that we see in both NSS and NNMB data. There can therefore be very little doubt that the decline is real. And far from offsetting the decline in cereals, consumption of pulses has also declined.

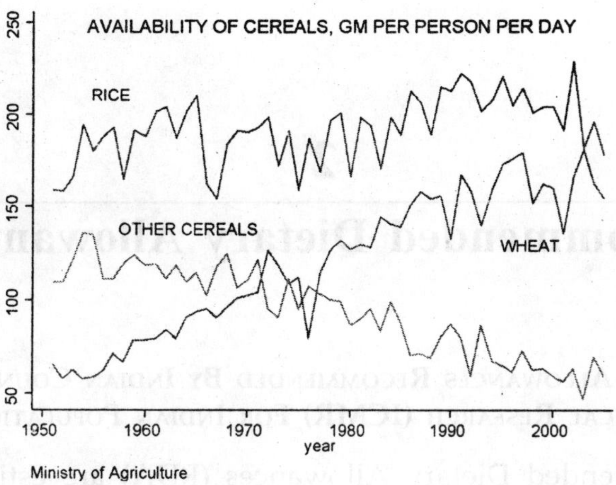

Figure 5: Availability of rice, wheat, and other cereals

Figure 5 shows the disaggregation of cereal availability into three main groups: rice, wheat, and other cereals. The last group is mainly the "coarse" cereal group consisting of maize, barley, *jowar* (sorghum), *ragi* (finger millet) and *bajra* (pearl millet). The most notable feature here is the steady long-term decline of the coarse cereals whose consumption has fallen by a half over the last half century; although there have been temporary increases, the fall in coarse cereals is long established. For many years, the place of coarse cereals was taken by an increase in consumption of wheat. However, the long-run increase in wheat consumption appeared to come to an end in the late 1990s. Rice consumption began to trend downward somewhat earlier, from about the early 1990s so that, in the last few years, there has been no increase in wheat consumption to offset the decline in the other two categories.

2

Recommended Dietary Allowances

Dietary Allowances Recommended By Indian Council of Medical Research (ICMR) For Indian Population

Recommended Dietary Allowances (RDA) are estimates of intakes of nutrients which individuals in a population group need to consume to ensure that the physiological needs of all subjects in that population are met.

Following the recommendations of the League of nations in 1937, an attempt to recommend dietary allowances for energy, protein, iron, calcium, vitamin A, thiamine, ascorbic acid and vitamin D for Indians was made in 1944 by the Nutrition Advisory Committee of the Indian Research Fund Association, now called Indian Council of Medical Research (ICMR).

Between 1950 and 1968, in the wake of recommendations for energy and protein requirements by the Food and Agricultural Organization (FAO) and based on the international data provided by the FAO/ WHO expert groups and those available in India, the recommendations for dietary requirements were revised.

Few years later, newer set of data generated by various researches and surveys conducted by renowned institutions like Avinashilingam Institute for Home science and Higher Education for Women – Deemed

University, Coimbatore, National Institute of Nutrition, Hyderabad, ICMR and National Nutrition Monitoring Bureau (NNMB), created a necessity to revise RDAs further.

In 1988 an expert committee constituted by ICMR modified the reference body weight for Indian adults and RDAs in respect of energy, fat, vitamin D and vitamin A. Recommendations on safe intake of fat in terms of both visible and invisible dietary fats were made. For the first time, recommendations for certain trace elements, electrolytes (sodium and potassium), magnesium and phosphorus, vitamin K and vitamin E and dietary fibre were considered.

A number of approaches such as

- dietary intake of nutrients
- growth
- nutrient balance
- minimal loss of nutrients and
- nutrient turnover

were utilized in arriving at the RDAs.

The RDA of an individual depends upon various factors which are as follows:

1. *Age*: Adults require more total calories than a child, whereas a growing child requires more calories per kg of body weight than an adult.
2. *Sex*: Males with high Basal Metabolic Rate (BMR) require more calories than females.
3. *Activity*: The type of activity also determines the energy requirements. The activities are classified as sedentary, moderate and heavy based on the occupation of an individual.
4. *Physiological Stress*: Nutrient requirements are increased in conditions of physiological stress such as pregnancy and lactation.

The RDAs are given for various age groups such as adult man and adult woman (for various activities), pregnant and lactating women, infants, children (1-9 years), boys and girls (10-12 yrs) and adolescents.

Planning Balanced Diets

Balanced Diet

A balanced diet is one which contains different types of foods such as cereals, pulses and vegetables in such quantities and proportion that the nutritional requirements are adequately met and a small provision is made for extra nutrients to withstand short duration of leanness.

- A balanced diet should provide 60-70 percent of calories from carbohydrate, 10-20 percent from protein and 20-25 percent from fat.
- Calorie allowance can be + 50, while for all other nutrients minimum RDA must be met.
- Energy from cereals should not be more than 75 percent.
- Include two cereals in one meal eg:- rice and wheat.
- To improve protein quality the ratio of cereal protein to pulse protein should be 4:1.
- Two to three serving of pulses should be taken a day.
- Include atleast one medium size fruit. The fruit can be given raw without much cooking.
- Five servings of fruits and vegetables should be included in a day
- The diet should include minimum 100ml milk per day.

— Foods rich in fibre should be included.

— One third of the nutritional requirements, at least calorie and protein should be met by lunch or dinner.

Essentials of Meal Planning

A major objective of planning meals is to achieve nutritional adequacy along with consideration of other factors such as food cost and economy, food habits, food preferences, acceptability of prepared foods and other factors.

Nutritional adequacy

The planned diet should meet the nutritional needs of the individual and the family as a whole. No single food can meet all the nutritional requirements. Therefore, to achieve a balance of nutrients a combination of different foods need to be included in the diet. The diet can be planned by including foods from the five food groups. Although all nutrients are important, the requirement for certain nutrients are proportionately higher in certain age groups. e.g:- Iron in adolescent girl and pregnant woman. Therefore identifying rich sources of various nutrients within the same food group is required. e.g:- whole cereals and rice flakes are rich in iron among cereals, milk and fish have high calcium content among animal foods.

Food cost and economy

The expenditure on food is an important part of a family's budget and it is influenced by

1. family size
2. number of children
3. age group

4. activity and
5. special needs of pregnancy, lactation and diseased condition.

The proportionate expenditure on food depends upon the income levels i.e. it increases with decrease in total income. Moreover in case of low income level, a higher proportion is spent on buying staples rather than protective foods like milk, vegetables and fruits. Therefore the aim should be to achieve maximum nutritional benefit at minimum cost. For example, pulse can be used as a source of protein instead of animal foods; less expensive cuts of meat can be used; families can have a small kitchen garden and grow vegetables and fruits to cut down their expenses on this food group and thus exercise economy in meal planning.

For achieving economy in meal planning, the following considerations are important.

— Knowledge of prevailing prices of food items.

— Knowledge of proportion of edible portion of different food stuffs as they vary widely. It may be high as 100 percent in foods like milk or low as 35-40 percent in leafy vegetables. This helps to decide the quantity of food to be purchased.

— Buying foods from fair price shops and retail outlets.

— Bulk purchase of nonperishables.

— Using seasonal foods as they are not only economical but also nutritious.

— Minimising nutrient losses during preparation and cooking.

— Making proper use of left overs and the commonly discarded foods eg: green leaves of vegetables like raddish leaves.

Acceptability of meals

Acceptability of meals is as important as meeting nutritional needs or planning within the budget. To make meals acceptable the following considerations are important.

Likes and dislikes

The likes and dislikes of all the family members should be kept in mind.

Variety

The meal should have variety in colour, texture, taste and flavour for better acceptability. Variety can be achieved by

i. selecting foods from each food group
ii. including a variety of vegetables to add colour
iii. avoid repeating the same food in different meals as well in the same meal in a different form.
iv. use different methods of cooking such as baking, boiling, frying to bring variety in texture.
v. use alternative garnishes and accompaniments.

Food habits and religious beliefs

Religious and socio cultural beliefs influence the choice of food. Certain foods are prohibited by certain religions. Also, the socio cultural factors either promote or prohibit the intake of particular foods in different families and communities.

Food availability and seasonal variation

As far as possible, seasonal and locally available foods should be used. Vegetables and fruits in season are not only cheap but have the highest nutrient content and best flavour.

Food fads

Wrong notions and beliefs regarding consumption of food is prevalent in different communities many of which are baseless and may deprive an important nutrient source. For example, fad like milk and fish should not be included in the same meal. These food fads need to be discouraged.

Portion sizes

While planning and preparing a meal, it must be ensured that the quantity prepared be easily consumed by the person of the given age, sex and activity. At the same time the quantity must meet the nutritional needs. These quantities are referred to as "one serving portion" or "portion sizes".

The balanced diets are given as multiples of these portion sizes. Table 1. gives the standard portion sizes for the various food groups.

Table 1: Portion sizes of foods and their nutrient content

Food groups	g/portion	Energy	Protein	Carbo hydrate	Fat
		(k.cal)	(g)	(g)	(g)
Cereals and Millets	30	100	3.0	20	0.8
Pulses	30	100	6.0	15	0.7
Egg	50	85	7.0	-	7.0
Meat / chicken/fish	50	100	9.0	-	7.0
Milk (ml)	100	70	3.0	5	3.0
Roots and Tubers	100	80	1.3	18	-
Green leafy vegetables	100	45	3.6	-	0.4
Other vegetables	100	30	1.7	-	0.2
Fruits	100	40	-	10	-
Sugar	5	20	-	5	-
Fats and Oils (Visible)	5	45	-	-	5.0

Steps in Meal Planning

The following steps may be adopted in planning meals.

Recommended Dietary Allowances

To plan a balanced diet the first step is to know the recommended dietary allowances for different age groups.

Food list

The next step is to prepare a food list ie., a list of quantities of various food groups to be included in the diet so that it is balanced and can meet the RDA. This can be done by

i. selecting foods from all the five food groups.

ii. deciding the quantities of the selected foods as multiples of portion sizes.

3

Nutrition in Pregnancy and Lactation

Nutrition requirements increase tremendously during pregnancy and lactation owing to the physiological changes. Wholesome nourishment before pregnancy has a greater impact on long term health than at any other time. A woman who has been well nourished before conception enters pregnancy with a good reserve of nutrients so that the needs of the growing foetus can be met without affecting her health. A well nourished foetus enters life with good physical and mental health. Moreover the reserve of nutrients laid before and during pregnancy help towards successful lactation after parturition.

Physiological Changes in Pregnancy

Foetal development is accompanied by many physiological, biochemical and hormonal changes which influence the nutrient needs and the efficiency with which the body utilizes them. The changes include

Increased Basal Metabolic Rate (BMR)

Due to foetal growth the BMR increases by about 5 percent in the 1st trimester reaching a high level of 12 percent during later stages of pregnancy.

Gastro Intestinal Changes

Gastro intestinal motility diminishes which may result in constipation. The acid and pepsin secretion in the stomach is less and additionally a relaxed lower oesophagal sphincter may cause regurgitation of stomach contents into the oesophagus leading to sensation of heartburn and vomiting. This becomes more pronounced with increasing pressure of the foetus.

In later half of pregnancy the efficiency of absorption of iron, calcium and B vitamins increases as a natural adaptation mechanism to meet the increased needs.

Hormonal Changes

During pregnancy there is increased secretion of the following hormones.

— Aldosterone by the adrenal gland.

— Progesterone which relaxes uterine muscles to expand to accommodate the growing foetus.

— Thyroxin.

— Parathormone.

Changes in Body Fluid

The blood volume expands by 50 percent and this increased amount of blood is required to carry nutrients to the foetus and remove metabolic wastes from the foetus.

With increase in blood volume the concentration of plasma proteins, haemoglobin, blood glucose and water soluble vitamins decrease. The decline in serum albumin level tends to accumulate extra cellular water during pregnancy.

Haemoglobin level drops to 11g / 100ml (normal range 12-13 g / 100 ml) despite an increase in total haemoglobin content ie., haemodilution occurs. Thus during pregnancy, women with haemoglobin levels less than 10 g / 100 ml are considered anaemic.

Altered Renal Function

Increased blood volume and increased production of waste products like creatinine, urea and other wastes due to foetal and maternal metabolism produces a high Glomerular Filtration Rate (GFR) and the renal tubules are unable to adjust completely to this load. Some percentage of nutrients which are normally completely reabsorbed are excreted. Compounds like glucose , aminoacids and water soluble vitamins may appear in trace amounts in urine.

Weight Gain During Pregnancy

Less than half of total weight gain resides in the foetus, placenta and amniotic fluid. The remainder is found in maternal reproductive tissues, fluid, blood and maternal stores (largely composed of fat). The increasing subcutaneous fat in abdomen and thighs serves as energy reserve during pregnancy and lactation.

By full term, average weight gain during pregnancy for a normal healthy woman with desirable body weight is 12.5kg ranging between 11 – 13 kg. The pattern of weight gain is as important as total weight gain. During first trimester there is little increase in weight (0.7 to 1.4kg). There after a steady gain of 0.4kg/ week is desirable. Table 1 gives an analysis of weight gain during pregnancy Weight reduction should never be undertaken during pregnancy.

Table 1: Analysis of weight gain (g) in Pregnancy

Component	Period of gestation			
	upto	upto	upto	upto

	10 weeks	20 weeks	30 weeks	40 weeks
Foetus and placenta	55	720	2350	4750
Uterus and breast	170	765	1170	1300
Blood	100	600	1300	1350
Extracellular water	—	—	—	1200
Fat	325	1915	3500	4200
Total	650	4000	8500	12600

Excessive weight gain places an extra strain on the organs and increases the incidence of toxaemia during pregnancy.

Need For Additional Nutrients

A well nourished mother with a good reserve of nutrients can meet the demands of the foetus without affecting her health. Such a mother gives birth to a healthier baby with less complications.

Malnutrition and Foetus

Chronic moderate malnutrition and anaemia during pregnancy may result in still birth and Low Birth Weight (LBW) babies weighing less than 2500g. A large number of such babies are premature (<37 weeks of gestation) and rest suffer from Intra Uterine Growth Retardation (IUGR). IUGR results in babies which are Small For Date (SFD) ie, infants born after 40 weeks of gestation but small because of malnutrition during intrauterine growth.

The risk of Low Birth Weight babies and the related neonatal mortality is associated with one or more of the following factors.

— Low socioeconomic status.

— Poor maternal nutritional status.

— Small stature of the mother.

— Low prepregnancy weight for height.

— Biological immaturity (mothers less than 17 years).
— Low weight gain during pregnancy.
— Smoking, consumption of alcohol, use of drugs.
— Infectious diseases.
— Lack of education, poor knowledge on sound nutrition.
— Lack of motivation towards wanted pregnancy.

Effect of Malnutrition on Placenta

The placenta of malnourished mothers have fewer cells than well nourished mothers. The reduction in the number of cells reduces the ability of the placenta to

i. synthesize substances required by the foetus
ii. transfer nutrients
iii. inhibit the passage of potentially harmful substances to the growing foetus

Effect of Malnutrition on Maternal Health

A malnourished mother supplies nutrients to the foetus at the expense of her own tissues. Multiple micronutrient deficiencies during pregnancy like vitamin A, zinc, iron and folic acid are common and are associated with complications during pregnancy and labour. This may lead to abortion and even death of the mother.

Effect of Malnutrition During Infancy

Inadequate nutrition during foetal life affects the health of the baby during infancy. Such infants develop nutritional deficiency diseases like rickets, anaemia or suffer from infectious diseases due to low resistance. Hence it is essential to meet the increased nutritional needs of a pregnant mother.

Nutritional Requirments During Pregnancy

Energy

Energy requirement during pregnancy is increased because of the additional energy required for

1. growth and activity of foetus
2. growth of placenta and maternal tissues
3. increase in maternal body size
4. steady rise in BMR

For a reference Indian woman weighing 50kg, the total energy cost of pregnancy has been estimated to be 73000 k.cal. This includes the energy required for deposition of 4 kg of body fat (36000 k.cal) to be utilized later during lactation. Considering the increased energy demand during lactation and beneficial effect of increased energy intake on birth weight of infants and also protein sparing action, an additional intake of 300k.cal.per day during pregnancy is recommended.

Protein

An additional protein intake of 15g/day i.e. a total of 65g is recommended. The additional protein is essential for

1) growth of the foetus
2) development of placenta
3) enlargement of uterus,mammary gland
4) increased maternal blood volume
5) formation of amniotic fluid
6) preparation for labour, delivery, post partum period and lactation by maternal tissues.

Fat

ICMR expert committee has suggested an intake of 30g of

visible fat/day during pregnancy. This is based on studies indicating that linoliec acid requirements during this stage is 4.5 percentage of total energy. Of this, some of the essential fatty acid needs are met with by the invisible fat. Therefore an intake of 30g of visible fat has been suggested to meet the essential fatty acid needs.

Calcium

The calcium requirement for an adult woman is 400mg/day. During pregnancy the need increases to 1000mg/day. The additional calcium is needed for the growth and development of bones as well as teeth of the foetus and also for the protection of calcium resources of the mother to meet the high demand of calcium during lactation.

The amount of calcium deposited in the full grown foetus is around 30g. Therefore an intake of 1g calcium per day which meets the needs of the mother and the additional needs of pregnancy has been recommended by the ICMR. Inadequate intake of calcium results in the mobilization of calcium from mother bones resulting in demineralization of maternal bones and osteoporosis.

Iron

The requirement of iron increases from 30mg/day to 38mg/day during pregnancy. The increased requirement of 8mg/day is due to

i. expansion of maternal tissues including red cell mass, iron content of placenta and blood loss during parturition.

ii. to build the iron store in foetal liver to last for atleast 4-6 months after birth. This is because the baby's first food milk is deficient in iron. Generally infants are born with a high level of iron, 18-22g/ 100ml.

Iodine

Due to increase in BMR, iodine needs are also enhanced during pregnancy.

Zinc

Deficiency of zinc adversely affects the outcome of pregnancy. Apart from being a component of insulin and enzyme systems, it also participates in the synthesis of DNA and RNA, playing a significant role in reproduction. Hence zinc deficiency leads to foetal mortality, foetal, malformations and reduced intra uterine growth rate. The risk of LBW babies doubles and preterm delivery increases three times due to low zinc intake during pregnancy.

Sodium

The increase in extra cellular fluid increases sodium requirement. Hence restriction in diet may cause biochemical and hormonal changes. When sodium level in blood drops (hyponatraemia), the kidney produces hormone renin which causes increased retention of sodium making it unavailable for normal body processes. When the system is overtaxed it results in sodium deficiency causing increased risk of eclempsia, prematurity and low birth weight infants. Normal sodium intake without restriction is advised during pregnancy. Sodium is restricted when there is oedema or hypertension.

Vitamins

Vitamin A

Vitamin A requirements during pregnancy have been computed based on the vitamin A content of liver of the newborn. The additional intake works out to 25mg/day throughout pregnancy. Since this constitutes a very small fraction of the RDA for normal women, no additional allowance during pregnancy is suggested.

Vitamin D

Vitamin D is essential as it enhances maternal calcium absorption. Its active form calcidiol and calcitriol can pass through placenta with ease and help in calcium metabolism of foetus. Since Vitamin D can be synthesised in adequate amounts by simple exposure to UV rays no recommendation for vitamin D has been made.

Other fat Soluble Vitamins

Vitamin K is required for synthesis of prothrombin which is essential for normal coagulation of blood. A liberal vitamin K level in the mother's blood proves helpful in preventing neonatal haemorrhage. Hence it has become a routine to administer natural form of this vitamin by injection either to the mother before delivery or to the neonate soon after birth.

Thiamine, Riboflavin, Niacin

The RDA for thiamine, riboflavin and niacin is estimated on the same basis as for a normal adult woman ie., 0.5mg/1000 kcal, 0.6mg/ 1000k.cal and 6.6mg/1000k.cal respectively. As the energy requirement increases during pregnancy, the requirement of these vitamins also increases correspondingly.

Pyridoxine

Pyridoxine needs are increased during pregnancy. The ICMR committee has suggested an intake of 2.5mg of vitamin B6 during pregnancy, an increase of 0.5 mg per day.

Vitamin B_{12}

Based on the vitamin B_{12} content of foetus, the demand for this vitamin is estimated to be nearly 0.3mg / day. ICMR has suggested an additional allowance of 0.5 mg recommending a total daily intake of 1.5 mg of Vitamin B_{12} during pregnancy.

Folic acid

Normal adult woman requires 100 mg of folic acid per day. ICMR recommendations during pregnancy are 400 mg/day. Folic acid is essential for

1) increased blood formation i.e. haematopoiesis
2) synthesis of essential components of DNA/RNA which increase rapidly during growth

Supplementation of folic acid before conception and during first twelve weeks of pregnancy is recommended to reduce the primary and secondary neural tube defects among new born babies.

Vitamin C

The foetal requirement for vitamin C is too small to justify the additional intake of this vitamin during pregnancy. Moreover the recommendation for a normal adult woman, 40mg / day, includes a margin of safety. ICMR, therefore, has not recommended any additional intake of vitamin C during pregnancy.

The balanced diet providing the required nutrients as per the RDA for a pregnant woman doing sedentary work is given in Table 2.

Table 2: Balanced Diet for a pregnant woman (Sedentary work)

S.No.	Food Group	quantity in g
1.	Cereals and millets	300

2.	Pulses	60
3.	Milk (ml)	500
4.	Roots and Tubers	100
5.	Green leafy vegetables	150
6.	Other vegetables	100
7.	Fruits	200
8.	Sugar	20
9.	Fats and oils (visible)	30

Diet During Pregnancy

The basic principle of meal planning remains the same, but since the nutritional requirements increase during pregnancy, emphasis should be in including nutrient dense foods ie., foods that give more nutrients per calorie consumed.

During early months, the mother often suffers from morning sickness due to the hormonal and physiological changes, when she should be given small amounts of foods with increased frequency. Solid carbohydrate rich foods like bread, biscuit and fruit given in the morning or before meals helps to relieve nausea. Also fried, rich, strongly flavoured and spicy foods need to be avoided.

To meet increased requirements the mother should consume extra food. The mother can be given nutritious snacks in between meals rather than three meals a day thus increasing the frequency of feeding. Her feeding pattern should be 5-6 meals a day. Protein needs can be met by including good quality protein foods like meat, milk, egg, fish. Protein can also be obtained from pulses like soyabean and groundnut at a lower cost. To improve protein quality, a combination of plant proteins, as that in cereals and pulses, with small amount of animal protein should be used.

To meet additional iron needs foodstuffs like whole grain cereals, rice flakes, puffed rice, dried fruits, green leafy vegetables, eggs, enriched cereals and organ meats can be given.

Food rich in dietary fibre like fresh fruits, vegetables, whole grain cereals with plenty of fluids need to be included. This is to ward off constipation which is a common problem during pregnancy.

Problems During Pregnancy

Nausea and Vomiting

Generally it is mild and occurs during early pregnancy and is commonly called "morning sickness" as it tends to occur early in the day but may occur at any time and can be improved by frequent small meals. If the condition develops to hyperemesis gravidarum, characterised by a severe prolonged persistent vomiting , then careful oral feeding and sometimes parenteral nutrition may be essential.

Constipation

The pressure of the enlarging uterus on the lower portion of the intestine in addition to the muscle relaxant effect of placental hormones on the gastro intestinal tract and physical inactivity may make elimination difficult. Limited activity and exercise, insufficient fluid intake and insufficient bulk in diet may also be the causes of constipation.

Intake of plenty of fluids, foods rich in fibre helps to relieve constipation. Sometimes the weight of the foetus and downward pressure on veins leads to development of haemorrhoids.

Heart Burn

Some pregnant women may complain of "feeling of fullness" or "heart burn" during later half of pregnancy.

This is usually due to the pressure of the enlarging uterus crowding the stomach which in combination with the relaxation of the oesophagal sphincter may cause regurgitation of stomach contents into the oesophagus. This may cause a burning sensation due to gastric acid mixed with the food mass. This feeling of fullness occuring due to gastric pressure, lack of space or gas formation can be avoided by taking small frequent meals and drinking fluids inbetween meals.

Oedema and Leg Cramps

Mild oedema due to physiological changes is usually present in the extremities in the third trimester. This may be caused by the pressure of the enlarging uterus on the veins returning fluid from the legs. This oedema does not require sodium restriction or other dietary changes. Also the common occurance of cramps during night manifested by sudden contractions of the muscle is thought to be related to decline in the serum calcium levels, which is in turn related to calcium imbalance.

Pica

Pica refers to the compulsion for persistent ingestion of unsuitable substances that have little or no nutritional value like starch, clay and chalk.

Anaemia

A pregnant woman is labelled anaemic if the blood haemoglobin is less than 10g/100ml from the 28th week onwards. A significant fall in birth weight due to increase in prematurity rate and intrauterine growth retardation can occur if the haemoglobin level goes below 8 g / 100 ml. The demand for folate is increased due to increased cellular proliferation. Low folate levels are due to deficient intake. Megaloblastic anaemia due to folate deficiency results in intensified nausea, vomiting and anorexia.

Pregnancy Induced Hypertension (PIH)

PIH is a syndrome characterized by hypertension, proteinuria and oedema, convulsions or coma. The condition develops in the third trimester. Pre-eclempsia and eclempsia are the two stages which differ with the degree of symptoms, eclampsia denoting a severe stage. PIH is defined by systolic pressure of 140 mm Hg or diastolic pressure of 90 mmHg or both. A rise in systolic pressure by 20-30 mm Hg or diastolic pressure of 10-15 mmHg or both in two or more occasions six hours apart is diagnostic of PIH.

The extent of proteinuria varies with the degree of PIH. Oedema of pre-eclampsia may be associated with dizziness, headache, visual disturbances, facial oedema, anorexia, nausea and vomiting. In severe state of eclampsia convulsions occur near time of delivery. Optimal nutrition is the fundamental aspect of treatment.

Gestational Diabetes Mellitus

Due to increased blood volume and corresponding metabolite load some glucose is excreted in urine. Most of these women revert to normal glucose tolerance after delivery. But they have a high chance of developing NIDDM after 40 years of age. The incidence of preclempsia is high in pregnant women with diabetes mellitus.

Ill Effects of Alcohol, Caffiene, Drugs and Tobacco

Alcohol consumption during pregnancy leads to abnormal physical and mental development of foetus defined as Foetal Alcoholic Syndrome (FAS). Infants with FAS are premature and have low birth weight. They have distinct physical characteristics like small head, short eye slits which make the eyes looking far apart, flat mid face, thin upper lip and high evidence of central nervous system dysfunction.

Caffiene can cross the placenta and enter foetal circulation. Pregnant women who are heavy coffee drinkers are considered at risk for miscarriages, premature deliveries and may give birth to small for date infants. Drugs used during pregnancy whether medicinal or recreational leads to numerous problems. Recreational drugs like heroin, LSD, marujuana lead to poor prenatal weight, short or prolonged labour and other perinatal problems. Self use of medicinal drugs especially during early stages of pregnancy may lead to malformation of the foetus.

Smoking during pregnancy results in placental abnormalities and foetal damage including prematurity and low birth weight. This is mainly due to reduced blood flow, which affects the oxygen and nutrient transport through the placenta.

Too early (teenage pregnancy) or too late (35 yrs and above) or too close (less than two years spacing) are not safe or conducive both to the health of the mother and infant.

Lactation

Adequate nutrition for the mother during lactation is also of vital importance as the infant is dependant on mothers milk for its nutrition for the first few months of life. As the mother has to nourish the fully developed and rapidly growing infant, she needs extra nutrients to meet the baby's increasing needs in addition to her own requirements. A satisfactory diet during pregnancy will ensure a good store of nutrients for satisfactory breast feeding. Inadequate nutrition during lactation is reflected on both the quality and quantity of milk secreted.

Physiology of Lactation

Hormonal changes markedly increase breast areola and nipple size. During pregnancy estrogen secreted by the placenta bring about rapid development of glands in the breasts. Large quantities of progesterone change the glandular cells to actual secreting cells.

By the time the baby is born breasts reach a degree of development capable of producing milk. Yet, oestrogen and progesterone, despite their developmental effects on breast inhibit the actual formation of milk until after the baby is born. Thus during pregnancy the placental hormones inhibit the secretion of lactating hormones by the pituitary gland.

With the sudden expulsion of placenta during delivery the source of placental hormones is removed and secretion of lactogenic hormones is increased which bring about production and secretion of milk.

The process of milk production and secretion occurs in two distinct stages.

Prolactin Reflex

When the baby sucks the breast, nerve impulses are passed up the spinal cord to the hypothalamus which stimulates anterior pituitary leading to the secretion of prolactin. Prolactin is carried via the blood stream to the alveoli in the breasts where it stimulates milk production.

Let down Reflex

When the baby sucks, nerve impulses are passed to the posterior pituitary producing another hormone, oxytocin. Oxytocin contracts the muscle cells around the alveoli, squeezing out milk and propelling it down to the nipples.

The let down reflex is highly sensitive to emotional and psychological disturbances as well as physical contact. The mother's emotions, the baby's cry or even the baby's thought might initiate this reflex. On the other hand, anxiety, fear and tension may inhibit this reflex. Hence the mother should be comfortable and relaxed while feeding the baby.

These two reflexes operate simultaneously and release milk. As long as pituitary produces these lactogenic hormones, it cannot produce sufficient Follicle Stimulating Hormone (FSH) and Leutenizing Hormone (LH) which bring about ovulation. Thus lactation brings about natural contraception.

Table 3 gives the summary of hormonal control of lactation.

Table 3: Summary of hormonal control of lactation

S.No.	Hormone	Source	Function
1	Estrogen	Ovary	Stimulates breast development
2	Progesterone	Placenta	Prepares breast for milk production by changing glandular cells to secreting cells
3	Prolactin	Anterior	pituitary Stimulates milk production
4	Oxytocin	Posterior	pituitary Facilitates release of milk from alveolus

Composition of Breast Milk

Soon after delivery small quantities of thick, yellowish, viscous liquid called colostrum is secreted which is rich in antibodies and Vitamin A. This should be given to the baby and not discarded. After a few days of lactation the mother secretes larger amounts of less viscous and whitish milk known as "mature milk" which is more or less a complete food nutritionally. A healthy mother secretes 850ml of milk daily for which her nutritional needs are increased enormously.

Nutrient Needs During Lactation

ICMR nutrient recommendations for a lactating mother is based on the composition of breast milk and the fact that 850 ml of milk is produced daily. However the milk secretion continues to increase in the early periods of lactation upto six months and then gradually decreases. Therefore the nutrient requirements are given for the two periods in lactation ie., 0-6 months and 6-12 months.

Energy

The lactating mother requires additional energy for the production of milk which is calculated from the volume of milk secreted, its energy content and the efficiency of conversion of food energy to milk energy. Based on the optimal output of 850 ml/day, energy content of 65 k.cal / 100 ml of breast milk and conversion efficiency of 80 percent, the additional allowance recommended during first six months of lactation is 550 k.cal / day. This is after taking into account the energy contribution from fat stores deposited during pregnancy. Most Indian mothers continue to lactate even after six months but the milk production is reduced. Hence ICMR has recommended an additional allowance of 400 k.cal / day for the period from 6 -12 months of lactation.

Protein

For production of milk, protein requirement also increases, as the produced milk contains 1.15g of proteins /100ml. The recommended additional protein intake during lactation is 25g per day for 0-6 months and 18g per day for 6-12 months.

Fat

ICMR has suggested an intake of 45g of visible fat per day. Although the total fat in breast milk is not influenced by the mothers diet, the composition of milk fat does. The fat also provides energy density to meet the higher energy requirement during lactation.

Calcium

Mothers milk contains 30-40 mg of calcium per 100 ml. Since about 850ml of milk is produced, around 300mg of calcium is secreted through milk per day. Therefore the additional intake of calcium is essential to enable the retention of 300mg of extra calcium daily. Since the dietary calcium retention in lactating women is 60 percent, ICMR has recommend 1000 mg of calcium per day for a lactating mother.

Iron

Since most mothers have lactational amenorrhea, it results in saving of nearly 1mg iron per day which otherwise would have been lost due to menstruation. This saving is more than sufficient to compensate for the negligible amount secreted in mother's milk and hence iron requirement during lactation is same as that of a normal adult woman ie, 30mg/day.

Vitamins

Vitamin A

The additional need of vitamin A during lactation is based on the amount secreted in mother's milk. On an average 300 mg of vitamin A is secreted per day. Hence ICMR has recommended an additional allowance of 350 mg of retinol ie.a total of 950 mg per day.

Thiamine, riboflavin and Niacin

As the calorie and protein requirements increase during lactation, the requirements of these vitamins also increase correspondingly. The amount of these vitamins computed on the basis of increased energy allowance would be sufficient to cover the amount secreted in breast milk. Hence the levels are computed on the same basis as that of adults i.e. 0.5mg/1000k.cal, 0.6mg / 1000k.cal and 6.6mg / 1000k.cal of thiamine, riboflavin and niacin respectively.

Pyridoxine

ICMR has recommended an additional intake of 0.5 mg i.e., total intake of 2.5 mg/day, same as that during pregnancy.

Folic acid

The folate content of breast milk is about 2.5 mg . Based on this, ICMR has recommended an additional allowance of 50µg/day of free folate ie., a total of 150µg free folate/ day.

Vitamin C (Ascorbic acid)

Well nourished Indian mother secretes about 20mg of Vitamin C per day during lactation. Considering this and the cooking losses averaging to 50 percent, ICMR has recommended an additional intake of 40mg/day ie. a total of 80mg of ascorbic acid per day.

Diet During Lactation

A lactating mother requires not only large quantities of body building and protective foods but also additional energy yielding foods to facilitate copious formation and secretion of breast milk. Besides adhering to the basic principles of meal planning the following guidelines need to be considered.

- Large amount of fluids are essential for milk production. Therefore adequate fluids such as milk, fruit juice, milk based beverages and even water must be encouraged.
- The choice of food is wide during lactation. No food need to be restricted except spicy and strong flavoured foods which might impart flavour to milk that may be repulsive to the baby and that may cause gastric distress to the mother.
- Almost all medicines taken during lactation are absorbed into mothers blood and are secreted in the milk. Hence any medicine during lactation must be avoided or taken under strict medical supervision.
- Since the nutrient needs are enhanced, the meal pattern may be changed to 5-7 meals a day by introducing in between snack between the meals.

When a mothers diet is inadequate, her milk yield is usually well maintained by drawing on her own reserve of nutrients and evidence of malnutrition is likely to appear in the mother before it does in her child. Many women in poor communities have a remarkable ability to breast feed their infants for long periods. This is probably due to repeated stimulation of the neurohumoral reflex by frequently putting the baby to the breast and letting it suckle at night.

4

Nutrition in Infancy

Infancy is a period of rapid growth. The development during infancy is rapid than any other period in the life time of an individual.

Growth and Development

The average birth weight of a newborn is 2.5 kg. The growth and development is accompanied by a number of physiological changes which include

Change in Body Size

A healthy normal infant doubles its birth weight by six months and triples the birth weight by the end of one year. Similarly there is increase in body length of the infant from 50-55 cm at birth to about 75 cm during the first year. With increase in body length the body proportion also changes. By the time the child is two years old the head circumference achieves nearly 2/3rd of its final size and there is an increase in chest circumference.

Change in Body Composition

Weight gain comprises of growth in muscles, organ tissue, skeletal tissue and skeletal structure. At birth the infant has water content as high as 75 percent in its body,12-15 percent fat and poorly developed muscles. By the end of one year the water content decreases to 60 percent and fat content increases to 24 percent and there is a corresponding decrease in lean body mass. Mineralization of skeletal system takes place and continues during childhood and later during adolosence.

Changes in Gastro Intestinal System

A full term infant is able to digest simple proteins, emulsified fat and simple carbohydrates. During the first few months gastric acidity and salivary secretion is low. As the child grows the digestibility improves and by the end of first year the child is able to digest all types of food.

Changes in Excretory System

Kidneys reach their full functioning capacity by the end of first year. During early months the glomerular filtration rate is low and hence excretion of high concentration of solutes is difficult.

Mental Development

There is a rapid increase in the number of brain cells in the first 5-6 months after birth. Thereafter the rate of cell division declines though it continues till the second year.

Changes in Circulatory System

The infants have a rapid heart rate of 120-140 per minute. At birth the level of haemoglobin is 18-22 g/100ml which provides sufficient reserve for expansion of blood volume and adequate oxygen carrying capacity to the growing tissues during the first 4-6 months.

Feeding Behaviour

Maturation of nervous system especially that which

controls muscular co-ordination brings about the change in feeding behaviour. At birth the baby is able to co ordinate sucking, swallowing and breathing. Although the eyes cannot focus, the baby is able to find its nourishment by rooting reflex. Till about three months the baby sucks by the up and down movement of the tongue which pushes out solid food if placed (extrusion reflex). By 3-4 months the tongue movements change and the child is able to swallow and by 6 months chewing movements also develop.

Growth Monitoring

Though the above mentioned growth and developmental changes are significant, satisfactory growth in an infant can be accurately assessed by growth monitoring.

"Growth monitoring is a regular measurement of growth which enables to visualize growth, or lack of it and obtain specific, relevant and practical guidance to ensure continued regular growth and health of children."

Though growth monitoring can be done in a number of ways the best way to do is by using a "Growth chart".

Immunization

Malnutrition during infancy leads to higher incidence of infant mortality. Besides malnutrition there are certain other factors which compound with it causing mortality. Infectious diseases are one of them and hence it is important to protect the children against these disease through immunization.

Immunization is given at different ages during the first year of life which give life long immunity to the child against six dreadful diseases namely tuberculosis, polio, diphtheria, pertusis, tetanus and measles. So immunization is important not only for nutritionally deprived but for all children. Table 1 presents the immunization schedule.

Table 1: Immunization Schedule

Age	Vaccine
Soon after birth	Hepatitus B 1st dose, OPV 1st dose, BCH
6 weeks	Hepatitis B 2nd dose
	DPT 1st dose
	OPV 2nd dose
10 weeks	DPT 2nd dose
	OPV 2nd dose
14 weeks	DPT 3rd dose
	OPV 4th dose
6 months	OPV 5th dose
	Hepatitis B 3rd dose
9 months	Measles
15 to 18 months	MMR
18 months	DPT, OPV 1st Booster
2 years	Typhoid vaccine
5 years	DPT, OPV 2nd Booster

Nutrition Requirements

As growth during infancy is rapid, meeting the nutritional requirements is very important. Nutritional requirements for infants is based on the composition and intake of breast milk of well nourished population combined with the contributions from supplementary foods introduced around 4-5 months of age as mothers milk alone is inadequate after that. The RDA for infants is given in table 2.

Table 2: ICMR recommended dietary allowances for Infants

Nutrients	0-6 months	6-12 months
Energy (k.cal)	108 / kg	98 / kg
Protein (gm)	2.05 / kg	1.65 / kg

Calcium (mg)	500	500
Vitamin A		
Retinol (mg) or	350	350
B carotene (mg)	1200	1200
Thiamine (mg)	55 / kg	50 / kg
Riboflavin (mg)	65 / kg	60 / kg
Niacin (mg)	710 / kg	650 / kg
Pyridoxine (mg)	0.1	0.4
Ascorbic acid (mg)	25	25
Folic acid (mg)	25	25
Vitamin B12 (mg)	0.2	0.2

Energy

The energy recommendations are based on the average secretion of 850 ml of milk per day by a well nourished mother. The infants require 108 k.cal/kg and 98 k.cal/kg during 0-6 months and 6-12 months of age respectively. Of the energy supplied 50 percent is used for basal energy, 25 percent for activity and 25 percent for growth. Extremely active children may utilize more energy and hence there will not be weight gain unless additional calories are given. After six months 70 percent of energy requirement is met by breast milk and for the rest supplementary foods have to be given.

Protein

Protein requirements should not only meet the need for maintenance but also for the rapid skeletal and muscular growth. The human milk provides all the amino acids essential for proper growth. Protein intake of healthy infants during first 6 months of age is 2g/kg body weight. Protein requirement decreases after 6 months as do the energy requirement. After six months the protein requirement is 1.65 g/kg body weight, the contribution being equal from the mothers milk and vegetable protein supplements.

Fat

Adequately breast fed infants receive 30g of fat /day of which 10 percent is linoleic acid and 1 percent linolenic acid. Breast milk also meets the essential fatty acid requirements. Foods used as substitutes when breast milk is inadequate or not available should provide this proportion of fat and also ensure that 5-6 percent of energy is in the form of essential fatty acids. During weaning, the diet should provide 25 percent of energy from fat, which should be a blend of visible and invisible fat to reduce bulk.

Calcium

Upto 6 months when the infant is solely breast fed 300mg of calcium daily is adequate. Large per cent of calcium in breast milk is retained by infant. As the baby grows, rapid calcification of bones take place which is essential to support the weight of the body by the time the baby walks. To meet these requirements ICMR has recommended 500mg of calcium/day throughout infancy.

Iron

The infants require iron for growth, expansion of blood volume and for improving iron stores in the body. Considering the availability and absorption of iron an allowance of 1mg / kg body weight/day for an infant had been recommended. However, the ICMR has not suggested any RDA for iron due to the following reasons

a. The infant is born with good iron stores sufficient to last for four months. The haemoglobin level which is about 17g / 100ml at birth falls to 11g/100ml during second week. The released iron from the haemoglobin breakdown is stored in the infant to be used subsequently.

b. Though mothers milk contains negligible iron, the amount of bio available iron is sufficient to meet the needs of exclusively breast fed infants.
c. Loss of iron in infants is not known correctly and hence the amount to be replaced cannot be assessed.

Vitamins

Vitamin A

On the basis of vitamin A ingested by breast fed infants in well nourished communities the ICMR has suggested RDA for vitamin A as 350 mg per day throughout infancy.

Other fat soluble vitamins

ICMR has not recommended any allowance for vitamin D, vitamin E and Vitamin K. The vitamin D requirement placed between 200-400 I.U can be obtained by adequate exposure to sunlight.

B Complex vitamins

RDA for B complex vitamins is expressed in terms of weight of an infant which in reality is based on calorie consumption.

Completely breast fed infants derive the required thiamine and riboflavin requirements from breast milk. ICMR has recommended 55mg/kg body weight and 50 mg/kg body weight of thiamine and 65mg/kg body weight and 60mg/kg body weight of riboflavin during 0-6 months and 6-12 months of age respectively.

Niacin requirements are computed on the same basis as adults i.e., 6.6mg of niacin / 1000 k.cal which when expressed in terms of body weight will be 710 mg/kg and 650 mg/kg body weight for infants 0-6 months and 6-12 months respectively.

Folic acid requirements are based on the folic acid level in breast milk. Breast fed infants normally receive about 25 to 30 mg/kg of folic acid per day most of which is absorbed. Hence the ICMR has recommended folic acid intake of 25mg/day for infants.

It was observed that infants receiving 0.2 mg/kg of vitamin B12/day show normal haemopoiesis whereas those receiving less than 0.05 mg/day exhibit deficiency symptoms. Hence a daily allowance of 0.2 mg of vitamin B_{12} is recommended.

Vitamin C:

ICMR has recommended an intake of 25mg of vitamin C per day. This allowance is arrived after considering beneficial effect of Vitamin C on non-haem iron absorption.

BREAST FEEDING

Infants who are exclusively breast fed for the first 4-6 months of life grow well and breast feeding is beneficial not only during this period but also during later years of life. The infant is put on breast within half an hour after a normal delivery.

Colostrum:

During first two or three days colostrum is secreted in small quantities of about 10-40 ml. The composition of colostrum is as follows:

Nutrient Quantity	/ 100 ml
Energy (k.cal)	58
Fat (g)	2.9
Calcium (mg)	31
Phosphorus (mg)	14

Iron (mg)	0.09
Protein (g)	2.7
Lactose (g)	5.3
Carotene (IU)	186
Vitamin A (IU)	296

Colostrum contains interferon like substance which has strong antiviral activity. It contains B_{12} binding protein making it unavailable for growth of E-coli and other bacteria. It also contains antibodies against viral infection. Enzymes lysozyme and peroxidase which promote cell maturation are found to be more in colostrum.

Advantages of Breast Feeding

Breast feeding is the simple and best method of feeding and has the following advantages

Nutritional factors

The composition of human milk is best suitable for infants. Table 3 shows a comparison of human milk, cow's milk and Buffalo's milk. It is observed that in human milk the protein content is lower but the content of carbohydrate, namely lactose is higher. The fat content is comparatively less. This is advantageous to the infant as low protein reduces pressure on kidney to excrete extra nitrogen. Also the protein is present as lactalbumin which is better digested than protein in cow's milk.

Table 3: Comparison of Human milk with cow's and buffalo's milk

Nutrient Per 100 ml	Human milk	Cow's Milk	Buffalo's Milk
Water (g)	88	87.5	81
Energy (k.cal)	65	67	117
Protein (g)	1.1	3.2	4.3

Carbohydrate (g)	7.4	4.4	5
Fat (g)	3.4	4.1	6.5
Calcium (mg)	28	120	210
Phosphorus (mg)	11	90	130
Iron (mg)	—	0.2	0.2
Carotene (mg)	137	174	160
Thiamine (mg)	0.02	0.05	0.04
Riboflavin (mg)	0.02	0.19	0.1
Vitamin C (mg)	3	2	1
Caseinogen lactalbumin ratio	1:2	3:1	—

Lactose provides natural sweetness and also helps in absorption of calcium and iron. Fat though less is highly emulsified and therefore better digested. Lipids in breast milk include unsaturated fatty acids, essential fatty acids, prostaglandin precursors, fat soluble vitamins, phospholipids and cholesterol. When compared to animal milk, breast milk provides higher amount of vitamin C which is not destroyed by heating as it happens with cow's milk. The bioavailability of iron, in the presence of iron binding protein lactoferrin is higher. Similarly calcium in breast milk though less when compared to cow's milk is better absorbed by the infant.

Hormones and growth factors:

Breast milk is a rich source of hormones like Thyroid Stimulating Hormone (TSH), thyroxin, insulin and prolactin. It also contains growth regulating factors, growth promoters and growth modulators.

Immunological factors:

The following factors in breast milk provide passive immunity –that does not require the activation of the infants own immune defenses.

a. *Macrophages*: They can digest bacteria and also develop immunity against infectious diseases.

b. *Lymphocytes*: Lymphocytes produce antiviral substances like interferon. Lymphocytes also produce lymphokynes and other growth factors which stimulate proliferation and differentiation in the lymphoid tissue and its capacity to react to antigens.

c. *Lactoferrin*: It is an iron binding protein that inhibits the growth of E.Coli and other bacteria by binding the iron needed for their growth.

d. *Lactobacillus bifidus factor*: It is an amino sugar and contains N-acetyl neuraminic acid. It encourages the growth of the microorganism Lactobacillus bifidus and produces acetic acid or lactic acid from lactose and depresses the growth of pathogenic and disease causing organisms.

e. *Enzymes*: Breast milk also supplies enzymes like lipase, amylase and lactoperoxidase which increase digestibility and also destroy the harmful microorganisms.

f. *Immunoglobulin*: They are defensive proteins which include all types of antibodies. Immunoglobulin A is found in relatively high levels which offers protection against polio virus, streptococus and pneumococcus.

Economic factors

Breast milk is the most economical food for the baby. Even after accounting the extra food cost required by the mother, breast milk is cheaper than any other type of artificial feed.

Psychological factors

Breast feeding is essential for a healthy, happy and

emotional relationship between the mother and the infant. While the mother gets a feeling of satisfaction, it gives a sense of security to the infant.

Natural contraceptive

During breast feeding there is a high level of protection, which prevents ovulation leading to lactational amenorrhea. This prevents the onset of another pregnancy due to suspension of menstruation and helps the uterus to return to its normal size. Breast feeding also prevents breast cancer.

Other advantages:

a. Infants jaw is more fully developed as he works harder to extract milk.
b. Breast milk is microbiologically sterile and hence less incidence of contamination and gastrointestinal problems.
c. Human milk is always fresh and at the right temperature.
d. It is convenient to administer at any time.
e. Low danger of incorrect formula or overfeeding.
f. Breast fed babies have better cognition and IQ later in life when compared to bottle fed babies.

In order to promote breast feeding and provide safe and adequate nutrition for the infant the Government of India has formulated the Indian National Code for protection and promotion of breast feeding. Subsequently the Infant Milk Substitute (IMS) act 1992 was passed to protect, promote and support breast feeding. According to this act there should be,

— no promotion of infant feeding products
— no display of artificial feeding products in health care facilitates

— the company personnel should not contact mothers for marketing and

— any brochures, booklets which advertise infant feeding products should not be permitted.

The World Alliance for Breast feeding Action (WABA) a network of organizations in collaboration with WHO and UNICEF, which also promote breast feeding, has declared August 1-7 as the world breast feeding week.

Artificial feeding

Though breast milk is the best milk and there can be no substitute for it, there are certain circumstances during which the infant need to be given artificial feeds.

Reasons related to mother

1. Illness of short duration like fever, cracked nipples or severe illness like tuberculosis, heart disease.
2. The mother is on steroids, anticoagulants or radioactive drugs.
3. Insufficient milk secretion.
4. Death of mother.

Reasons related to infant

1. Extreme prematurity.
2. Acute infections.
3. Congenital deformities like 'cleft palate' and gastrointestinal tract obstructions.

In the absence of breast milk, animal milk or toned milk is given as a substitute which need not be diluted but in cases when the infant is not able to digest, milk can be diluted using boiled water in the ratio of 3:1. When the baby is fed on animal milk, supplements of iron and vitamin C are essential.

Artificial milk formulae in dry form prepared from animal milk are available in the market which have been modified in nutrient content so as to resemble breast milk. These formulas are fortified with iron. Whenever the infant is fed with an artificial food utmost care in handling and preparing the feed is essential. This includes cleanliness of utensils, bottles and nipples.

Weaning and Supplementary Food

Weaning is the process of gradually introducing foods other than breast milk in the child's feeding schedule. The foods that are introduced in addition to breast milk are called supplementary foods. Introducing supplementary foods not only ensures the fulfillment of nutrient needs of the infant (which cannot be met by breast milk alone after 6 months) but also introduces the child gradually to the family eating pattern. The nutrient density of the weaning foods should be 0.25k.cal to 0.4k.cal/g. Hence calorie dense foods should be given. Weaning food should provide atleast 10 percent of energy as protein.

Types of Supplementary Foods

Liquid supplements

Milk:

Initially milk can be given diluted with water in the ratio of 3:1, then the amount of water can be gradually reduced so that the infant consumes undiluted milk within a few weeks.

Fruit juices:

Fresh juices of tomato, grapes, oranges and sweet lime can be given. When this is introduced between 4-6 months a teaspoon of it can be diluted with little water and given. Gradually the quantity can be increased and undiluted juices (85ml of orange juice) can be given.

Soups:

Soups of green leafy vegetables can be given. The leafy vegetable is washed well with water and prepared in the form of soup by boiling it with a minimal amount of water and a little salt and onion. First the soups may be strained and later on unstrained soups can be given.

Semi Solid Supplements

Semi solid supplements may be given at 5 - 6 months. The first solid food commonly offered is a cereal or a starchy vegetable like potato, well cooked and mashed. In case of cereals small quantities of milk and sugar are added. Calorie dense foods can be prepared by using malted wheat or ragi.

Cooked mashed vegetables like potatoes, carrots, green leafy vegetables can be introduced starting with small quantities, which supply vitamins and add colour to the diet. Fruits should be mashed and steamed except for banana until one year after which fruits can only be stewed.

Yolk of egg can be given at 6-7 months. Half a teaspoon of yolk can be started with and if tolerated, gradually increased to one yolk. Yolk can also be introduced as soft custard. Egg white because of its allergic manifestation is given only after 10 months. Thereafter whole egg can be given as poached or soft boiled.

Ground and cooked meat, boiled fish may be given with little flavouring and salt. Pulses well cooked along with the cereals as kichidi or pongal can be given or can be made into porridge. Pulse and meat preparations can be given on alternate days, so that the baby receives each of them 3 or 4 times a week.

Solid supplements

When the baby starts cutting teeth solid supplements are given. Cooked cereals, pulses and vegetables can be given. Solids like idli, chappathi, rice and dhal can be given after the child gets used to semisolids. Meat may be minced fine instead of ground.

Vegetables chopped and boiled, leafy vegetables, soft and boiled raw carrots and fruit segments without skin and seeds can be given. When fed with solid supplements, plenty of water should be given to the child. Small amount of boiled, cooled water has to be given 2 to 3 times a day and more often during hot weather.

Table 4 presents the quantity of different foods to be included in the diet of 6-12 months old infant. Care should be taken in preparing the foods in a special way according to the age of the infant.

Table 4: Balanced Diet for Infants (6-12 months)

S.No.	Food groups	quantity (gm)
1.	Cereals and millets	45
2.	Pulses	15
3.	Milk (ml)	500
4.	Roots and tubers	50
5.	Green leafy vegetables	25
6.	Other vegetables	25
7.	Fruits	100
8.	Sugar	25
9.	Fats/oils (visible)	10

Points to be considered in Weaning

1. Only one food should be introduced at a time.
2. Small quantities of food should be given at the beginning and the amount gradually increased as he develops a liking for it.

3. The child should never be fed by force. If the child shows dislike for a particular food, it should be removed from the diet and tried again after a week or two. If the dislike persists the food can be replaced by a substitute.
4. Food given should not be spicy. Fried foods should also be avoided.
5. Variety in child's diet is important to make it more appealing. As soon as the baby accepts a particular food well the next one may be started so that in time he / she learns to accept a good variety of foods. As the child grows the colour, flavour, texture and shape of food should be given special consideration so as to attract the child's attention.
6. To inculcate good eating habits and to encourage the child to eat all types of food, the parents should not show any personal dislike towards any food.

Low cost weaning foods

Several low cost weaning foods have been developed by the Institutes like Central Food Technology Research Institute (CFTRI), Mysore, National Institute of Nutrition (NIN) Hyderabad, Avinashilingam Deemed university (ADU), Coimbatore and Gandhigram Rural Institute. Indian multi purpose food, malt food, Balahar, Kuzhandhai Amudhu, win feed are a few of them. They are very nutritious and can be easily prepared at home.

Feeding a Pre-term Baby

The preterm babies are those who are born before 37 weeks of gestation. Goal of feeding the preterm is to achieve a growth rate that approaches the normal growth rate of foetus in uterus. The preterm is at a disadvantage in many aspects of nutrition. The problem facing the preterm are, poor sucking and swallowing reflexes, relatively high caloric requirement with small stomach capacity, and incompetent cardiooesophageal sphincter leading to aspiration, decreased absorption of essential nutrients.

The caloric need of non-growing preterm babies during the first week of life are 60 kcal / kg / day. After first one or two weeks of life most preterm babies require 120 - 150 kcal / kg / day to maintain satisfactory growth. High calories may be necessary in babies who are not gaining weight, post - operative patients and extreme preterms.

Fluid needs of the preterm babies are relatively high during the first week of life. The intake of fluids varies from 90 - 100 ml / kg / day for 7 - 10 days. Additional fluids may be required when the baby is under the phototherapy or a radiant warmer.

Very low birth weight babies may have difficulty in tolerating the lactose the first few days. Glucose polymers are well tolerated. Preterm babies require 3 - 4 g of protein per kilogram of body weight for rapid growth. Certain amino acids essential for the preterm such as cystine, taurine, alanine and arginine are present in breast milk.

Very low birth weight babies poorly digest and absorb saturated triglycerides. Vegetable oils containing unsaturated long chain fatty acids are better absorbed. Better still are medium chain triglycerides because their digestion and absorption are not dependent on bile salt level.

Calcium and phosphorus supplements may be needed to prevent rickets or osteopenia in preterms. Iron deficiency can occur by 6 - 12 weeks and hence 2.5 mg / kg / day of iron starting from 6 - 8 weeks of age may be given. All low birth weight babies should receive vitamin supplementation in addition to the amount present in human milk.

The preterm babies are best fed with unprocessed human milk obtained from their mothers. It has been shown that milk of mothers delivering premature babies has higher caloric, fat, protein and sodium content which is suitable for the nutritional needs of low birth weight babies. Antimicrobial property of breast milk is of great importance to the preterm baby. If the baby does not gain weight satisfactorily with breast milk alone, dietary supplements like vegetable oils (corn oil, groundnut oil) may be used which increase the calorie value without increasing its volume.

When human milk feeding is not possible one must resort to animal milk or formula feeds.

Nutrition During Preschool Age (1-6 Years)

The rapid growth during infancy is followed by a generally slow growth between one to six years. The child becomes more active and the social and environmental influences have a great impact on his food behaviour and eating pattern. Development of full dentition by the end of two years increase the range of foods that can safely be eaten. The need for nutrients is increased as growth and development continues.

Growth Pattern

During the second year, the increase in height is about 10cm and weight gain is 2 to 2.5 kg. After two years annual gain in height and weight is only six to seven cm and 1.5 to 2 kg respectively. However there is a wide variance in the physical development of children.

As growth proceeds, changes occur in proportion of water, muscle tissue, fat deposits and skeletal structure. The body water gradually decreases and there is addition of adipose tissue and that of minerals to the bones.

Psychosocial changes also take place. As he steps into the second year he develops a sense of individuality which is distinct and is reflected in his food behaviour. With advancing age there is an increasing sense of independence, initiative, imagination and curiosity.

Preschool age is also a period of imitation and sex identification, with boys imitating their fathers and girls their mothers. Such behaviour is reflected at meal times and therefore the parents play an important role in inculcating healthy and positive attitude towards food.

Nutritional Allowances

Energy

Energy is required for growth and activity. The rate of growth fluctuates with age. Upto 10 years, there is no difference in sex for dietary allowance. The energy requirements are 1240 k.cal for 1-3 years and 1690 k.cal for 4-6 years. Improper weaning may lead to protein and energy malnutrition.

Protein

The increasing muscle mass requires a positive nitrogen balance. The basal losses and the additional requirement for growth have been considered in determining the allowances for protein. The protein requirement is 22g and 30g for age groups 1-3 years and 4 – 6 years respectively.

Fat

Adequate fat is required to provide the extra calories as well as to add calorie density and reduce bulk in the diet. The linoleic acid requirement is 3 percent of energy. To provide sufficient energy density and improve palatability of the diet 25g of visible fat per day has been suggested.

Calcium

Calcium requirements are assessed based on the calcium accretion in the body during period of growth. This deposition is not uniform throughout the growing period but is relatively higher during early childhood and during adolescence. Moreover all dietary calcium is not absorbed. Hence to ensure a positive balance, 400mg of calcium per day is recommended.

Iron

Iron requirements during childhood need to cover the basal loss of iron from the body, amount needed for growth and for increase in the haemoglobin concentration by about 1g/ dl. Based on this the requirements are given as 12 mg/day and 18 mg/day for 1 – 3 years and 4 – 6 years respectively.

Vitamins

Vitamin A

It has been observed that the incidence of vitamin A deficiency is high and serum vitamin A levels are low in Indian children whose intake of Vitamin A is less than 100mg/day. However, when food supplements providing a total of 300mg/day are given over a period of six months the deficiency symptoms disappear. Based on this observation and including a safety allowance, ICMR has suggested an intake 400 mg of vitamin A/day.

B complex vitamins

The recommended intake for B vitamins is based on the energy intake and is calculated as for adults i.e., 0.5mg/ 1000k.cal, 0.6mg/ 1000k.cal and 6.6mg/1000k.cal for thiamine, riboflavin and niacin respectively.

Folic acid and pyridoxine requirements are computed from interpolation of values for infants and adults. The requirement for children is slightly higher than that of infants.

Vitamin C

ICMR has suggested the same level of vitamin C as for adults i.e, 40 mg/day for preschool children.

The quantities of various food groups to be included in a balanced diet for preschool children is given in Table 5.

Table 5: Balanced diet for Preschool Children

S.No.	Food groups	quantity (g)	
		1 - 3 years	4 - 6 years
1.	Cereals and Millets	120	210
2.	Pulses	30	45
3.	Milk (ml)	500	500
4.	Roots and tubers	50	100
5.	Green leafy vegetables	50	50
6.	Other vegetables	50	50
7.	Fruits	100	100
8.	Sugar	25	30
9.	Fats / oils (visible)	20	25

Need Good Food Habits

The preschool years are ones that create a number of concerns about food intake. Nearly two out of three preschool children in India are malnourished. The different household factors affecting the child's nutrition are

- The economic status which determines the food available and thus the energy density of food.
- The mother's experience and knowledge which influences the food preparation and food intake by the child.

— Demand on mother's time to prepare the food
— Poor sanitation and water supply
— Poor living conditions
— Contamination of food leading to infectious diseases
— Parental influence in showing dislike for a particular food.

These factors in turn affect the food intake leading to severe malnutrition and this has a profound impact on the growth and performance during later years.

In addition to these the preschoolers may show certain likes and dislikes which when not properly interpreted may lead to undernutrition. They may show interest in certain foods that may last from few months to few years. Food preferences may change from time to time. Also certain foods are liked by them only when cooked in a particular way.

Appetite is also erratic, with the result that the child may eat one meal well refusing the next. So there must be no hurrying at meal times, the atmosphere should be pleasant, peaceful and lacking distraction. There should be regularity of meal times. The child should be taught to eat everything on his plate.

Proper evacuation of faeces shall be maintained by daily diet of fruits, vegetables and whole grains. They prefer simple unmixed dishes that are neither too cold nor too hot. Familiar foods are better liked and hence new foods should be given in small portions along with well accepted ones.

A balance should be maintained between hard and soft foods. Colourful foods add variety and stimulate interest. Finger foods such as cutlets, hard boiled eggs, small sandwiches, rolls and whole fruits are handy.

At the table, physical comfort while sitting, unbreakable bowls and cutlery with blunt edges will help the child in his/her efforts to feed himself.

Hence it is essential that good food habits are inculcated during childhood considering their food preferences.

Prevalence of Protein Energy Malnutrition (PEM)

Protein energy malnutrition, micronutrient deficiencies such as vitamin A deficiency and iron deficiency anaemia are common among preschool children.

The primary cause of malnutrition is a faulty and inadequate diet. Besides diet and socio economic factors various environmental factors aggravate the dietary deficiencies. These include

- chronic infection
- poor environmental sanitation
- poor insanitary living conditions and
- poor personal hygiene.

Protein Energy Malnutrition

PEM is defined as a range of pathological conditions arising from coincident lack of varying proportions of protein and calorie, occurring most frequently in infants and young children and often associated with infection.

The symptoms vary with the degree of malnutrition. Symptoms of different types of PEM is as follows.

1. *Kwashiorkor* : Oedema of face and lower limbs, failure to thrive, anorexia, diarrhoea, dermatitis, apathy, sparse, soft and thin hair, angular stomatitis, cheilosis and anaemia.

2. *Marasmus* : Failure to thrive, irritability and apathy, diarrhoea, dehydration. The child is shrunk and there is little or no subcutaneous fat.

3. *Marasmic kwashiorkor* : These children exhibit symptoms of both marasmus and kwashiorkor.
4. *Nutritional dwarfing* : Characterised by a marked retardation of growth.

The peak prevalence of protein energy malnutrition is observed in the age group of 2-3 years and marasmus between 1-2 years. Over 80 percent of under five are estimated to be malnourished and 1-2 percent suffer from severe malnutrition. Also, more than 50 percent of deaths in children is attributed to malnutrition either directly or indirectly.

The NNMB survey (1988 - 1990) of rural children reveals that only 10 percent are normal with weights above 90 percent of the standard weights. A majority of the children exhibit mild or moderate malnutrition while 7-8 percent are severely malnourished.

About 1-2 percent of preschool children suffer from severe forms of PEM namely kwashiorkor and marasmus and more than half of the Indian preschool children suffer from sub clinical undernutrition manisfested by low weight for age. About 65 percent of them are stunted which indicates undernutrition of long duration.

Vitamin A deficiency

Inadequate dietary intake of vitamin A or its precursor (b - carotene) is the most contributory factor for vitamin A deficiency.

Blindness due to xerophthalmia is an important public health problem among children in India. The term xerophthalmia includes all ocular manifestations of vitamin A deficiency like Night blindness, conjunctival xerosis, Bitot's spot and corneal xerosis.

Vitamin A deficiency is exhibited as Bitot's spots in 3 percent of preschool children and 30-40 thousand children become blind every year. Vitamin A deficiency increases the risk of disease and death.

Iron deficiency anaemia

This is caused by the dietary lack of iron or inadequate absorption and utilization of iron. The symptoms include

— skin appears pale
— fingernails become thin and flat and eventually results in koilonychia (spoon – shaped nails)
— atrophy of papillae of tongue, glossitis
— angular stomatitis and dysphagia
— gastritis resulting in achlorohydria

Long term deficiency symptoms result in malfunctioning of various systems. The general symptom are lassitude, fatigue, breathlessness on exertion, palpitation, dizziness, headache, dimness of vision, insomnia and angina.

More than 50 percent of preschool children suffer from iron deficiency anaemia. The high prevalence of these nutrient deficiency diseases stress the need for a balanced, nutritious diet during preschool years.

5

Nutrition During School Age (6-12 Years)

The school age, six to twelve years, is a latent period of growth. During this stage growth is slow and body changes occur gradually. The nutritional requirement is the same for boys and girls upto nine years after which girls out do boys and there is a change in some of the nutrient requirements for boys and girls.

Growth Pattern

Though rate of growth is slow during school years, adequate reserves are laid down during this period for the rapid growth during adolescence. Hence the age from 6-12 years is being called the "lull before the storm".

Usually girls have a higher deposition of body fat as compared to boys of the same age but have less percentage of muscle tissues. During childhood boys are taller and heavier at each stage than girls but at the age of 11 to12 years girls become heavier and taller.

As the child enters school he/she develops ability to work out problems and participate in group activities. This is a period of emotional stress, competitive behaviour and dreaming which brings a drastic change in the previous learning and personality pattern. There is a change from dependence of parental standards towards those set by peer group.

Nutritional Allowance

Energy and Protein

The requirements for calories and proteins increase during school age. The calorie requirements remain almost the same for girls throughout. Boys 10-12 years of age require more calories as adequate reserves are being laid for growth spurt during adolescence. The protein requirements are slightly higher for girls than boys between 10-12 years for the approaching menarche.

Fat

In terms of visible fat the ICMR has recommended an intake of 5-6 percentage of total energy from linoliec acid. Considering this the minimum visible fat required has been estimated to be 12g / day but ICMR has suggested the desirable visible intake for school going children as 22g/day.

Minerals

The 10-12 year old children require more calcium than adults to meet the demand for skeletal growth.

The iron requirements are increased as blood volume increases. Also the mean increase in body weight from second year to the twelth year in boys and tenth year in girls is 2.5 to 2.7 kg per year which is equivalent to iron requirement of 0.3mg/day. The iron requirement is further increased by the gradual rise in the haemoglobin concentration and losses. The requirement for iron in girls 10-12 years is lower than 7-9 years because the iron absorption during 10-12 yrs is more which is 5 percent whereas it is only 3 percent in 7-9 years.

Vitamins

Vitamin A requirements of children have been computed from the requirement figures for infants (50mg/kg) and adults (93mg/kg) taking into account the growth rate at different ages. The RDA of vitamins A and C are same as adult RDA. The requirement for B vitamins are in proportion with the calorie requirements.

Table 1 gives the recommended dietary allowances of school going children.

Table 1: ICMR Recommended dietary allowances of school going children

		Age (in years)	
Nutrients	7-9	10-12	
		Boys	Girls
Energy k.cal	1950	2190	1970
Protein (g)	41	54	57
Fat (g)	25	22	22
Calcium (mg)	400	600	600
Iron (mg)	26	34	19
Vitamin A			
Retinol (mg) or	600	600	600
b Carotene (mg)	2400	2400	2400
Thiamine (mg)	1.0	1.1	1.0
Riboflavin (mg)	1.2	1.3	1.2
Niacin (mg)	13	15	13
Pyridoxine (mg)	1.6	1.6	1.6
Ascorbic acid (mg)	40	40	40
Folic acid (mg)	60	70	70
Vitamin B12 (mg)	0.2-1	0.2-1	0.2-1

Diet

By school age the children establish a particular pattern of food intake. This may slightly differ from what is followed at home due to peer influence. The child may try new foods which they normally do not consume.

Breakfast is a very important meal. Children are generally restless and spent very little time at the table. Skipping breakfast affects their performance level and the calorie and nutrients lost cannot be made up at any other time during the day. Menus must include dishes that are quick to eat yet nutritionally adequate. Also there should be variety in colour, texture and taste. Table 2 presents the recommended quantities of food to be consumed by the school going children.

Table 2: Balanced diet for school going children

			Quantity gms	
			10 - 12 yrs	
S.No.	Food groups	7-9 yrs	Boys	Girls
1.	Cereals and millets	270	330	270
2.	Pulses	60	60	60
3.	Milk (ml)	500	500	500
4.	Roots and tubers	100	100	100
5.	Green leafy vegetables	100	100	100
6.	Other vegetables	100	100	100
7.	Fruits	100	100	100
8.	Sugar	30	35	30
9.	Fats / oils (visible)	25	25	25

Packed Lunch

Packed lunch have become a necessity for school children as it is not possible to have lunch at home. Packed lunch is a lunch in a tiffin box to be eaten by the child while away from home. Points to be considered while planning packed lunches are

1. It should meet one third of the day's nutritional requirements.
2. It should include food from all the five food groups though the number of dishes may be less.

3. At least one serving of green leafy vegetables should be included.
4. Food stuffs providing good quality protein like egg, milk or milk product like paneer or curd would improve overall protein quality in combination with vegetable protein.
5. Variety should be present.
6. Preferably the food packed should be different from that prepared for breakfast.
7. The dishes should be packed at right consistency so as to avoid leakage or food becoming dry during lunch which may not be appetising to the child.

One fruit or vegetable salad may be included every day.

Following are two examples of a packed lunch.

1. Vegetable pulao, onion raita, boiled egg, orange.
2. Sambar rice, amaranath porial, vegetable salad and butter milk.

School Lunch Programmes

Increasing urbanization and number of working mothers have made school days longer. Improper and hurried meals at home have become a routine. Whereas among rural population, young children are sent for work to earn a living and the drop out rate is higher in children at primary and secondary school level. These factors have created a necessity to provide lunch at schools which will provide nutritious food to children and also reduce the dropout rate.

The school lunch programmes operate with the following objectives To

1. provide food to the undernourished child and improve the nutritional status.

2. increase school enrolment and attendance.
3. inculcate good food habits.
4. incorporate nutrition education as part of the curriculum.
5. improve the educational performance of the students.
6. encourage use of locally available nutritious foods.
7. encourage community participation in the feeding programmes.

The two major nutrition intervention programmes currently in operation for the population below poverty line in Tamil Nadu are Nutritious Noon Meal Programme of the Government of Tamil Nadu and the Integrated Child Development Services (ICDS) sponsored by the ministry of social welfare, Government of India.

Developing Good Eating Habits and Prevention of Dental Caries

The adequacy of food in terms of nutrients not only depends on food available to the children but also on the food environment and models set for them by their peers, siblings, parents and other elders in the family.

Use of convenience foods by mothers and entry of fast foods have had a great impact on the food preferences of children. Hence nutrition knowledge of parents incorporated into meal planning is important in imparting positive attitudes towards food. The environment at the eating place also affects the nutrient intake while a comfortable and pleasant atmosphere is conducive to good eating. Arguments and family fights while eating affects the food intake adversely.

Advertising and television have a very strong influence on type of food chosen by children. Exposure to these and catchy slogans like 'chocolate', 'yummy', 'rich' tempt children to go in for processed foods and distort their liking and curiousity for natural flavour and colour of foods.

Tooth decay can be caused by caries. This can occur in children who are susceptible to and whose integrity of tooth structure may be affected by nutritional deficiency. Vitamin A is necessary for enamel and Vitamin C is essential for dentine. Calcium, phosphorus and vitamin D are needed for calcification. Fluorine decreases susceptibility of caries. Fermentable carbohydrate which adheres to the tooth is the major cause of tooth decay. The stickier the food and longer it stays in the mouth the greater is the effect. Thorough cleaning of mouth after each meal and developing the habit of brushing twice a day, early morning and before bed, might prevent dental caries.

6

Nutrition During Adolescence

The transition from childhood to adulthood is called adolescence. This period (13-18 years) is characterized by rapid growth and development at all levels i.e., physical, physiological, psychological and social as described below.

Growth Spurt

The second and final growth spurt occurs during this period. The process of physical development from a child to an adult is called puberty. The growth spurt occurs in girls at approximately 11-14 years and in boys 13-16 years. Growth in girls in terms of height and weight is maximum prior to menarche. It is very rare that girls gain height after menarche, which is hardly 2-3 cm. In boys growth continues till late teens. They tend to gain weight at a faster rate and by 18-20 years, they have achieved their full height.

Physical Physiological, Physiological and Psychological Changes

Body Composition

Body composition changes during the period of maturation. The changes occur due to hormonal influence which regulate the development of sex characteristics.

The skeletal growth continues for a longer period of time for boys than girls. Usually the skeleton reaches its full maturity by 17 years for girls and by 20 years for boys. As mineralization increases the water content decreases.

Girls tend to deposit more fat whereas boys add more muscle mass. The result of pubertal changes is that boys have more lean body mass, skeletal weight and less adipose tissue as a ratio of total body mass. This difference in body composition for boys and girls is reflected in their nutrient requirements.

Sexual Maturity

The growth spurt is accompanied by sexual maturity. In girls there is development of breasts, auxiliary and pubic hair and menarche. In boys the pubertal changes include deepening of voice, broadening of shoulders, development of auxiliary and pubic hair, growth of penis and testicles.

Psycho Social Changes

As this period is a transition to adulthood, they try to develop self identity. The desire to be accepted in their peer group changes their food habits, dressing and group conduct. This in turn brings psychological, emotional and social stress.

NUTRIENT ALLOWANCES

The recommended dietary allowances for adolescents is presented in Table 1.

Energy

The metabolic demands of growth and energy expenditure increases the calorie needs. The ICMR committee has suggested that energy should be provided on the basis of ideal weight for age. The energy requirements for boys is more than that of girls which is 2450 k.cal. and 2640 k.cal for boys 13-15 years and 16-18 years respectively and 2060 k.cal for girls of 13 to 18 years. The difference in energy requirements can be attributed to the rapid increase in weight for boys.

Protein

The protein requirements are computed in the same way as for adults. The protein needs represent 12-14 percent of the total energy requirements. This meets the need for growth, for pubertal changes in both sexes and for developing lean body mass in boys.

Table 1: ICMR recommended dietary allowances for Adolescents

	Boys		Girls	
Nutrients	13-15 yrs	16-18 yrs	13-15 yrs	16-18 yrs
Energy (k.cal)	2450	2640	2060	2060
Protein (g)	70	78	65	63
Fat (g)	22	22	22	22
Calcium (mg)	600	500	600	500
Iron (mg)	41	50	28	30
Vitamin A				
Retinol (mg) or	600	600	600	600
b Carotene (mg)	2400	2400	2400	2400
Thiamine (mg)	1.2	1.3	1.0	1.0
Riboflavin (mg)	1.5	1.6	1.2	1.2
Niacin (mg)	16	17	14	14
Pyridoxine (mg)	2.0	2.0	2.0	2.0
Vitamin C (mg)	40	40	40	40
Folic acid (mg)	100	100	100	100
Vitamin B12 (mg)	0.2-1.0	0.2-1.0	0.2-1.0	0.2-1.0

Calcium

Bone growth requires calcium. Calcium requirements are

based on calcium accretion during the period of growth. About 150 mg of calcium should be retained for increasing bone mass. Hence the allowance for boys is more than girls because of their increased skeletal growth.

Iron

The increase in body mass during adolescence correspond to 4.3 kg/year in boys and 4 kg/year in girls. The haemoglobin concentration increases by 2g /dl in boys and 1g/dl in girls. Therefore the iron required for growth alone is 0.7 mg / day in boys and 0.45 mg/day in girls. Moreover there is additional loss of iron in girls during menstruation which is significant from 13 years onwards which amounts to 0.45 to 0.5 mg/day. Hence considering the additional requirement for

- growth spurt
- expansion of blood volume
- increase in haemoglobin concentration
- additional iron to compensate menstrual losses in girls and
- adding the basal loss of iron,

the requirements for iron have been arrived at 41 mg/day and 28 mg/day for boys and girls 13 – 15 years of age, and 50 mg /day and 30 mg / day for boys and girls 16-18 years of age respectively. The higher requirement of iron for boys than girls may be attributed to the low percentage of iron absorption in adolescent boys (3 percent) than adolescent girls (5 percent).

Vitamins

The requirement for B vitamins namely thiamine, riboflavin and niacin increases in direct proportion with increase in calorie intake. Folic acid and vitamin B_{12}

requirements also increase when there is rapid tissue synthesis as they participate in synthesis of DNA and RNA. Transamination to synthesize non-essential amino acids requires more vitamin B_6. The structural and functional integrity of newly formed cells depends on the availability of vitamins A, C and E. Table 2 gives the balanced diet for adolescents.

Table 2: Balanced diet for adolescents (13 – 18 years)

S.No.	Food Groups	Quantity (g)	
		Boys	Girls
1.	Cereals and Millets	420	300
2.	Pulses	60	60
3.	Milk (ml)	500	500
4.	Roots and Tuber	200	100
5.	Green leafy vegetables	100	100
6.	Other vegetables	100	100
7.	Fruits	100	100
8.	Sugar	35	30
9.	Fats / oils (visible)	25	25

For Non-Veg 30 g of pulse can be exchanged with 50 g of meat / chicken /fish/ egg.

Change in Eating Habits

Psychological pressures on adolescents influence their eating habits. Boys generally tend to have a better appetite than girls and this helps them to meet their nutritional demands. The adolescent girls are at a disadvantage due to the following reasons.

1. with considerable amount of fat deposits and less physical activity than boys, girls may gain weight.
2. figure consciousness due to social pressure may force her into a self imposed crash diet for weight

loss or self starvation leading to eating disorders like bulimia and anorexia nervosa.

The adolescents also develop a liking for fast foods which are nutritionally inadequate and rich in saturated fats and may skip meals at times.

Hence adolescents should be educated to consume a balanced nutritional diet including iron rich, calcium rich, protein rich foods and avoiding junk foods providing empty calories.

The adolescents should be advised not to miss meals and that, emotions should not dominate during meal times.

EATING DISORDERS

Binge Eating

Binge eating is a eating disorder characterized by the consumption of a large amount of food in a small amount of time and may start at any age often not recognized till adulthood. The individual suffering from this is either overweight or obese and suffer from consequent disorders like high blood pressure, hypercholesterolemia and type II diabetes.

Food habits of binge eating:

a. Frequent dieting with erratic increase and decrease in weight.

b. Eating only when hungry or eating to the point of extreme discomfort or consuming large amount during a short time.

c. Avoiding eating at a social gathering or eating only small amounts in front of others.

d. Either avoiding physical activity or anything that may invite attention or increased awareness about one's own body.

They show psychological changes and the signs include

a. Depression, loneliness, guilt or shame and having a low self esteem.

b. Not able to control when eating and unable to stop binges.

c. Being preoccupied with dieting, body weight or food.

Both psychological and nutritional counselling is extremely important for binge eaters.

Anorexia Nervosa

Anorexia nervosa is an eating disorder characterized by refusal to eat and loss of body weight. This is more common among adolescent girls when they try to avoid eating food due to over consciousness of their figure and social stress.

They appear extremely thin or emaciated due to rapid weight loss and complaint of nausea, vomiting or bloating after consuming normal food. Girls suffer from loss of mensturation.

They refuse to eat, deny hunger or eat tiny portions of food. They rigidly avoid specific foods like meat and milk.

They exercise heavily and show a different behaviour while eating such as using special utensils while eating or cutting food into fine pieces or eating very small spoons at a time.

Bulimia Nervosa

This is in quite contrast with anorexia nervosa. Bulimia nervosa is a eating disorder characterized by periods of bingeing and purging and developing unrealistic ideas about food.

The bulimic adolescents eat large quantities of food and then binge. The consequences are

— dental enamel erosion
— dental cavities
— swollen cheeks
— callus on back of hands
— fatigue and weakness due to malnutrition
— irregular menstrual period.

Figure 1 gives the viscious cycle of eating disorders

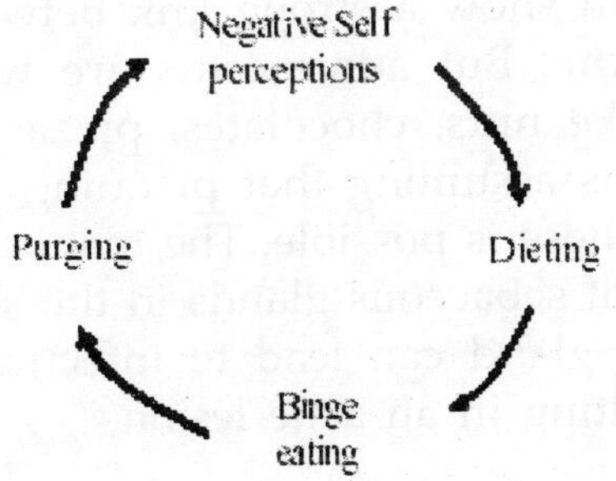

Figure 1: Viscious Cycle of Eating Disorders

Nutrition Related Problems

Anaemia

There is an increasing trend towards a decrease in age of menarche both in upper affluent class and rural communities making adolescent girls susceptible to anaemia. About 20-25 percent of adolescent girls suffer from anaemia irrespective of their social class. The impact is more profound in rural girls because of non-availability of healthy foods. Likes and dislikes and eating disorders also lead to anaemia.

Obesity

It affects 10-20 percent of adolescent population. Lack of exercise rather than excess calorie consumption is the cause. Concern about personal appearance may make adolescents more reluctant to participate in activities like sports. Obesity may also be due to hormonal imbalance, emotional stress or family habits.

Acne Vulgarise

Acne is a common concern among adolescents and about 80 percent of teens experience it. Scientific studies have been unable to show a strong link between any dietary factor and acne. But adolescents are warned to avoid junk foods like nuts, chocolates, pizzas, chips, candies and ice creams assuming that planning a well balanced diet without these is possible. The main culprit of acne is over activity of sebaceous glands in the skin. Blockage in a duct in the gland can lead to infection and localized pressure resulting in an acne lesion.

Malnutrition Due to Teenage Pregnancy

Teenage mothers are considered to be at high risk as maternal death and infant mortality rates are higher among them. The biological immaturity has a greater impact on pregnancy. Malnutrition sets in when the pregnant adolesent girl fails to meet the demands of not only her growth but also that of the foetus. This has a direct bearing on the outcome of pregnancy. Lactation failure is also common. Teenage mothers fail to breast feed their infants adequately resulting in high infant morbidity rate.

Good nutrition and fostering healthy eating habits during adolescence paves way for a healthy adulthood.

7

Nutrition for Adults

By the time an individual reaches adulthood, body growth especially in terms of height and body status stop to a certain extent, but tissue breakdown and repair of body tissues continues even among adults. Therefore adequate amount of essential nutrients need to be provided for maintenance of physical and mental health in adults. Though adulthood does not feature psychological and social stress as in school age or adolescence, the family and social responsibilities of the individual increases. This is when they tend to lead an independent living and many, both men and women, are breadwinners for their family. Entry into married life adds to their responsibilities, especially women who should be prepared to bear the physiological stress during pregnancy and lactation.

There may also be changes in lifestyle pattern based on their occupation, which may change their eating habits. The physical and mental stress due to their job, family and social pressure make adequate nutrition a necessity to safeguard the health of this highly productive age group.

Dietary Allowances

Since individual variations are high, the ICMR has

suggested the recommended allowances based on reference Indian man and woman.

Reference Indian man has been defined as "an adult man between 20 – 39 years of age, weighing 60 kg. He is free from diseases and physically fit for active work. On each working day he is employed for eight hours in occupation that usually involves moderate activity. While not at work he spends eight hours in bed, four to six hours in sitting and moving about and two hours in walking, active recreation or house hold duties". For such a reference man the ICMR has taken an average height of 163 cm.

Reference Indian woman is defined as "an adult woman between 20 – 39 years of age, weighing 50 kg. She may be engaged for eight hours in general house hold work, in light industry or in any other moderately active work. Apart from eight hours in bed, she spends four to six hours in sitting and moving around (light activity) and two hours in walking, active recreation or household duties". For such as reference woman the ICMR has taken a height of 151 cm.

Energy

The energy requirement of an individual has been defined as "the level of energy intake from food that will balance energy expenditure when the individual has body size and composition and level of physical activity, consistent with long term good health and that will allow for maintenance of economically necessary and socially desirable activity". The components of energy expenditure include

a. Basal Metabolic Rate (BMR)

b. Regulatory thermogenesis which includes the metabolic response to food ingested and stimuli such as cold, stimulants and drugs.

c. Nature and duration of activity. The allowances for those engaged in heavy work should be higher than those doing either sedentary or moderate work.

Protein

Studies on Indian adults have revealed that the minimum intake of dietary protein to maintain nitrogen equilibrium, on an average, is 0.58 g/kg body weight. After allowing for sweat losses the intake works out to 0.7 g/kg. The corresponding safe level of intake has been computed to be 0.88 g/kg body weight. Hence the ICMR has recommended 1.0 g protein per kg body weight for both men and women. Since protein needs are not affected by activity the RDA for an protein is 60 g/day and 50 g/day for adult man and adult woman respectively.

Fat

The two factors that need to be considered while assessing fat requirements are

a. The invisible fat in the diet which supplies majority of the essential fatty acid requirements.

b. A certain amount of visible fat is required to meet requirements of two essential fatty acids i.e., linoliec and linolenic fatty acids.

The requirement of linoleic acid has been estimated to be 3 percent of total energy requirement, which can be met by 12 g of visible fat. To provide energy density and palatability to the diet the ICMR has suggested 20 g visible fat per day. The type of visible fat used is also important. Oils containing high amount of saturated fatty acids may increase the linoleic acid requirements and are detrimental to health. Hence combination of oils with equal proportion of saturated, monounsaturated and polyunsaturated fatty acids has been recommended.

Calcium and Phosphorus

In adults calcium is required for replacing calcium lost from body through urine, faeces, sweat and bile. Of the dietary calcium only 20 to 30 percent is absorbed and this is facilitated by vitamin D. Long term balance studies have shown that a positive calcium balance can be achieved by an intake of 300 to 500 mg of calcium daily. ICMR has suggested 400 mg calcium / day for both men and women.

Along with this, a desirable intake of phosphorus is recommended as the functions of calcium and phosphorus is closely linked. The elemental Ca:P ratio in the diet should be maintained at 1:1.

Iron

The loss of iron through sweat, gastrointestinal tract and urine is estimated to be 14 mg/kg body weight. Apart from this women have additional loss due to menstruation which varies between 0.5 to 1mg per day (an addition of 16 mg/kg taken as the upper limit). Based on these the iron requirements are arrived at as 28 mg for men and 30 mg for women per day respectively.

Vitamins

a. Vitamin A

Studies have revealed that 600 mg of retinol daily would be sufficient to maintain a normal serum vitamin A level at 20 mg / 100 ml. Hence the ICMR has suggested 600 mg of retinol for both men and women equivalent to 2400 mg of b carotene. Since Indian diets contain both retinol and b carotene it is advisable to express the Vitamin A content of diet in terms of retinol equivalents.

Retinol equivalent = mg of retinol + ¼ mg of b - carotene.

b. B Complex vitamins

The requirement for B Vitamins is based on calorie intake i.e. 0.5 mg / 1000 k.cal, 0.6mg / 1000 k.cal and 6.6 mg / 1000 k.cal for thiamine, riboflavin and niacin respectively. The RDA for pyridoxine is 2.0 mg/day for both adult man and woman.

The minimal daily requirement of folic acid among Indians is 75 mg of folate. In this view the safe level of intake has been suggested to be 100 mg of folate per day. Due to lack of precise data on bioavailability of food folates ICMR has recommended 100 mg of free folate per day for adults.

c. Vitamin C (Ascorbic Acid)

The concentration of Vitamin C in circulating leukocytes reflects the tissue concentration. Based on this a daily intake of 20 mg vitamin C is sufficient to maintain satisfactory ascorbic acid status. Considering 50 percent loss of vitamin C during cooking ICMR has recommended RDA of 40 mg vitamin C per day for both men and women.

A sample vegetarian menu for a adult woman doing sedentary work is given below.

Meal	Menu	Raw Amounts
Early morning	Milk /Coffee / Tea	Milk - 100 ml
		Sugar - 10 g
Break fast	Upma - 11/2 cup, fruit	Cereal - 75 g
		Fruit - 50 g
Lunch	Rice - 1 cup	Cereal - 100g
	Phulkas - 2 No's	
	Dhal - ½ cup	Pulse - 20 g
	Amaranth poriyal 1cup	Green leafe vegetable-100 g
	Vegetable Raita	Vegetable - 50 gm

	Curd - ½ cup	Milk - 100 ml
Tea	Samosa - 2 no	Cereal - 50 g
		Potato - 50 g
	Tea 1 cup	Milk - 100 ml
		Sugar - 10 g
Dinner	Dosai 3 no	Cereal - 75 g
	Sambar ½ cup	Pulse - 40 g
	Vegetable salad	Vegetable - 100 g
		Fruit Fruit - 50 g
Bed time	Milk	Milk - 100 ml
		Sugar - 5 g

Nutrition Related Problem Among Adults

Being a productive age group, adequate nutrition is important for adults to maintain their productivity. Inadequate nutrition, besides leading to various nutrient related problems also results in subsequent physical and psychological disturbances leading to absenteeism from work, poor concentration, lethargy and emotional distress. All these affect not only the economy of the family but superimposes the same on other family members and the viscious cycle continues.

The various nutrient related problems that commonly occur among adults are as follows:

Anaemia

Anaemia is a common nutritional problem especially among Indian women. Women in the reproductive age group are the most affected. The causes of anaemia may be

— Inadequate diet in quality and quantity, deficient in folate, Iron, B Complex vitamins and vitamin C.

— Excessive menstruation

— Poverty
— Lack of awareness of food values
— Poor environmental hygiene and sanitation

Obesity

This can occur at any age and in either sex as long as the person is under positive energy balance. Besides genetic inheritance and physical inactivity, faulty eating habits contributes to obesity. These include nibbling between meals, eating more, eating fast with less chewing and housewives eating leftovers.

The concept of a balanced nutritious diet should be introduced even in the work place starting with the industrial canteens where more number of high calorie snack items are sold. These can be substituted with nutritious snacks prepared using green leafy vegetables and other vegetables and with limited frying.

Diabetes Mellitus

Type II diabetes is more prevalent among adults. Obese individuals are identified to be at risk. Malnutrition related diabetes occurs in young people between 15 to 30 years of age who are lean and undernourished. Acute stress more common among working women and executives is another cause.

Underweight

Adults with Body Mass Index (BMI) of less than 18.5 have reduced capacity for sustaining heavy work and therefore decreased productivity.

Coronary Heart Disease (CHD)

Those in the high socioeconomic group who adapt a sedentary life style and have a high intake of saturated fatty acids tend to develop CHD. The incidence is high in obese individuals.

8

Nutrition During Old Age

Individuals above the age of 60 years constitute the elderly. However the increasing number of healthy and active people among the elderly has led to the need for more defenitive age groupings. Thus the specific age groups of 65-75, 75-85 and older are often referred to as the young old, old and the oldest old respectively. Today the elderly constitute about seven percent of the total population and the projected figure is ten percent by 2016. Hence health and well being of the elderly is given more importance and has paved way for a specific field of study called 'Geriartric Nutrition".

Aging

Aging is a irreversible biochemical change that occurs throughout an individuals life cycle and continues until death. Genes are the major determinants of nature of aging. Health and good nutrition may delay the process of aging. Aging varies among individuals depending on their nutritional status and living environmental conditions.

In old age, the nutritional status is determined by the state of nutrition of an individual cell. Conditions like dietary deficiency, improper digestion and absorption, insufficient distribution of nutrients, accumulation of excess waste products lead to poor nourishment of cells.

With increasing age, cell functioning is slowed down and the response to harmones and synthesis of enzymes decreases. These changes are associated with a decrease in the number of functioning cells. Since the cells are interdependent, if one cell dies, others of the same or different organ lose their ability to function resulting in malfunctioning of the organ. This in turn gradually affects the total body function leading to death.

Physiological and Psychological Changes

The process of aging is associated with various changes, which are as follows.

Physical Changes

Old people develop physical changes due to the process of maturation like graying of hair, wrinkled skin, decline in height and a bowed posture. There may be loss of vision and decrease in sense of learning. Their physical strength and vigour also decreases.

Physiological Changes

The physiological decline in body functions during aging is not uniform. It varies among different organs. The capacity of the system may not decline but their ability to respond to a challenge or to maintain homeostasis is lowered. The physiological changes that occur in various systems are as follows.

Taste and smell

There is a decrease in the number of taste buds and papillae on the tongue. The ability to taste salt is very much decreased whereas that to sugar in less altered. Besides there is a reduction in olfactory sensitivity which decreases the ability to detect the flavour. This decreases the palatability of the food resulting in poor intake.

Diminished taste and smell decreases the sensory stimulation that may impair metabolic processes.

Salivary Glands

Decrease in salivary secretion or lack of salivation (xerostomia) causes a feeling of dry mouth, which makes chewing and swallowing difficult. Hence crunchy, dry and sticky foods are avoided by old people.

Teeth

They may lose teeth or have ill fitting dentures which makes chewing difficult. They may omit fresh vegetables and fruits. This may lead to vitamin and mineral deficiency accompanied by decreased gastrointestinal motility and problems in elimination like constipation.

Gastrointestinal function

The secretion of digestive enzymes and digestive juices decline. This results in incomplete digestion, or food remaining longer in stomach for digestion. The secretion of hydrochloric acid, intrinsic factor and pepsin decreases which affects absorption of calcium, protein, iron and vitamin B_{12}.

Above 60 years of age the rate of emptying of liquids is rapid which again leads to decreased absorption of nutrients. The pH of proximal small bowel increases and there is bacterial over growth in the bowel.

In the small intestine there is decreased secretion of enzyme lactase, which can be a risk factor for developing osteoporosis. Thinning of gastrointestinal layer decreases gastric motility and prolonged transit through the colon leading to constipation.

Liver and biliary function

There is a decrease in blood flow to the liver. This may

lead to minor structural and biochemical changes. Gall bladder becomes sluggish in releasing bile, which impairs fat metabolism and increases susceptibility to gall stones. The activity of drug metabolising enzymes decrease and therefore lower drug doses need to be prescribed during old age.

Metabolic Function

There is a decrease in metabolic rate and impaired glucose tolerance, which necessitate dietary modifications. The body protein levels also decrease.

Neurological Function

There is a decrease in neuromuscular coordination. They may develop a state of confusion. There is a decreased synthesis of seratonin. Carnitine derived from the aminoacids lysine and methionine may be effective in slowing down mental deterioration. Carotenoids play a protective role related to aging and cognitive function.

Cardiovascular function

Changes in blood vessels such as narrowing of the lumen, thickening of the arterial walls and replacement of elastic muscle fibres with non elastic fibres lead to increased rigidity of vessels (atherosclerotic changes) which reduces their capacity to carry nutrients to the cells. There is decreased myocardial contractibility and increased peripheral resistance, increasing the prevalence of hypertension.

Renal function

There is a decrease in Glomerular Filtration Rate (GFR) affecting the elimination of waste products and reabsorption of electrolytes. Moreover, the body's ability to regenerate nephrons ceases after 40 years of age.

Hence increased solute load on each nephron may lead to necrosis and kidney damage.

Skeletal tissue

Demineralisation of bones is more rapid than mineralisation. The bones become increasingly vulnerable to fractures and the vertebrae may collapse. This results in decline in height and a stooped or bowed posture. This posture may affect respiratory function.

Pulmonary function

Pulmonary capacity declines by about 40 percent throughout life. Among elderly this may not have an impact on health but may impose restriction on energetic exercise.

Harmonal changes

Activity of various glands like thyroid, adrenal cortex, islets of langerhans is decreased resulting in changes in metabolism and metabolic functions. The hormonal imbalance affects the calcium metabolism leading to osteoporosis and bone loss. Menopause in women decreases their iron requirements.

Psychological Change

Loneliness

With increasing urbanization and generation gap, nuclear family systems have emerged. The elderly are considered irrelevant and redundant by their own families and are left lonely. Loneliness leads to depression and in turn loss of appetite. They tend to follow irregular meal times leading to malnutrition.

Economic aspects

Among many elderly individuals financial constraints often limit their food intake.

Anxiety

Emotional stress and deprivation leads to alterations in food habits and attitude towards food. In addition, hormonal changes associated with anxiety depress the flow of digestive juices which may result in impaired digestion and absorption.

Loss of self esteem and independence

With retirement the elderly may experience a loss of self esteem. With decreasing physical strength, mobility and diminishing financial resources their dependence on others increase. They sometimes feel powerless leaving the task of decision making to youngsters. This may cause depression and frustration among elderly.

Nutritional Needs

Energy

The energy requirement decreases due to

a. decreased physical activity

b. reduction in lean body mass and increase in adipose tissue,

c decrease in resting metabolic rate by 15-20 percent due to changes in body composition and physical inactivity.

The calorie intake should be adjusted to maintain weight. The energy requirements for different age groups 60 years and above are given in table 1.

Table 1: Energy requirement (k.cal / 24 hrs) of male and female 60 years and above with different body weights

Sex	Body weight Kg	Energy requirement for sedentary activity k.cal
Male	60	1976

	65	2072
	70	2176
	75	2280
Females	60	1864
	65	1944
	70	2024

Protein

The protein requirement do not change during old age. It is the same as adults i.e. 1g / kg of body weight. Since the calories are reduced without decrease in proteins the diet should be protein rich when compared to a normal adult diet.

Carbohydrate

Since the calorie requirement is reduced the carbohydrate content should also be proportionately reduced. Due to impaired glucose tolerance and gastro intestinal disturbances like constipation, emphasis should be on taking complex carbohydrates.

Fat

The fat requirements are also reduced corresponding to the energy requirements. The intake of saturated fat should be less and that of unsaturated fat more.

Minerals

Calcium needs increases during old age due to increasing mobilization of calcium from bones and incidence of osteoporosis. During old age 1000mg of calcium is recommended per day because of the following reasons.

a. Limited availability of calcium from foods.

b. To compensate age related bone loss and to improve calcium balance.

c. To prevent fractures and tooth decay.

d. To compensate decreased efficiency in calcium absorption.

Aging does not affect iron needs. Hence iron needs are same as that for adults. Mild anaemia may affect the health of old people due to inefficient circulation. Therefore iron intake should be adequate during old age.

Vitamins

a. Vitamin A requirements remain the same i.e., 600 mg of retinol

b. Inadequate exposure to sunshine may affect vitamin D levels in which case supplementation may be required.

c. Vitamin C requirements increase due to stress and medications. The antioxidant vitamins such as vitamin E, carotenoids and vitamin C have been identified to promote health of the elderly.

d. Vitamin B_6 requirements are also increased due to atrophic gastritis which interferes with absorption. Liver dysfunction is an additional risk factor for Vit. B_6 deficiency.

Besides these various nutrients, water should be consumed in plenty as such or as fluids like buttermilk, fruit juice and soups. Intake of sufficient fluids reduce the load on kidneys and relieves from constipation by stimulating peristalisis.

The quantity of food stuffs to be included in a balanced diet for elderly is given in Table 2.

Table 2: Balanced diet for an elderly person for a day

Food Stuff	Quantity (raw) g	
	Males	Females

Cereals	350	225
Pulses	50	40
Vegetables	200	150
Green Leafy vegetables	50	50
Roots and Tubers	100	100
Fruits	200	200
Milk and Milk Products	300	300
Sugar	20	20
Fats and oils	25	20

Nutrition Related Problem of Elderly

The elderly are at risk of poor nutrition due to economic pressure, poor dentition, aging tissues and inadequate diet, which may be compounded with the incidence of chronic disease. The commonly prevalent nutrition related problems among the aged include;

Osteoporosis

Osteoporosis is characterized by decreasing bone mass and density. As a result the bones become porous, light and fragile becoming more vulnerable to fractures. The incidence of osteoporosis is more common in women after menopause.

Obesity

Many of the elderly are obese. They fail to make adjustments in their energy intake corresponding to decreased energy needs.

Anaemia

Anaemia characterized by feeling of fatigue, anxiety, lack of energy is common. Iron inadequacy is caused by low dietary intake, decreased absorption or lack of haem iron, vitamin C or blood loss. Pernicious anaemia due to vitamin B12 deficiency is common among elderly women.

The diet for elderly should include foods rich in haem iron and vitamin B12.

Malnutrition

The causes of malnutrition during old age are

a) economic constraints

b) physical inactivity

c) cumulative effect of chronic disease and medication

d) social isolation

e) lack of knowledge in preparing meals adequate to meet their needs

Constipation

Aging disturbs the natural rythmic contraction of colon due to

a) loss of tone

b) stress

c) medications

d) lack of exercise

e) low fibre diet

f) insufficient fluid intake.

These result in constipation. Excess use of laxatives or enemas may also cause constipation.

Diabetes Mellitus

The incidence of Non Insulin Dependent Diabetes Mellitus (NIDDM) is increased due to impaired glucose tolerance and decreased sensitivity of cells to insulin.

Cardiovascular Disease

The incidence of hypertension and other cardiovascular diseases like atherosclerosis, acute myocardial infarction, angina pectoris, and congestive heart failure is high due to changes in cardio vascular function. These may impose dietary restrictions, change in texture of diet and use of diuretics and hypotensives. These inturn may affect the dietary intake and health of the individual.

Modifications in the Diet

The various physical, physiological and psychological changes during oldage necessitate the following modifications in the diet.

1. The problems of dentition or loss of teeth create the need to include foods with soft texture and that are easily chewable.
2. Foods should be easily digestible as there is a decrease in production of digestive enzymes.
3. Fat should be restricted to prevent obesity and susceptibility to cardiovascular diseases. Foods rich in saturated fat should be avoided.
4. Energy rich foods like sweets, fried foods and starchy foods need to be avoided.
5. Foods rich in calcium like milk and milk products should be given to compensate bone loss and reduce osteoporosis.
6. Fresh fruits, vegetables and green leafy vegetables should be included liberally which supply vitamins, minerals and fibre and are rich in antioxidants. Fruits and vegetables may be given as fresh juices, purees, soups and salads.
7. Coffee, tea and carbonated beverages should be restricted as they may result in insomnia (lack of sleep) due to over stimulation.
8. Small frequent meals may be given instead of three large meals which will aid in complete digestion.

9. Plenty of fluids need to be included to prevent constipation and dehydration.
10. Salt intake should be reduced.

Good nutrition during old age is of immense significance and care should be taken to see that the diets are nutritionally adequate, well balanced and suitable for consumption.

First of October is celebrated as world elders day.

Recipes for the Elderly

With changing socio economic environment sometimes the elderly people are forced to live on their own and cook their own food. Hence they need some simple but nutritious recipes to maintain good health.

The recipes should

— be nutritious
— be easy to cook
— involve minimum time for cooking or no cooking
— be ready to eat

A few easy to cook and ready to eat recipes have been formulated by National Institute of Nutrition, Hyderabad which are as follows.

	Easy to cook		Ready to eat
1.	Dalia (made from dhal)	1.	Coconut laddu Green Gram Broken wheat
2.	Ragi Ambli	2.	Groundnut Chikki
3.	Rava Upma	3.	Black gram dhal laddu
4.	Kichedi	4.	Groundnut biscuits
5.	Curd Salad	5.	Cheera
6.	Suji Kheer		
7.	Rice		
8.	Methi Paratha		
9.	Pohe (Rice flakes upma)		

9

Vitamin A

Vitamin A in Human Metabolic Processes

Vitamin A (retinol) is an essential nutrient needed in small amounts by humans for the normal functioning of the visual system; growth and development; and maintenance of epithelial cellular integrity, immune function, and reproduction. These dietary needs for vitamin A are normally provided for as preformed retinol (mainly as retinyl ester) and provitamin A carotenoids.

Preformed vitamin A in animal foods occurs as retinyl esters of fatty acids in association with membrane-bound cellular lipid and fat-containing storage cells. Provitamin A carotenoids in foods of vegetable origin are also associated with cellular lipids but are embedded in complex cellular structures such as the cellulose-containing matrix of chloroplasts or the pigment-containing portion of chromoplasts. Normal digestive processes free vitamin A and carotenoids from food matrices, which is a more efficient process from animal than from vegetable tissues. Retinyl esters are hydrolysed and the retinol and freed carotenoids are incorporated into lipid-containing, water-miscible micellar solutions. Products of fat digestion (e.g. fatty acids, monoglycerides, cholesterol, and phospholipids) and secretions in bile (e.g. bile salts and hydrolytic enzymes) are essential for the efficient solubilization of retinol and especially for solubilization of the very lipophilic carotenoids (e.g. α-and βcarotene, β-cryptoxanthin, and lycopene) in the aqueous intestinal milieu.Micellar solubilization is a prerequisite to their efficient passage into the lipidrich membrane of intestinal mucosal cells (i.e. enterocytes). Diets critically low in dietary fat (under about 5–10 g daily) or disease conditions that interfere with normal digestion and absorption leading to steatorrhoea (e.g. pancreatic and liver diseases and frequent gastroenteritis) can therefore impede the efficient absorption of retinol and carotenoids. Retinol and some carotenoids enter the intestinal mucosal brush border by diffusion in accord with the concentration gradient between the micelle and plasma membrane of enterocytes. Some carotenoids pass into the enterocyte and are solubilized into chylomicrons without further change whereas some of the provitamin A carotenoids are converted to retinol by a cleavage enzyme in the brush border Retinol is trapped intracellularly by re-esterification or binding to specific intracellular binding proteins. Retinyl esters and unconverted carotenoids together with other lipids are incorporated into chylomicrons, excreted into intestinal lymphatic channels, and delivered to the blood through the thoracic duct.

Tissues extract most lipids and some carotenoids from circulating chylomicrons, but most retinyl esters are stripped from the chylomicron remnant, hydrolysed, and taken up primarily by parenchymal liver cells. If not immediately needed, retinol is re-esterified and retained in the fat-storing cells of the liver (variously called adipocytes, stellate cells, or Ito cells). The liver parenchymal cells also take in substantial amounts of carotenoids. Whereas most of the body's vitamin A reserve remains in the liver, carotenoids are also deposited elsewhere in fatty tissues throughout the body. Usually, turnover of carotenoids in tissues is relatively slow, but in times of low dietary carotenoid intake, stored carotenoids are mobilized. A recent study in one subject using stable isotopes suggests that retinol can be derived not only from conversion of dietary provitamin carotenoids in enterocytes—the major site of bioconversion—but also from hepatic conversion of circulating provitamin carotenoids. The quantitative contribution to vitamin A requirements of carotenoid converted to retinoids beyond the enterocyte is unknown.

Following hydrolysis of stored retinyl esters, retinol combines with a plasma-specific transport protein, retinol-binding protein (RBP). This process, including synthesis of the unoccupied RBP (apo-RBP), occurs to the greatest extent within liver cells but it may also occur in some peripheral tissues. The RBP-retinol complex (holo-RBP) is secreted into the blood where it associates with another hepatically synthesized and excreted larger protein, transthyretin. The transthyretin-RBP-retinol complex circulates in the blood, delivering the lipophilic retinol to tissues; its large size prevents its loss through kidney filtration. Dietary restriction in energy, proteins, and some micronutrients can limit hepatic synthesis of proteins specific to mobilization and transport of vitamin A. Altered kidney functions or fever associated with infections (e.g. respiratory infections or diarrhoea) can increase urinary vitamin A loss.

Holo-RBP transiently associates with target tissue membranes, and specific intracellular binding proteins then extract the retinol. Some of the transiently sequestered retinol is released into the blood unchanged and is recycled (i.e. conserved). A limited reserve of intracellular retinyl esters is formed that subsequently can provide functionally active retinol and its oxidation products (i.e. isomers of retinoic acid) as needed intracellularly. These biologically active forms of vitamin A are associated with specific cellular proteins which bind with retinoids within cells during metabolism and with nuclear receptors that mediate retinoid action on the genome. Retinoids modulate the transcription of several hundreds of genes. In addition to the latter role of retinoic acid, retinol is the form required for functions in the visual and reproductive systems and during embryonic development. Holo-RBP is filtered into the glomerulus but recovered from the kidney tubule and recycled. Normally vitamin A leaves the body in urine only as inactive metabolites resulting from tissue utilization and in bile secretions as potentially recyclable active glucuronide conjugates of retinol. No single urinary metabolite has been identified which accurately reflects tissue levels of vitamin A or its rate of utilization. Hence, at this time urine is not a useful biological fluid for assessment of vitamin A nutriture.

Biochemical Mechanisms for Vitamin A

A functions Vitamin A functions at two levels in the body: the first is in the visual cycle in the retina of the eye; the second is in all body tissues where it systemically maintains the growth and soundness of cells. In the visual system, carrierbound retinol is transported to ocular tissue and to the retina by intracellular binding and transport proteins. Rhodopsin, the visual pigment critical to dim-light vision, is formed in rod cells after conversion of all-*trans*-retinol to retinaldehyde, isomerization to the 11-*cis*-form, and binding to opsin. Alteration of rhodopsin through a cascade of photochemical reactions results in the ability to see objects in dim light. The speed at which rhodopsin is regenerated is related to the availability of retinol. Night blindness is usually an indicator of inadequate available retinol, but it can also be due to a deficit of other nutrients that are critical to the regeneration of rhodopsin, such as protein and zinc, and to some inherited diseases, such as retinitis pigmentosa.

The growth and differentiation of epithelial cells throughout the body are especially affected by vitamin A deficiency (VAD). In addition, goblet cell numbers are reduced in epithelial tissues and as a consequence, mucous secretions (with their antimicrobial components) diminish. Cells lining protective tissue surfaces fail to regenerate and differentiate, hence they flatten and accumulate keratin. Both factors—the decline in mucous secretions and loss of cellular integrity—reduce the body's ability to resist invasion from potentially pathogenic organisms. Pathogens can also compromise the immune system by directly interfering with the production of some types of protective secre-tions and cells. Classical symptoms of xerosis (drying or non-wetability) and desquamation of dead surface cells as seen in ocular tissue (i.e. xerophthalmia) are the external evidence of the changes also occurring to various degrees in internal epithelial tissues.

Current understanding of the mechanism of vitamin A action within cells outside the visual cycle is that cellular functions are mediated through specific nuclear receptors. Binding with specific isomers of retinoic acid (i.e. all*trans*-and 9-*cis*-retinoic acid) activates these receptors. Activated receptors bind to DNA response elements located upstream of specific genes to regulate the level of expression of those genes. These retinoid-activated genes regulate the synthesis of a large number of proteins vital to maintaining normal physiologic functions. There may, however, be other mechanisms of action that are as yet undiscovered.

Consequences of Vitamin A Deficiency

VAD is not easily defined. WHO defines it as tissue

concentrations of vitamin A low enough to have adverse health consequences even if there is no evidence of clinical xerophthalmia. In addition to the specific signs and symptoms of xerophthalmia and the risk of irreversible blindness, nonspecific symptoms include increased morbidity and mortality, poor reproductive health, increased risk of anaemia, and contributions to slowed growth and development. However, these nonspecific adverse effects may be caused by other nutrient deficits as well, making it difficult to attribute non-ocular symptoms specifically to VAD in the absence of biochemical measurements reflective of vitamin A status.

Geographic Distribution and Magnitude

In 1995, WHO estimated the global distribution of VAD and categorized countries according to the seriousness of VAD as a public health problem on the basis of both clinical and moderate and severe subclinical (prevalence of low blood levels of retinol) indicators of deficiency. It was estimated that about 3 million children have some form of xerophthalmia and, on the basis of blood levels, another 250 million are subclinically deficient. The magnitude of the subclinical estimate is currently being re-evaluated to establish quantitatively a benchmark for measuring prevalence trends. The actual number of subclinical deficiencies based on the prevalence of low serum levels of retinol, however, remains uncertain because of the confounding and poorly quantified role of infections.

Epidemiological studies repeatedly report clustering of VAD, presumably resulting from concurrent occurrences of several risk factors. This clustering may occur among both neighbourhoods and households.

Age and Sex

VAD can occur in individuals of any age. However, it is a disabling and potentially fatal public health problem for children under 6 years of age. VADrelated blindness is most prevalent in children under 3 years of age. This period of life is characterized by high requirements for vitamin A to support rapid growth, and the transition from breast-feeding to dependence on other dietary sources of the vitamin. In addition, adequate intake of vitamin A reduces the risk of catching respiratory and gastrointestinal infections. The increased mortality risk from concurrent infections extends at least to 6 years of age and is associated with both clinical and subclinical VAD. There is little information regarding the health consequences of VAD in school-age children. The prevalence of Bitot's spots (i.e. white foamy patches on the conjunctiva) may be highest in this age group but their occurrence may reflect past more than current history of VAD. Women of reproductive age are also thought to be vulnerable to VAD during pregnancy and lactation because they often report night blindness and because their breast milk is fre-quently low in vitamin A. Not all night blindness in pregnant women, however, responds to vitamin A treatment.

There is no consistent, clear indication in humans of a sex differential in vitamin A requirements during childhood. Growth rates, and presumably the need for vitamin A, from birth to 10 years for boys are consistently higher than those for girls. In the context of varied cultural and community settings, however, variations in gender-specific child-feeding and care practices are likely to subsume a small sex differential in requirements to account for reported sex differences in the prevalence of xerophthalmia. Pregnant and lactating women require additional vitamin A to support maternal and fetal tissue growth and lactation losses, additional vitamin A which is not needed by other post-adolescent adults.

Risk Factors

VAD is most common in populations consuming most of their vitamin A needs from provitamin carotenoid sources and where minimal dietary fat is available. About 90% of ingested preformed vitamin A is absorbed, whereas the absorption efficiency of provitamin A carotenoids varies widely, depending on the type of plant source and the fat content of the accompanying meal. Where possible, an increased intake of dietary fat is likely to improve the absorption of vitamin A in the body.

In areas with endemic VAD, fluctuations in the incidence of VAD throughout the year reflect the balance between intake and need. Periods of general food shortage (and specific shortages in vitamin A-rich foods) coincide with peak incidence of VAD and common childhood infectious diseases (e.g. diarrhoea, respiratory infections, and measles). Seasonal food availability influences VAD prevalence directly by influencing access to provitamin A sources; for example, the scarcity of mangoes in hot arid months followed by the glutting of the market with mangoes during harvest seasons. Seasonal growth spurts in children, which frequently follow seasonal post-harvest increases in energy and macronutrient intakes, can also affect the balance. These increases are usually obtained from staple grains (e.g. rice) and tubers (e.g. lightcoloured yams) that are not, however, good sources of some micronutrients (e.g. vitamin A) to support the growth spurt.

Food habits and taboos often restrict consumption of potentially good food sources of vitamin A (e.g. mangoes and green leafy vegetables). Culturespecific factors for feeding children, adolescents, and pregnant and lactating women are common. Illness- and childbirth-related proscriptions of the use of specific foods pervade many traditional cultures. Such influences alter short- and long-term food distribution within families. However, some cultural practices can be protective of vitamin A status and they need to be identified and reinforced.

Morbidity and Mortality

The consequences of VAD are manifested differently in different tissues. In the eye, the symptoms and signs, together referred to as xerophthalmia, have a long, well-recognized history and have until recently been the basis for estimating the global burden from the disease. Although ocular symptoms and signs are the most specific indicators of VAD, they occur only after other tissues have impaired functions that are less specific and less easily assessed.

The prevalence of ocular manifestations (i.e. xerophthalmia or clinical VAD) is now recognized to far underestimate the magnitude of the problem of functionally significant VAD. Many more preschool-age children, and perhaps older children and women who are pregnant or lactating, have their health compromised when they are subclinically deficient. In young children, subclinical deficiency, like clinical deficiency, increases the severity of some infections, particularly diarrhoea and measles, and increases the risk of death. Moreover, the incidence and prevalence of diarrhoea may also increase with subclinical VAD. Meta-analyses conducted by three independent groups using data from several randomized trials provide convincing evidence that community-based improvement of the vitamin A status of deficient children aged 6 months to 6 years reduces their risk of dying by 20–30% on average. Mortality in children who are blind from keratomalacia or who have corneal disease is reported to be from 50% to 90%,and measles mortality associated with VAD is increased by up to 50%. Limited data are available from controlled studies of the possible link between morbidity history and vitamin A status of pregnant and lactating women.

There are discrepancies in the link between incidence and severity of infectious morbidity of various etiologies and vitamin A status. A great deal of evidence supports an association of VAD with severity of an infection once acquired, except for respiratory diseases, which are non-responsive to treatment. The severity of pneumonia associated with measles, however, is an exception because it decreases with the treatment of vitamin A supplementation.

Infectious diseases depress circulating retinol and contribute to vitamin A depletion. Enteric infections may alter the absorptive surface area, compete for absorption-binding sites, and increase urinary loss. Febrile systemic infections also increase urinary loss and metabolic utilization rates and may reduce apparent retinol stores if fever occurs frequently.In the presence of latent deficiency, disease occurrence is often associated with precipitating ocular signs. Measles virus infection is especially devastating to vitamin A metabolism, adversely interfering with both efficiencies of utilization and conservation. Severe protein–energy malnutrition affects many aspects of vitamin A metabolism, and even when some retinyl ester stores are still present, malnutrition—often coupled with infection—can prevent transport-protein synthesis, resulting in immobilization of existing vitamin A stores.

The compromised integrity of the epithelium, together with the possible alteration in hormonal balance at severe levels of deficiency, impairs normal reproductive functions in animals. Controlled human studies are, of course, lacking. In animals and humans, congenital anomalies can result if the fetus is exposed to severe deficiency or large excesses of vitamin A at critical periods early in gestation (first trimester) when fetal organs are being formed. Reproductive performance, as measured by infant outcomes, in one community-based clinical intervention trial, however, was not influenced by vitamin A status.

The growth of children may be impaired by VAD. Interventions with vitamin A only have not consistently demonstrated improved growth in community studies because VAD seldom occurs in isolation from other nutrient deficiencies that also affect growth and may be more limiting.

A lack of vitamin A can affect iron metabolism when deficiencies of both nutrients coexist and particularly in environments that favour frequent infections. Maximum haemoglobin response occurs when iron and vitamin A deficiencies are corrected together. VAD appears to influence the availability of storage iron for use by haematopoietic tissue. However, additional research is needed to clarify the mechanisms of the apparent interaction.

Units of Expression

In blood, tissues, and human milk, vitamin A levels are conventionally expressed in mg/dl or mmol/l of all-*trans*-retinol. Except for postprandial conditions, most of the circulating vitamin A is retinol whereas in most tissues (such as the liver), secretions (such as human milk), and other animal food sources, it exists mainly as retinyl esters, which are frequently hydrolysed before analytical detection.

To express the vitamin A activity of carotenoids in diets on a common basis, a Joint FAO/WHO Expert Group in 1967 introduced the concept of the retinol equivalent (RE) and established the following relationships among food sources of vitamin A:

1 mg retinol = 1 RE

1 mg b-carotene = 0.167 mg RE

1 mg other provitamin A = 0.084 mg RE.

Carotenoids

These equivalencies were derived from balance studies to account for the less efficient absorption of carotenoids (at that time thought to be about one third that of retinol) and their bioconversion to vitamin A (one half for b-carotene and one fourth for other provitamin A carotenoids). It was recognized at the time that the recommended conversion factors (i.e. 1 :6 for vitamin A:bcarotene and 1 : 12 for vitamin A : all other provitamin carotenoids) were only best approximations for a mixed diet, which could under- or overestimate bioavailability depending not only on the quantity and source of carotenoids in the diet, but also on how the foods were processed and served (e.g. cooked or raw, whole or pureed, with or without fat). In 1988, a Joint FAO/WHO Expert Consultation confirmed these conversion factors for operational application in evaluating mixed diets. In reaching its conclusion, the Consultation noted the controlled depletion–repletion studies in adult men using a dark adaptation endpoint that reported a 2 :1 equivalency of supplemental bcarotene to retinol,and the range of factors that could alter the equivalency ratio when dietary carotenoids replaced supplements.

Recently there has been renewed interest in re-examining conventional conversion factors by using more quantitative stable isotope techniques for measuring whole-body stores in response to controlled intakes and by following post-absorption carotenoids in the triacylglycerol-rich lipoprotein fraction. The data are inconsistent but suggest that revision toward lower absorbability of provitamin A carotenoids is warranted. These studies indicate that the conditions that limit carotenoids from entering enterocytes rather than conversion once in the enterocyte are more significant than previously thought.

Other evidence questions the validity of factors used earlier, which suggests that 6mg of food-sourced β-carotene is equivalent to 2mg pure β carotene in oil, and equivalent to 1mg dietary retinol. Currently, however, only one study has used post-absorptive serum carotenoids to directly compare, in healthy, adequately nourished adult humans in Holland, the absorption of carotene in oil with that of dietary β-carotene from a mixed diet predominately containing vegetables. The investigators reported that about 7mg of β-carotene from the mixed predominately vegetable diet is equivalent to 1mg pure β-carotene when it is provided in oil. Assuming that 2mg β-carotene in the enterocyte is equivalent to 1mg retinol, the conversion factor would be 1:14 for β-carotene and 1:28 for other provitamin A carotenoids. Other researchers using a similar methodology have reported factors from a variety of specific food sources that fall within this range. Lowest bioavailability is reported for leafy green vegetables and raw carrots and highest for fruit/tuber diets. In view of the data available to date, conversion factors from usual mixed vegetable diets of 1 : 14 for β carotene and 1 : 28 for other provitamin A carotenoids as suggested by Van het Hof et al. are recommended. Where green leafy vegetables or fruits are more prominent than in the usual diet in Holland, adjustment to higher or lower conversion factors could be considered. For example, in the United States of America where fruits constitute a larger portion of the diet, the Food and Nutrition Board of the Institute of Medicine suggests retinol activity equivalency (RAE) factors of 12 :1 for β-carotene and 24 :1 for other provitamin A carotenoids.

Retinol equivalents in a diet are calculated as the sum of the weight of the retinol portion of preformed vitamin A plus the weight of β-carotene divided by its conversion factor, plus the weight of other provitamin A carotenoids divided by their conversion factor. Most recent food composition tables report β-carotene and, sometimes, other provitamin A carotenoids as mg/g edible portion. However, older food composition tables frequently report vitamin A as international units (IUs). The following conversion factors can be used to calculate comparable values as mg:

1 IU retinol = 0.3 mg retinol

1 IU β-carotene = 0.6 mg β-carotene

1 IU retinol = 3 IU β-carotene.

It is strongly recommended that weight or molar units replace the use of IUs to decrease confusion and overcome limitations in the non-equivalence of the IU values for retinol and β-carotene. For example, after converting all values from food composition tables to weight units, the vitamin A equivalency of a mixed diet should be determined by dividing the weight by the recommended weight equivalency value for preformed and specific provitamin A carotenoids. Hence, if a diet contained 150mg retinol, 1550mg β-carotene, and 1200mg other provitamin A carotenoids, the vitamin A equivalency of the diet would be:

150 mg + (1550 mg. 14) + (1200 mg. 28) = 304 mg retinol equivalency.

Sources and Supply Patterns of Vitamin A

Dietary Sources

Preformed vitamin A is found almost exclusively in animal products, such as human milk, glandular meats, liver and fish liver oils (especially), egg yolk, whole milk, and other dairy products. Preformed vitamin A is also used to fortify processed foods, which may include sugar, cereals, condiments, fats, and oils. Provitamin A carotenoids are found in green leafy vegetables (e.g. spinach, amaranth, and young leaves from various sources), yellow vegetables (e.g. pumpkins, squash, and carrots), and yellow and orange non-citrus fruits (e.g. mangoes, apricots, and papayas). Red palm oil produced in several countries worldwide is especially rich in provitamin A. Some other indigenous plants also may be unusually rich sources of provitamin A. Such examples are the palm fruit known in Brazil as *buriti,* found in areas along the Amazon River (as well as elsewhere in Latin America),and the fruit known as *gac* in Viet Nam, which is used to colour rice, particularly on ceremonial occasions. Foods containing provitamin A carotenoids tend to have less biologically available vitamin A but are more affordable than animal products. It is mainly for this reason that carotenoids provide most of the vitamin A activity in the diets of economically deprived populations.

Dietary Intake and Patterns

Although vitamin A status cannot be assessed from dietary intake alone, dietary intake assessment can provide evidence of risk of an inadequate status. However, quantitative collection of dietary information is fraught with measurement problems. These problems arise both from obtaining representative quantitative dietary histories from individuals, communities, or both, and from interpreting these data while accounting for differences in bioavailability, preparation losses, and variations in food composition data among population groups. This is especially difficult in populations consuming most of their dietary vitamin A from provitamin carotenoid sources. Simplified guidelines have been developed recently in an effort to improve the collection of reliable dietary intake information from individuals and communities.

World and Regional Supply and Patterns

In theory, the world's food supply is sufficient to meet global requirements for vitamin A. Great differences exist, however, in the availability of sources (animal and vegetable) and in per capita consumption of the vitamin among different countries, age categories, and socioeconomic groups. VAD as a global public health problem is therefore largely due to inequitable food distribution among and within countries and households in relation to the need for ample bioavailable vitamin A sources.

FAO global estimates for 1984 indicate that preformed vitamin A constituted about one third of total dietary vitamin A activity. World availability of vitamin A for human consumption at that time was approximately 220mg of preformed retinol per capita per day and 560mg RE from provitamin carotenoids (about 3400mg carotenoids for a 1 :6 conversion factor) per person per day, a total of about 790mg RE. These values are based on supply estimates and not consumption estimates. Losses commonly occur during food storage and processing, both industrially and in the home.

The estimated available regional supply of vitamin A from a more recent global evaluation shown in Table 1 illustrates the variability in amounts and sources of vitamin A. This variability is linked to access to the available supply of foods containing vitamin A, which varies with household income, with poverty being a yardstick for risk of VAD. VAD is most prevalent in South-East Asia, Africa, and the Western Pacific, where vegetable sources contribute nearly 80% or more of the available supply of retinol equivalents. Furthermore, in South-East Asia the total available supply is about half of that of most other regions and is particularly low in animal sources. In contrast, the Americas, Eastern Mediterranean, and Europe have a supply ranging from 700 to 1000mg RE/day, one third of which comes from animal sources. Based on national data from the United States Continuing Survey of Food Consumption and the third National Health and Nutrition Examination Survey mean dietary intakes of children aged 0–6 years were estimated to be 864 ± 497 and 921 ± 444mg RE per day, respectively. In the Dietary and Nutritional Survey of British Adults,the median intake of men and women aged 35–49 years was 1118mg RE and 926mg RE, respectively, which corresponded to serum retinol concentrations of 2.3mmol/l and 1.8mmol/l, respectively. In a smaller scale survey in the United Kingdom, median intakes for non-pregnant women who did not consume liver or liver products during the survey week were reported to be 686mg RE per day.

The available world supply figures in Table 1 were recently recalculated using a bioavailability ratio of 1 :30 for retinol to other provitamin A carotenoids. This conversion factor was justified on the basis of one published controlled intervention study conducted in Indonesia and a limited number of other studies not yet published in full.

Table 1: Available supply of vitamin A, by WHO region

Region	Animal sources (mg RE/day)	Vegetable sources (mg RE/day)	Total (mg RE/day)
Africa	122	654 (84)	776
The Americas	295	519 (64)	814
South-East Asia	53	378 (90)	431
Europe	271	467 (63)	738
Eastern Mediterranean	345	591 (63)	936
Western Pacific	216	781 (78)	997
Total	212	565 (72)	777

Applying the unconfirmed conversion factor to the values in Table 1 would lead to the conclusion that regional and country needs for vitamin A could not be met from predominantly vegetarian diets. However, this is inconsistent with the preponderance of epidemiological evidence. Most studies report a positive response when vegetable sources of provitamin A are given under controlled conditions to deficient subjects freed of confounding parasite loads and provided with sufficient dietary fat. Emerging data are likely to justify a lower biological activity for provitamin A carotenoids because of the mix of total carotenoids found in food sources in a usual meal. The present Consultation concluded that the 1 :6 bioconversion factor originally derived on the basis of balance studies should be retained until there is firm confirmation of more precise methodologies from ongoing studies.

Indicators of Vitamin A Deficiency

Clinical Indicators

Ocular signs of VAD are assessed by clinical examination and history, and are quite specific in preschool-age children. However, these are rare occurrences that require examination of large populations in order to obtain incidence and prevalence data. Subclinical VAD being the more prevalent requires smaller sample sizes for valid prevalence estimates.

A full description of clinical indicators of VAD, with coloured illustrations for each, can be found in the WHO field guide. The most frequently occurring is night-blindness, which is the earliest manifestation of xerophthalmia. In its mild form it is generally noticeable after stress from a bright light that bleaches the rhodopsin (visual purple) found in the retina. VAD prolongs the time to regenerate rhodopsin, and thus delays adaptation time in dark environments. Night-blind young children tend to stumble when going from bright to dimly-lit areas and they, as well as night-blind mothers, tend to remain inactive at dusk and at night.

No field-applicable objective tool is currently available for measuring nightblindness in children under about 3 years of age. However, it can be measured by history in certain cultures. In areas where night-blindness is prevalent, many cultures coin a word descriptive of the characteristic symptom that they can reliably recall on questioning, making this a useful tool for assessing the prevalence of VAD. It must be noted that questioning for night-blindness is not always a reliable assessment measure where a local term is absent. In addition, there is no clearly defined blood retinol level that is directly associated with occurrence of the symptom, such that could be used in conjunction with questioning. Vitamin A-related night-blindness, however, responds rapidly (usually within 1–2 days) to administration of vitamin A.

Subclinical Indicators

Direct measurement of concentrations of vitamin A in the liver (where it is stored) or in the total body pool relative to known specific vitamin A-related conditions (e.g. night-blindness) would be the indicator of choice for determining requirements. This cannot be done with the methodology currently available for population use. There are several more practical biochemical methods for estimating subclinical vitamin A status but all have limitations. Each method is useful for identifying deficient populations, but not one of these indicators is definitive or directly related quantitatively to disease occurrence. The indicators of choice are listed in Table 2. These indicators are less specific to VAD than clinical signs of the eye and less sensitive than direct measurements for evaluating subclinical vitamin A status. WHO recommends that where feasible at least two subclinical biochemical indicators, or one biochemical and a composite of non-biochemical risk factors, should be measured and that both types of indicators should point to deficiency in order to identify populations at high risk of VAD. Cut-off points given in Table 2 represent the consensus gained from practical experience in comparing populations with some evidence of VAD with those without VAD. There are no field studies that quantitatively relate the prevalence of adverse health symptoms (e.g. incidence or prevalence of severe diarrhoeal disease) and relative levels of biologic indicator cut-off values. Furthermore, each of the biochemical indicators listed is subject to confounding factors which may be unrelated to vitamin A status (e.g. infections).

Although all biochemical indicators currently available have limitations, the preferred biochemical indicator for population assessment is the distribution of serum levels of vitamin A (serum retinol). Only at very low blood levels (<0.35mmol/l) is there an association with corneal disease prevalence. Blood levels between 0.35 and 0.70mmol/l are likely to characterize subclinical deficiency,but subclinical deficiency may still be present at levels between 0.70 and 1.05mmol/l and occasionally above 1.05mmol/l.

Table 2: Indicators of subclinical VAD in mothers and in children aged 6–71 months

Indicator	Cut-off to indicate deficiency
Night-blindness (24–71 months)	≥1% report a history of night-blindness
Biochemical	
Breast-milk retinol	≤1.05mmol/l (≤8mg/g milk fat)
Serum retinol	≤0.70mmol/l
Relative dose response	≥20%
Modified relative dose response	Ratio ≥0.06

The prevalence of values below 0.70mmol/l is a generally accepted population cutoff for preschool-age children to indicate risk of inadequate vitamin A status and above 1.05mmol/l to indicate an adequate status. As noted elsewhere, clinical and subclinical infections can lower serum levels of vitamin A on average by as much as 25%, independently of vitamin A intake. Therefore, at levels between about 0.5 and 1.05mmol/l, the relative dose response or the modified relative dose response test on a subsample of the population can be useful for identifying the prevalence of critically depleted body stores when interpreting the left portion of serum retinol distribution curves.

Vitamin A Requirements

The mean requirement for an individual is defined as the minimum daily intake of vitamin A, expressed as mg retinol equivalents (mg RE), to prevent xerophthalmia in the absence of clinical or subclinical infection. This intake should account for the proportionate bioavailability of preformed vitamin A (about 90%) and provitamin A carotenoids from a diet that contains sufficient fat (e.g. at least 10 g daily). The required level of intake is set to prevent clinical signs of deficiency, allow for normal growth, and reduce the risk of vitamin A-related severe morbidity and mortality within any given population. It does not allow for frequent or prolonged periods of infections or other stresses.

The safe level of intake for an individual is defined as the average continuing intake of vitamin A required to permit adequate growth and other vitamin A-dependent functions and to maintain an acceptable total body reserve of the vitamin. This reserve helps offset periods of low intake or increased need resulting from infections and other stresses. Useful indicators include a plasma retinol concentration above 0.70mmol/l, which is associated with a relative dose response below 20%, or a modified relative dose response below 0.06. For lactating women, breast-milk retinol levels above 1.05mmol/l (or above 8mg/g milk fat) are considered to reflect minimal maternal stores because levels above 1.05mmol/l are common in populations known to be healthy and without evidence of insufficient dietary vitamin A.

Infants and Children

Vitamin A requirements for infants are calculated from the vitamin A provided in human milk. During at least the first 6 months of life, exclusive breast-feeding can provide sufficient vitamin A to maintain health, permit normal growth, and maintain sufficient storės in the liver.

Reported retinol concentrations in human milk vary widely from country to country (0.70–2.45mmol/l). In some developing countries, the vitamin A intake of breast-fed infants who grow well and do not show signs of deficiency ranges from 120 to 170mg RE/day. Such intakes are considered adequate to cover infant requirements if the infant's weight is assumed to be at least at the 10th percentile according to WHO standards.

However, this intake is unlikely to build adequate body stores, given that xerophthalmia is common in preschool-age children in the same communities with somewhat lower intakes. Because of the need for vitamin A to support the growth rate of infancy, which can vary considerably, a requirement estimate of 180mg RE/day seems appropriate.

The safe level for infants up to 6 months of age is based on observations of breast-fed infants in communities in which good nutrition is the norm. Average consumption of human milk by such infants is about 750ml/day during the first 6 months. Assuming an average concentration of vitamin A in human milk of about 1.75mmol/l, the mean daily intake would be about 375mg RE, which is therefore the recommended safe level. From 7–12 months, human milk intake averages 650ml/day, which would provide 325mg of vitamin A daily. Because breast-fed infants in endemic vitamin A-deficient populations are at increased risk of death from 6 months onward, the requirement and recommended safe intake levels are increased to 190mg RE/day and 400mg RE/day, respectively.

The requirement (with allowance for variability) and the recommended safe intake for older children may be estimated from those derived for late infancy (i.e. 20 and 39mg RE/kg body weight/day).On this basis, and including allowances for storage requirements and variability, requirements for preschool-age children would be in the range of 200–400mg RE daily. In poor communities where children 1–6 years old are reported to have intakes of about 100–200mg RE/day, signs of VAD do occur; in southern India these signs were relieved and risk of mortality was reduced when the equivalent of 350–400mg RE/day was given to children weekly.In the United States, most preschool-age children maintain serum retinol levels of 0.70mmol/l or higher while consuming diets providing 300–400mg RE/day (from the databank for the third National Health and Nutrition Examination Survey.

Adults

Estimates for the requirements and recommended safe intakes for adults are also extrapolated from those derived for late infancy, i.e. 4.8 and 9.3mg RE/kg body weight/day. Detailed account of how the requirement for vitamin A is arrived at is provided in the FAO/WHO report of 1988 and is not repeated here because no new studies have been published that indicate a need to revise the assumptions on which those calculations were based. The safe intakes recommended are consistent with the per capita vitamin A content in the food supply of countries that show adequate vitamin A status in all sectors of the population. Additional evidence that the existing safe level of intake is adequate for adults on a population basis is provided by an analysis of dietary data from the 1990 survey of British adults in whom there was no evidence of VAD. In another survey in the United Kingdom, the median intake of vitamin A among non-pregnant women who did not consume liver or liver products during the survey week was 686mg RE/day. This value is substantially above the estimated mean requirement for pregnant women and falls quite short of the amount at which teratology risk is reported. About one third of the calculated retinol equivalents consumed by the British women came from provitamin A sources (20% from carrots).

Pregnant Women

During pregnancy, women need additional vitamin A to sustain the growth of the fetus and to provide a limited reserve in the fetal liver, as well as to maintain their own tissue growth. Currently, there are no reliable figures available for the specific vitamin A requirements for these processes.

Newborn infants need around 100mg of retinol daily to meet their needs for growth. During the third trimester the fetus grows rapidly and, although obviously smaller in size than the infant born full term, the fetus presumably has similar needs. Incremental maternal needs associated with pregnancy are assumed to be provided from maternal reserves in populations of adequately nourished healthy mothers. In populations consuming vitamin A at the basal requirement, an additional increment of 100mg/day during the full gestation period should enhance maternal storage during early pregnancy and allow for adequate amounts of vitamin A to be available for the rapidly growing fetus in late pregnancy. However, this increment may be minimal for women who normally ingest only the basal requirement of vitamin A, inasmuch as the needs and growth rate of the fetus will not be affected by the mother's initial vitamin A reserves.

A recent study in Nepal,where night-blindness is prevalent in pregnant women, provided 7000mg RE (about 23300IU) weekly to pregnant and lactating women (equivalent to 1000mg RE/day). This level of intake normalized serum levels of vitamin A and was associated with a decrease in prevalence of night-blindness and a decrease in maternal mortality. However, the findings of this study need to be confirmed. In the interim period it seems prudent, recognizing that a large portion of the world's population of pregnant women live under conditions of deprivation, to increase by 200mg RE the recommended safe level to ensure adequacy of intake during pregnancy. Because therapeutic levels of vitamin A are generally higher than preventive levels, the safe intake level recommended during pregnancy is 800mg RE/day. Women who are or who might become pregnant should carefully limit their total daily vitamin A intake to a maximum of 3000mg RE (10000IU) to minimize risk of fetal toxicity.

Lactating Women

If the amount of vitamin A recommended for infants is supplied by human milk, mothers who are breast-feeding should intake at least as much vitamin A in their diets as is needed to replace the amount lost through breast-feeding. Thus, the increments in basal and safe recommended intakes during lactation are 180mg RE and 350mg RE, respectively. After the infant reaches the age of 6 months or when solid foods are introduced, the mother's need for additional amounts of vitamin A lessens.

Elderly

There is no indication that the vitamin A requirements of healthy elderly individuals differ from those of other adults. It should be remembered, however, that diseases that impede vitamin A absorption, storage, and transport might be more common in the elderly than in other age groups.

Toxicity

Because vitamin A is fat soluble and can be stored, primarily in the liver, routine consumption of large amounts of vitamin A over a period of time can result in toxic symptoms, including liver damage, bone abnormalities and joint pain, alopecia, headaches, vomiting, and skin desquamation. Hypervitaminosis A appears to be due to abnormal transport and distribution of vitamin A and retinoids caused by overloading of the plasma transport mechanisms.

The smallest daily supplement associated with liver cirrhosis that has been reported is 7500mg taken for 6 years. Very high single doses can also cause transient acute toxic symptoms that may include bulging fontanelles in infants; headaches in older children and adults; and vomiting, diarrhoea, loss of appetite, and irritability in all age groups. Rarely does toxicity occur from ingestion of food sources of preformed vitamin A. When this occurs, it usually results from very frequent consumption of liver products. Toxicity from food sources of provitamin A carotenoids is not reported, except for the cosmetic yellowing of skin.

Infants, including neonates,administered single doses equivalent to 15000–30000mg retinol (50000–100000IU) in oil generally show no adverse symptoms. However, daily prophylactic or therapeutic doses should not exceed 900mg, which is well above the mean requirement of about 200mg/day for infants. An increase in bulging fontanelles occurred in infants under 6 months of age in one endemically deficient population given two or more doses of 7500mg or 15000mg preformed vitamin A in oil,but other large-scale controlled clinical trials have not reported increased bulging after three doses of 7500mg given with diphtheria-pertussis-tetanus immunizations at about 6, 10, and 14 weeks of age. No effects were detected at 3 years of age that related to transient vitamin A-induced bulging that had occurred before 6 months of age.

Most children aged 1–6 years tolerate single oral doses of 60000mg (200000IU) vitamin A in oil at intervals of 4–6 months without adverse symptoms. Occasionally diarrhoea or vomiting is reported but these symptoms are transient with no lasting sequelae. Older children seldom experience toxic symptoms unless they habitually ingest vitamin A in excess of 7500mg (25000IU) for prolonged periods of time.

When women take vitamin A at daily levels of more than 7500mg (25000 IU) during the early stages of gestation, fetal anomalies and poor reproductive outcomes are reported. One report suggests an increased risk of teratogenicity at intakes as low as 3000mg (10000IU), but this is not confirmed by other studies.Women who are pregnant or might become pregnant should avoid taking excessive amounts of vitamin A. A careful review of the latest available information by a WHO Expert Group recommended that daily intakes in excess of 3000mg (10000IU), or weekly intakes in excess of 7500mg (25000IU) should not be taken at any period during gestation. High doses of vitamin A (60000mg, or 200000IU) can be safely given to breastfeeding mothers for up to 2 months postpartum and up to 6 weeks to mothers who are not breastfeeding.

10

Vitamin D

Vitamin D in Human Metabolic Processes

Vitamin D is required to maintain normal blood levels of calcium and phosphate, which are in turn needed for the normal mineralization of bone, muscle contraction, nerve conduction, and general cellular function in all cells of the body. Vitamin D achieves this after its conversion to the active form 1,25-dihydroxyvitamin D [1,25-$(OH)_2$D], or calcitriol. This active form regulates the transcription of a number of vitamin D-dependent genes which code for calcium-transporting proteins and bone matrix proteins.

Vitamin D also modulates the transcription of cell cycle proteins, which decrease cell proliferation and increase cell differentiation of a number of specialized cells of the body (e.g. osteoclastic precursors, enterocytes, keratinocytes). This property may explain the actions of vitamin D in bone resorption, intestinal calcium transport, and skin. Vitamin D also possesses immunomodulatory properties that may alter responses to infections in vivo. These cell differentiating and immunomodulatory properties underlie the reason why vitamin D derivatives are now used successfully in the treatment of psoriasis and other skin disorders.

Vitamin D Metabolism

Vitamin D, a seco-steroid, can either be made in the skin from a cholesterollike precursor (7-dehydrocholesterol) by exposure to sunlight or can be provided pre-formed in the diet. The version made in the skin is referred to as vitamin D_3 whereas the dietary form can be vitamin D_3 or a closely-related molecule of plant origin known as vitamin D_2. Because vitamin D can be made in the skin, it should not strictly be called a vitamin, and some nutritional texts refer to the substance as a prohormone and to the two forms as colecalciferol (D_3) and ergocalciferol (D_2).

From a nutritional perspective, the two forms are metabolized similarly in humans, are equal in potency, and can be considered equivalent. It is now firmly established that vitamin D_3 is metabolized first in the liver to 25-hydroxyvitamin D (calcidiol) and subsequently in the kidneys to 1,25-$(OH)_2$D (calcitriol) to produce a biologically active hormone. The 1,25-$(OH)_2$D compound, like all vitamin D metabolites, is present in the blood complexed to the vitamin D-binding protein, a specific a-globulin. Calcitriol is believed to act on target cells in a similar way to a steroid hormone. Free hormone crosses the plasma membrane and interacts with a specific nuclear receptor known as the vitamin D receptor, a DNA-binding, zinc-finger protein with a relative molecular mass of 55 000. This ligand-receptor complex binds to a specific vitamin D-responsive element and, with associated transcription factors (e.g. retinoid X receptor), enhances transcription of mRNAs which code for calcium-transporting proteins, bone matrix proteins, or cell cycle-regulating proteins. As a result of these processes, 1,25-$(OH)_2$D stimulates intestinal absorption of calcium and phosphate and mobilizes calcium and phosphate by stimulating bone resorption. These functions serve the common purpose of restoring blood levels of calcium and phosphate to normal when concentrations of the two ions are low.

Lately, interest has focused on other cellular actions of calcitriol. With the discovery of 1,25-$(OH)_2D$ receptors in many classically non-target tissues such as brain, various bone marrow-derived cells, skin, and thymus, the view has been expressed that 1,25-$(OH)_2D$ induces fusion and differentiation of macrophages. This effect has been widely interpreted to mean that the natural role of 1,25-$(OH)_2D$ is to induce osteoclastogenesis from colony forming units (i.e. granulatory monocytes in the bone marrow). Calcitriol also suppresses interleukin-2 production in activated T-lymphocytes, an effect which suggests the hormone might play a role in immunomodulation in vivo. Other tissues (e.g. skin) are directly affected by exogenous administration of vitamin D, though the physiologic significance of these effects is poorly understood. The pharmacologic effects of 1,25-$(OH)_2D$ are profound and have resulted in the development of vitamin D analogues, which are approved for use in hyperproliferative conditions such as psoriasis.

Clinical assays measure 1,25-$(OH)_2D_2$ and 1,25-$(OH)_2D_3$, collectively called 1,25-$(OH)_2D$. Similarly, calcidiol is measured as 25-OH-D but it is a mixture of 25-OH-D_2 and 25-OH-D_3. For the purposes of this document, 1,25-$(OH)_2D$ and 25-OH-D will be used to refer to calcitriol and calcidiol, respectively.

Calcium Homeostasis

In calcium homeostasis, 1,25-$(OH)_2D$ works in conjunction with parathyroid hormone (PTH) to produce its beneficial effects on the plasma levels of ionized calcium and phosphate. The physiologic loop (Figure 1) starts with the calcium receptor of the parathyroid gland.

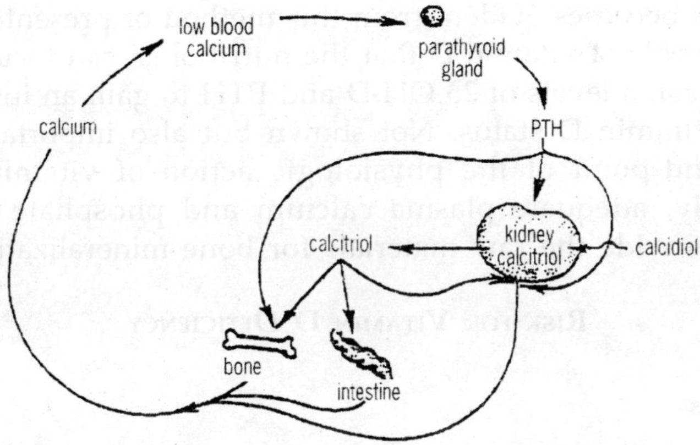

Figure 1: Calcium homeostasis

When the level of ionized calcium in plasma falls, PTH is secreted by the parathyroid gland and stimulates the tightly regulated renal enzyme 25-OH-D-1-a-hydroxylase to make more 1,25-$(OH)_2$D from the large circulating pool of 25-OH-D. The resulting increase in 1,25-$(OH)_2$D (with the rise in PTH) causes an increase in calcium transport within the intestine, bone, and kidney. All these events raise plasma calcium levels back to normal, which in turn is sensed by the calcium receptor of the parathyroid gland. The further secretion of PTH is turned off not only by the feedback action of calcium, but also by a short feedback loop involving 1,25-$(OH)_2$D directly suppressing PTH synthesis in the parathyroid gland.

Although this model oversimplifies the events involved in calcium homeostasis, it clearly demonstrates that sufficient 25-OH-D must be available to provide adequate 1,25-$(OH)_2$D synthesis and hence an adequate level of plasma calcium; and similarly that vitamin D deficiency will result in inadequate 25-OH-D and 1,25-$(OH)_2$D synthesis, inadequate calcium homeostasis, and a constantly elevated PTH level (i.e. secondary hyperparathyroidism).

It becomes evident from this method of presentation of the role of vitamin D that the nutritionist can focus on the plasma levels of 25-OH-D and PTH to gain an insight into vitamin D status. Not shown but also important is the end-point of the physiologic action of vitamin D, namely, adequate plasma calcium and phosphate ions that provide the raw materials for bone mineralization.

Risk for Vitamin D Deficiency

Infants

Infants constitute a population at risk for vitamin D deficiency because of relatively large vitamin D needs brought about by their high rate of skeletal growth. At birth, infants have acquired in utero the vitamin D stores that must carry them through the first months of life. A recent survey of French neonates revealed that 64% had 25-OH-D values below 30 nmol/l, the lower limit of the normal range. Breast-fed infants are particularly at risk because of the low concentrations of vitamin D in human milk. This problem is further compounded in some infants fed human milk by a restriction in exposure to ultraviolet (UV) light for seasonal, latitudinal, cultural, or social reasons. Infants born in the autumn months at extreme latitudes are particularly at risk because they spend the first 6 months of their life indoors and therefore have little opportunity to synthesize vitamin D in their skin during this period. Consequently, although vitamin D deficiency is rare in developed countries, sporadic cases of rickets are still being reported in many northern cities but almost always in infants fed human milk.

Infant formulas are supplemented with vitamin D at levels ranging from 40 international units (IU) or 1mg/ 418.4kJ to 100IU or 2.5mg/418.4kJ, that provide approximately between 6mg and 15mg of vitamin D, respectively. These amounts of dietary vitamin D are sufficient to prevent rickets.

Adolescents

Another period of rapid growth of the skeleton occurs at puberty and increases the need not for the vitamin D itself, but for the active form 1,25-$(OH)_2$D. This need results from the increased conversion of 25-OH-D to 1,25-$(OH)_2$D in adolescents. Unlike infants, however, adolescents usually spend more time outdoors and therefore usually are exposed to levels of UV light sufficient for synthesizing vitamin D for their needs. Excess production of vitamin D in the summer and early autumn months is stored mainly in the adipose tissue and is available to sustain high growth rates in the winter months that follow. Insufficient vitamin D stores during this period of increased growth can lead to vitamin D insufficiency.

Elderly

Over the past 20 years, clinical research studies of the basic biochemical machinery for handling vitamin D have suggested an age-related decline in many key steps of vitamin D action (24), including the rate of skin synthesis, the rate of hydroxylation (leading to the activation to the hormonal form), and the response of target tissues (e.g. bone). Not surprisingly, a number of independent studies from around the world have shown that there appears to be vitamin D deficiency in a subset of the elderly population, characterized by low blood levels of 25-OH-D coupled with elevations in plasma PTH and alkaline phosphatase. There is evidence that this vitamin D deficiency contributes to declining bone mass and increases the incidence of hip fractures. Although some of these studies may exaggerate the extent of the problem by focusing on institutionalized individuals or inpatients with decreased sun exposures, in general they have forced health professionals to re-address the vitamin D intake of this segment of society and look at potential solutions to correct the problem. .

Pregnant and Lactating Women

Elucidation of the changes in calciotropic hormones occurring during pregnancy and lactation has revealed a role for vitamin D in the former but not definitively in the latter. Even in pregnancy, the changes in vitamin D metabolism which occur, namely an increase in the maternal plasma levels of 1,25-$(OH)_2$D due to a putative placental synthesis of the hormone, do not seem to impinge greatly on the maternal vitamin D requirements. The concern that modest vitamin D supplementation might be deleterious to the fetus is not justified. Furthermore, because transfer of vitamin D from mother to fetus is important for establishing the neonate's growth rate, the goal of ensuring adequate vitamin D status with conventional prenatal vitamin D supplements probably should not be discouraged.

In lactating women there appears to be no direct role for vitamin D because increased calcium needs are regulated by the PTH-related peptide, and recent studies have failed to show any change in vitamin D metabolites during lactation. As stated above, the vitamin D content of human milk is low. Consequently, there is no great drain on maternal vitamin D reserves either to regulate calcium homeostasis or to supply the need of human milk. Because human milk is a poor source of vitamin D, rare cases of nutritional rickets are still found, but these are almost always in breast-fed infants deprived of sunlight exposure. Furthermore, there is little evidence that increasing calcium or vitamin D supplementation to lactating mothers results in an increased transfer of calcium or vitamin D in milk. Thus, the current thinking, based on a clearer understanding of the role of vitamin D in lactation, is that there is little purpose in recommending additional vitamin D for lactating women. The goal for mothers who breast-feed their infants seems to be merely to ensure good nutrition and sunshine exposure in order to ensure normal vitamin D status during the perinatal period.

Recommended Intakes

Lack of Accuracy in Estimating Dietary Intake and Skin Synthesis

The unique problem of estimating total intake of a substance that can be provided in the diet or made in the skin by exposure to sunlight makes it difficult to derive adequate total intakes of vitamin D for the general population. Moreover, accurate food composition data are not available for vitamin D, accentuating the difficulty in estimating dietary intakes. Whereas two recent United States national surveys have avoided even attempting this task, the second National Health and Nutrition Examination Survey (NHANES II) estimated vitamin D intakes to be 2.9mg/day and 2.3mg/day for younger and older women, respectively. A recent study of elderly women by Kinyamu et al. concurred with this assessment, finding an intake of 3.53mg/day. Skin synthesis is equally difficult to estimate, being affected by such imponderables as age, season, latitude, time of day, skin exposure, and sunscreen use. In vitamin D-replete individuals, estimates of skin synthesis are put at around 10mg/day, with total intakes estimated at 15mg/day.

Use of Plasma 25-OH-D as a Measure of Vitamin D Status

Numerous recent studies have used plasma 25-OH-D as a measure of vitamin D status, and there is a strong presumptive relationship of this variable with bone status. Thus, it is not surprising that several nutritional committees (e.g. the Food and Nutrition Board of the United States National Academy of Sciences' Institute of Medicine in conjunction with Health Canada) have chosen to use a biochemical basis for estimating required intakes and have used these estimates to derive recommended intakes. The method used involves the estimation of the mean group dietary intake of vitamin D required to maintain the plasma 25-OH-D levels above 27 nmol/l, which is the level necessary to ensure normal bone health. Previously, many studies had established 27nmol/l as the lower limit of the normal range (e.g. NHANES III). This dietary intake of vitamin D for each population group was rounded to the nearest 50 IU (1.25mg) and then doubled to cover the needs of all individuals within that group irrespective of sunlight exposure. This amount was termed *adequate intake* (AI) and was used in place of the recommended dietary allowance (RDA), which had been used by United States agencies since 1941. The present Expert Consultation decided to use these figures as recommended nutrient intakes (RNIs) because it considered this to be an entirely logical approach to estimating the vitamin D needs for the global population.

Because many studies had recommended increases in vitamin D intakes for the elderly, it might have been expected that the proposed increases in suggested intakes from 5mg/day (the RDA in the United States and the RNI in Canada) to between 10 and 15mg/day (AI) would be welcomed. However, a recent editorial in a prominent medical journal attacked the recommendations as being too conservative. Furthermore, an article in the same journal reported the level of hypovitaminosis D to be as high as 57% in a population of ageing (mean age, 62 years) medical inpatients in the Boston area.

Of course, such inpatients are by definition sick and should not be used to calculate intakes of healthy individuals. Indeed, the new NHANES III study of 18323 healthy individuals from all regions of the United States suggests that approximately 5% had values of 25-OH-D below 27 nmol/l (Table 1). Although the data are skewed by sampling biases that favour sample collection in the southern states in winter months and northern states in the summer months, even subsets of data collected in northern states in September give the incidence of low 25-OH-D in the elderly in the 6–18% range, compared with 57% in the institutionalized inpatient population mentioned above. Ideally, such measurements in a healthy population should be made at the end of the winter months before UV irradiation has reached a strength sufficient to allow skin synthesis of vitamin D.Thus, the NHANES III study may still underestimate the incidence of hypovitaminosis D in a northern elderly population in winter.

Table 1: Frequency distribution of serum or plasma 25-OH-D: preliminary unweighted results from the third National Health and Nutrition Examination Survey, 1988–1994

Percentile	25-OH-D (ng/ml)c
1st	7.6
5th	10.9
10th	13.2
50th	24.4
90th	40.1
95th	45.9
99th	59.0

Nevertheless, in lieu of additional studies of selected human populations, it would seem that the recommendations of the Food and Nutrition Board are reasonable guidelines for vitamin D intakes, at least for the near future. This considered approach allows for a period of time to monitor the potential shortfalls of the new recommendations as well as to assess whether the suggested guidelines can be achieved, a point that was repeatedly raised about the vitamin D RDA.

Recommended Intakes for Vitamin D

In recommending intakes for vitamin D, it must be recognized that in most locations in the world in a broad band around the equator (between latitudes 42°N and 42°S), the most physiologically relevant and efficient way of acquiring vitamin D is to synthesize it endogenously in the skin from 7-dehydrocholesterol by sun (UV) light exposure. In most situations, approximately 30 minutes of skin exposure (without sunscreen) of the arms and face to sunlight can provide all the daily vitamin D needs of the body. However, skin synthesis of vitamin D is negatively influenced by factors which may reduce the ability of the skin to provide the total needs of the individual:

- *latitude and season*: both influence the amount of UV light reaching the skin;
- *the ageing process*: thinning of the skin reduces the efficiency of this synthetic process;
- *skin pigmentation*: the presence of darker pigments in the skin interferes with the synthetic process because UV light cannot reach the appropriate layer of the skin;
- *clothing*: virtually complete covering of the skin for medical, social, cultural, or religious reasons leaves insufficient skin exposed to sunlight;
- *sunscreen use*: widespread and liberal use of sunscreen, though reducing skin damage by the sun, deleteriously affects synthesis of vitamin D. Because

not all of these problems can be solved in all geographic locations, particularly during winter at latitudes higher than 42° where synthesis is virtually zero, it is recommended that individuals not synthesizing vitamin D should correct their vitamin D status by consuming the amounts of vitamin D appropriate for their age group.

Toxicity

The adverse effects of high vitamin D intakes—hypercalciuria and hypercalcaemia —do not occur at the recommended intake levels discussed above. In fact, it is worth noting that the recommended intakes for all age groups are still well below the lowest observed adverse effect level of 50mg/day and do not reach the "no observed adverse effect level" of 20mg/day. Outbreaks of idiopathic infantile hypercalcaemia in the United Kingdom in the post-World War II era led to the withdrawal of vitamin D fortification from all foods in that country because of concerns that they were due to hypervi-taminosis D. There are some suggestions in the literature that these outbreaks of idiopathic infantile hypercalcaemia may have involved genetic and dietary components and were not due strictly to technical problems with overfortification as was assumed. In retrospect, the termination of the vitamin D fortification may have been counterproductive as it exposed segments of the United Kingdom community to vitamin D deficiency and may have discouraged other nations from starting vitamin D fortification programmes. This is all the more cause for concern because hypovitaminosis D is still a problem worldwide, particularly in developing countries, at high latitudes and in countries where skin exposure to sunlight is discouraged.

11

Calcium

Calcium is a divalent cation with an atomic weight of 40. In the elementary composition of the human body, it ranks fifth after oxygen, carbon, hydrogen, and nitrogen, and it makes up 1.9% of the body by weight. Carcass analyses show that calcium constitutes 0.1–0.2% of early fetal fat-free weight, rising to about 2% of adult fat-free weight. In absolute terms, this represents a rise from about 24 g (600 mmol) at birth to 1300 g (32.5 mol) at maturity, requiring an average daily positive calcium balance of 180mg (4.5mmol) during the first 20 years of growth (Figure 1).

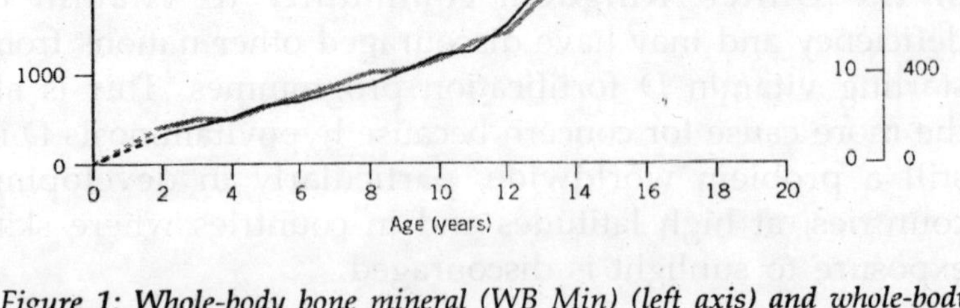

Figure 1: Whole-body bone mineral (WB Min) (left axis) and whole-body calcium (WB Ca) (right axis) as a function of age as determined by total-body dual-energy X-ray absorptiometry

Nearly all (99%) of total body calcium is located in the skeleton. The remaining 1% is equally distributed between the teeth and soft tissues, with only 0.1% in the extracellular fluid (ECF). In the skeleton it constitutes 25% of the dry weight and 40% of the ash weight. The ECF contains ionized calcium at concentrations of about 4.8mg/100ml (1.20 mmol/l) maintained by the parathyroid–vitamin D system as well as complexed calcium at concentrations of about 1.6mg/100ml (0.4 mmol/l). In the plasma there is also a protein-bound calcium fraction, which is present at a concentration of 3.2mg/100ml (0.8 mmol/l). In the cellular compartment, the total calcium concentration is comparable with that in the ECF, but the free calcium concentration is lower by several orders of magnitude.

Biological Role of Calcium

Calcium salts provide rigidity to the skeleton and calcium ions play a role in many, if not most, metabolic processes. In the primitive exoskeleton and in shells, rigidity is generally provided by calcium carbonate, but in the vertebrate skeleton, it is provided by a form of calcium phosphate which approximates hydroxyapatite [Ca10(OH)2(PO4)6] and is embedded in collagen fibrils.

Bone mineral serves as the ultimate reservoir for the calcium circulating in the ECF. Calcium enters the ECF from the gastrointestinal tract by absorption and from bone by resorption. Calcium leaves the ECF via the gastrointestinal tract, kidneys, and skin and enters into bone via bone formation (Figure 2). In addition, calcium fluxes occur across all cell membranes. Many neuromuscular and other cellular functions depend on the maintenance of the ionized calcium concentration in the ECF. Calcium fluxes are also important mediators of hormonal effects on target organs through several intracellular signalling pathways, such as the phosphoinositide and cyclic adenosine monophosphate systems. The cytoplasmic calcium concentration is regulated by a series of calcium pumps, which either concentrate calcium ions within the intracellular storage sites or extrude them from the cells (where they flow in by diffusion). The physiology of calcium metabolism is primarily directed towards the maintenance of the concentration of ionized calcium in the ECF.

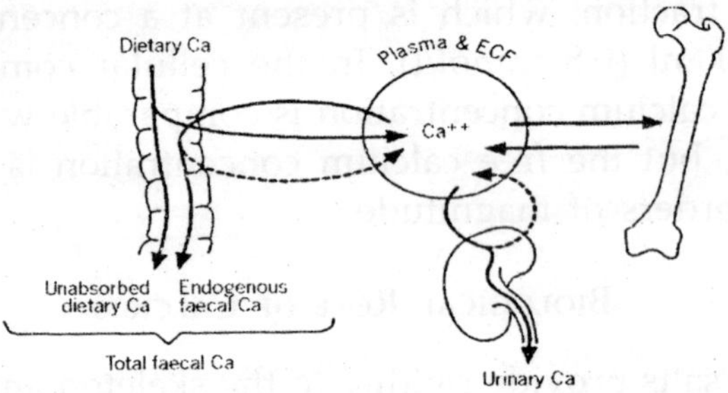

Figure 2: Major calcium movements in the body

This concentration is protected and maintained by a feedback loop through calcium receptors in the parathyroid glands, which control the secretion of parathyroid hormone. This hormone increases the renal tubular reabsorption of calcium, promotes intestinal calcium absorption by stimulating the renal production of 1,25-dihydroxyvitamin D or calcitriol [1,25-$(OH)_2$ D], and, if necessary, resorbs bone. However, the integrity of the system depends critically on vitamin D status; if there is a deficiency of vitamin D, the loss of its calcaemic action leads to a decrease in the ionized calcium and secondary hyperparathyroidism and hypophosphataemia. This is why experimental vitamin D deficiency results in rickets and osteomalacia whereas calcium deficiency gives rise to osteoporosis.

Determinants of Calcium Balance

Calcium Intake

In a strictly operational sense, calcium balance is determined by the relationship between calcium intake and calcium absorption and excretion. A striking feature of the system is that relatively small changes in calcium absorption and excretion can neutralize a high intake or compensate for a low one. There is a wide variation in calcium intake between countries, generally following the animal protein intake and depending largely on dairy product consumption. The lowest calcium intakes occur in developing countries, particularly in Asia, and the highest in developed countries, particularly in North America and Europe (Table 1).

Calcium Absorption

Ingested calcium mixes with digestive juice calcium in the proximal small intestine from where it is absorbed by a process which has an active saturable component and a diffusion component.When calcium intake is low, calcium is mainly absorbed by active (transcellular) transport, but at higher intakes, an increasing proportion of calcium is absorbed by simple (paracellular) diffusion. The unabsorbed component appears in the faeces together with the unabsorbed component of digestive juice calcium known as endogenous faecal calcium. Thus, the faeces contain unabsorbed dietary calcium and digestive juice calcium that was not reabsorbed (Figure 2).

True absorbed calcium is the total amount of calcium absorbed from the calcium pool in the intestines and therefore contains both dietary and digestive juice components. Net absorbed calcium is the difference between dietary calcium and faecal calcium and is numerically the same as true absorbed calcium minus endogenous faecal calcium.

Table 1: Daily protein and calcium intakes in different regions of the world, 1987–1989

	Protein (g)			Calcium (mg)		
Region	Total	Animal	Vegetable	Total	Animal	Vegetable
North America	108.7	72.2	36.5	1031	717	314
Europe	102.0	59.6	42.4	896	684	212
Oceania	98.3	66.5	31.8	836	603	233
Other developed	91.1	47.3	43.8	565	314	251
USSR	106.2	56.1	50.1	751	567	184
All developed	103.0	60.1	42.9	850	617	233
Africa	54.1	10.6	43.5	368	108	260
Latin America	66.8	28.6	38.2	477	305	171
Near East	78.7	18.0	60.7	484	223	261
Far East	58.2	11.0	47.2	305	109	196
Other developing	55.8	22.7	33.1	432	140	292
All developing	59.9	13.3	46.6	344	138	206

At zero calcium intake, all the faecal calcium is endogenous and represents the digestive juice calcium which has not been reabsorbed; net absorbed calcium at this intake is therefore negative to the extent of about 200mg (5mmol). When the intake reaches about 200mg (5mmol), dietary and faecal calcium become equal and net absorbed calcium is zero. As calcium intake increases, net absorbed calcium also increases, steeply at first but then, as the active transport becomes saturated, more slowly until the slope of absorbed on ingested calcium approaches linearity with an ultimate gradient of about 5–10%. The relationship between intestinal calcium absorption and calcium intake, derived from 210 balance experiments performed in 81 individuals collected from the literature, is shown in Figure 3.

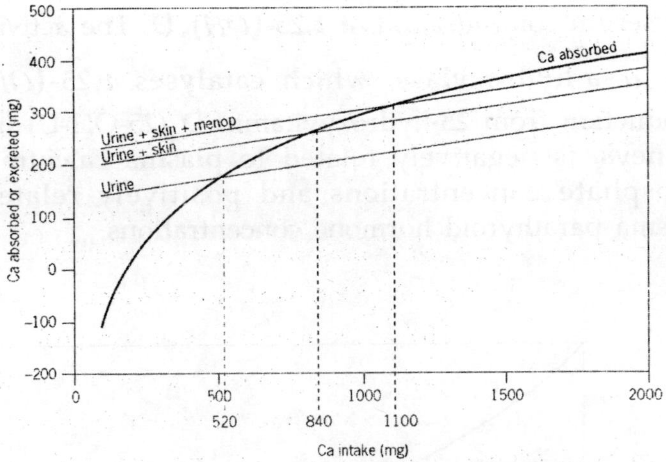

Figure 3: The relationship between calcium intake and calcium absorbed (or excreted) calculated from 210 balance experiments in 81 subjects

True absorption is an inverse function of calcium intake, falling from some 70% at very low intakes to about 35% at high intakes (Figure 4). Percentage net absorption is negative at low intake, becomes positive as intake increases, reaches a peak of about 35% at an intake of about 400 mg, and then falls off as intake increases further. True and net absorption converge as intake rises because the endogenous faecal component that separates them becomes proportionately smaller.

Many factors influence the availability of calcium for absorption and the absorptive mechanism itself. In the case of the former, factors include the presence of substances which form insoluble complexes with calcium, such as the phosphate ion. The relatively high calcium–phosphate ratio of 2.2 in human milk compared with 0.77 in cow milk may be a factor in the higher absorption of calcium from human milk than cow milk.

Intestinal calcium absorption is mainly controlled by the serum concentration of 1,25-$(OH)_2$ D. The activity of the α-a-hydroxylase, which catalyses 1,25-$(OH)_2$ D production from 25-hydroxyvitamin D (25-OH-D) in the kidneys, is negatively related to plasma calcium and phosphate concentrations and positively related to plasma parathyroid hormone concentrations.

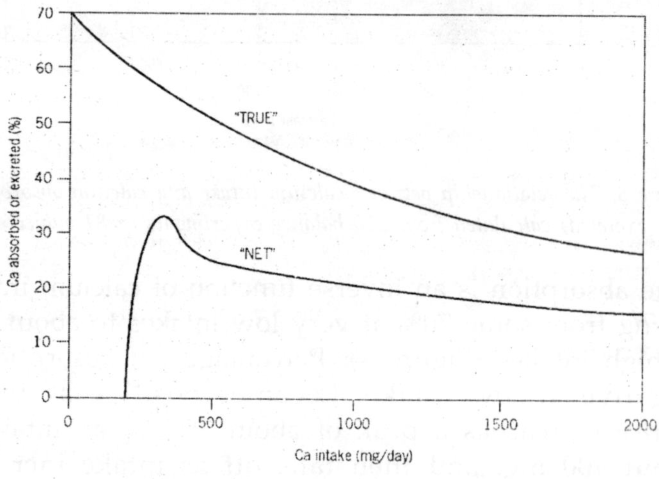

Figure 4: True and net calcium absorption as percentages of calcium intake

Thus the inverse relationship between calcium intake and fractional absorption described above is enhanced by the inverse relationship between dietary calcium and serum 1,25-$(OH)_2$ D. Phytates, present in the husks of many cereals as well as in nuts, seeds, and legumes, can form insoluble calcium phytate salts in the gastrointestinal tract. Excess oxalates can precipitate calcium in the bowel but are not an important factor in most diets.

Urinary Calcium

Urinary calcium is the fraction of the filtered plasma water calcium which is not reabsorbed in the renal tubules. At a normal glomerular filtration rate of 120ml/min and an ultrafiltrable calcium concentration of 6.4mg/100ml (1.60 mmol/l), the filtered load of calcium is about 8mg/min (0.20mmol/min) or 11.6 g/day (290 mmol/day). Because the average 24-hour calcium excretion in subjects from developed countries is about 160–200mg (4–5mmol), it follows that 98–99% of the filtered calcium is usually reabsorbed in the renal tubules. However, calcium excretion is extremely sensitive to changes in filtered load. A decrease in plasma water calcium of only 0.17mg/100ml (0.043 mmol/l), which is barely detectable, was sufficient to account for a decrease in urinary calcium of 63 mg (1.51mmol) when 27 subjects changed from a normal- to a low-calcium diet. This very sensitive renal response to calcium deprivation combines with the inverse relationship between calcium intake and absorption to stabilize the plasma ionized calcium concentration and to preserve the equilibrium between calcium entering and leaving the ECF over a wide range of calcium intakes. However, there is always a significant obligatory loss of calcium in the urine (as there is in the faeces), even on a low calcium intake, simply because maintenance of the plasma ionized calcium and, therefore, of the filtered load, prevents total elimination of calcium from the urine. The lower limit for urinary calcium in developed countries is about 140 mg (3.5mmol) but depends on protein and salt intakes. From this obligatory minimum, urinary calcium increases on intake with a slope of about 5–10%. In Figure 3, the relationship between urinary calcium excretion and calcium intake is represented by the line which intersects the absorbed calcium line at an intake of 520mg.

Insensible Losses

Urinary and endogenous faecal calcium are not the only forms of excreted calcium; losses through skin, hair, and nails also need to be taken into account. These are not easily measured, but a combined balance and isotope procedure has yielded estimates of daily insensible calcium losses in the range of 40–80mg (1–2mmol), which are unrelated to calcium intake. Thus, the additional loss of a mean of 60 mg (1.5 mmol) as a constant to urinary calcium loss raises the level of dietary calcium at which absorbed and excreted calcium reach equilibrium from 520 to 840 mg (13 to 21 mmol) (Figure 3).

Calcium Requirements and Recommended Nutrient Intakes

Although it is well established that calcium deficiency causes osteoporosis in experimental animals, the contribution that calcium deficiency makes to osteoporosis in humans is much more controversial, in part due to the great variation in calcium intakes across the world (Table 1), which does not appear to be associated with any corresponding variation in the prevalence of osteoporosis. This issue is dealt with at greater length in the section on nutritional factors; in this section we will simply define what is meant by calcium requirement and how it may be calculated.

The calcium requirement of an adult is generally recognized to be the intake required to maintain calcium balance and therefore skeletal integrity. The mean calcium requirement of adults is therefore the mean intake at which intake and output are equal; at present this can only be determined by balance studies conducted with sufficient care, and over a sufficiently long period of time to ensure reasonable accuracy and then corrected for insensible losses. The reputation of the balance technique has been harmed by a few studies with inadequate equilibration times and short collection periods, but this should not be allowed to detract from the value of the meticulous work of those who have collected faecal and urinary samples for weeks or months from subjects on well-defined diets. This meticulous work has produced valuable balance data, which are clearly valid; the mean duration of the 210 experiments from eight publications used in this report to derive the recommended intakes was 90 days with a range of 6–480 days. (The four 6-day balance studies in the series used a non-absorbable marker and are therefore acceptable.)

The usual way of determining mean calcium requirement from balance studies is by linear regression of calcium output (or calcium balance) on intake and calculation of the mean intake at which intake and output are equal (or balance is zero). This was probably first done in 1939 by Mitchell and Curzon, who arrived at a mean requirement of 9.8 mg/kg/day or about 640mg/day (16 mmol) for a mean body weight of 65 kg. The same type of calculation was subsequently used by many others who arrived at requirements ranging from 200mg/day (5mmol/day) in male Peruvian prisoners to 990mg/day (24.75mmol) in premenopausal women, but most values were about 600mg/day (15mmol) without allowing for insensible losses. However, this type of simple linear regression yields a higher mean calcium requirement (640 mg in the 210 balance experiments used here) (Figure 5a) than the intercept of absorbed and excreted calcium (520 mg) (Figure 3) because it tends to underestimate the negative calcium balance at low intake and overestimate the positive balance at high intake. A better reflection of biological reality is obtained by deriving calcium output from the functions given previously and then regressing that output on calcium intake. This yields the result shown in Figure 5b where balance is more negative (i.e. the regression line is above the line of equality) at low intakes and less positive (i.e. the regression line is below the line of equality) at high intakes than in the linear model, and yields a zero balance at 520 mg, which is the same as that arrived at in Figure 3 when excreted and absorbed calcium were equal.

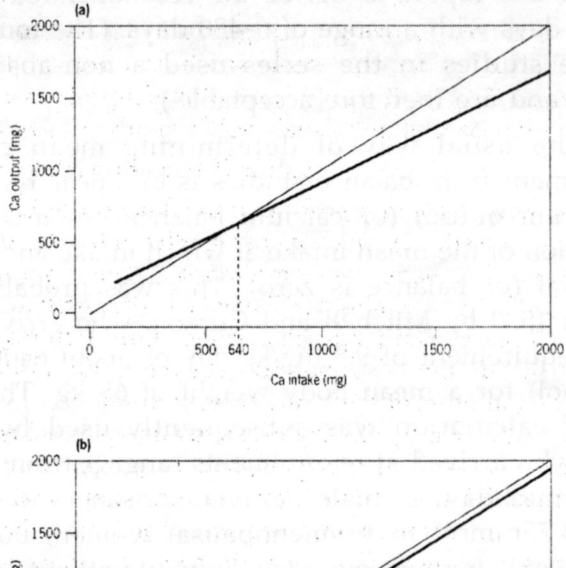

Figure 5: Calcium output as a (a) linear and (b) non-linear function of calcium intake calculated from the same balances as Figure 3

An alternative way of calculating calcium requirement is to determine the intake at which the mean maximum positive balance occurs.

This has been done with a two-component, split, linear regression model in which calcium balance is regressed on intake to determine the threshold intake above which no further increase in calcium retention occurs. This may well be an appropriate way of calculating the calcium requirement of children and adolescents (and perhaps pregnant and lactating women) who need to be in positive calcium balance and in whom the difference between calcium intake and output is therefore relatively large and measurable by the balance technique. However, in normal adults the difference between calcium intake and output at high calcium intakes represents a very small difference between two large numbers, and this calculation, therefore, carries too great an error to calculate their requirement.

The Expert Consultation concurred that the most satisfactory way of calculating calcium requirement from current data is by using the intake level at which excreted calcium equals net absorbed calcium, which has the advantage of permitting separate analysis of the effects of changes in calcium absorption and excretion. This intercept has been shown in Figure 3 to occur at an intake of about 520 mg, but when insensible losses of calcium of 60mg (1.5mmol) are taken into account, the intercept rises to 840mg, which was considered to be as close as it is possible to get at present to the calcium requirement of adults on Western-style diets. The intercept rises to about 1100mg due to an increase in obligatory urinary calcium losses of 30mg (0.75mmol) at menopause. A value of 1100 mg was thus proposed as the mean calcium requirement of postmenopausal women. However, this type of calculation cannot be easily applied to other high-risk populations (such as children) because there are not sufficient published data from these groups to permit a similar analysis of the relationship between calcium intake, absorption, and excretion. An alternative is to estimate how much calcium each population group needs to absorb to meet obligatory calcium losses and desirable calcium retention, and then to calculate the intake required to provide this rate of calcium absorption.

Risk for Calcium Deficiency

It is clear from Figure 1 that a positive calcium balance (i.e. net calcium retention) is required throughout growth, particularly during the first 2 years of life and during puberty and adolescence. These age groups therefore constitute populations at risk for calcium deficiency, as do pregnant women (especially in the last trimester), lactating women, postmenopausal women, and, possibly, elderly men.

Recommendations for Calcium Requirements

Infants

In the first 2 years of life, the daily calcium increment in the skeleton is about 100mg (2.5mmol). The urinary calcium of infants is about 10mg/day (0.25mmol/day) and is virtually independent of intake; insensible losses are likely to be similar in magnitude. Therefore, infants need to absorb some 120mg (3mmol) of calcium daily to allow for normal growth. What this represents in dietary terms can be calculated from calcium absorption studies in newborn infants. These studies suggest that the absorption of calcium from cow milk by infants is about 0.5 SD above the normal adult slope and from human milk is more than 1 SD above the normal adult slope. If this information is correct, different recommendations need to be made for infants depending on milk source. With human milk, an absorption of 120mg (3mmol) of calcium requires a mean intake of 240mg (6mmol) (Figure 6) and a recommended intake of say 300 mg (7.5mmol), which is close to the amount provided in the average daily milk production of 750 ml. With cow milk, calcium intake needs to be about 300 mg (7.5mmol) to meet the requirement (Figure 6) and the recommended intake 400mg (10mmol) (Table 2).

Children

The accumulation of whole-body calcium with skeletal growth is illustrated in Figure 1. It rises from about 120 g (3 mol) at age 2 years to 400 g (10mol) at age 9 years. These values can be converted into a daily rate of calcium accumulation from ages 2 to 9 years of about 120mg (3mmol), which is very similar to the amount calculated by Leitch and Aitken from growth analyses. Although urinary calcium must rise with the growth-related rise in glomerular filtration rate, a reasonable estimate of the mean value from ages 2 to 9 years might be 60 mg (1.5mmol).

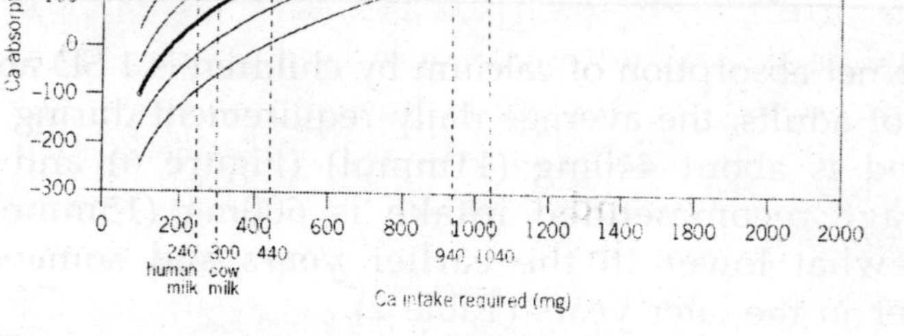

Figure 6: Calcium intakes required to provide the absorbed calcium necessary to meet calcium requirements at different stages in the lifecycle

When this is added to a daily skeletal increment of 120mg (3mmol) and a dermal loss of perhaps 40mg (1.0mmol), the average daily net absorbed calcium needs to be 220mg (5.5 mmol) during this period.

Table 2: Recommended calcium allowances based on North American and western European data

Group	Recommended intake (mg/day)
Infants and children	
0-6 months	
Human milk	300
Cow milk	400
7-12 months	400
1-3 years	500
4-6 years	600
7-9 years	700
Adolescents	
10-18 years	1300
Adults	
Females	
19 years to menopause	1000
Postmenopause	1300
Males	
19-65 years	1000
65+ years	1300
Pregnant women (last trimester)	1200
Lactating women	1000

If the net absorption of calcium by children is 1 SD above that of adults, the average daily requirement during this period is about 440mg (11mmol) (Figure 6) and the average recommended intake is 600mg (15mmol)—somewhat lower in the earlier years and somewhat higher in the later years (Table 2).

Adolescents

As can be seen in Figure 1, a striking increase in the rate of skeletal calcium accretion occurs at puberty—from about ages 10 to 17 years. The peak rate of calcium retention in this period is 300–400 mg (7.5–10 mmol) daily ; it occurs earlier in girls but continues longer in boys. To maintain a value of 300mg (7.5 mmol) for the skeleton—taking into account 100 mg (2.5mmol) for urinary calcium, and 40 mg (1.0 mmol) for insensible losses—the net absorbed calcium during at least part of this period needs to be 440mg (11mmol) daily. Even with the assumption of high calcium absorption (+2 SD), this requires an intake of 1040 mg (26.0 mmol) daily (Figure 6) and a recommended intake of 1300mg (32.5mmol) during the peak growth phase (Table 2). It is difficult to justify any difference between the allowances for boys and girls because, as mentioned above, although the growth spurt starts earlier in girls, it continues longer in boys. This recommended intake (which is close to that derived differently by Matkovic and Heaney is not achieved by many adolescents even in developed countries, but the effects of this shortfall on their growth and bone status are unknown.

Adults

As indicated earlier and for the reasons given, the Consultation concluded that the mean apparent calcium requirement of adults in developed countries is about 520mg (13mmol) but that this is increased by insensible losses to some 840mg (21mmol) (Figure 3). This reasoning forms the basis of the recommended intake for adults of 1000mg (Table 2).

Menopausal Women

The most important single cause of osteoporosis—at least in developed countries —is probably menopause, which is accompanied by an unequivocal and sustained rise in obligatory urinary calcium of about 30 mg (0.75mmol) daily. Because calcium absorption certainly does not increase at this time, and probably decreases, this extra urinary calcium represents a negative calcium balance which is compatible with the average bone loss of about 0.5–1.0% per year after menopause. There is a consensus that these events are associated with an increase in bone resorption but controversy continues about whether this is the primary event, the response to an increased calcium demand, or both. The results of calcium trials are clearly relevant.Before 1997, there had been 20 prospective trials of calcium supplementation in 857 postmenopausal women and 625 control subjects; these trials collectively showed a highly significant suppression of bone loss through calcium supplementation. Another meta-analysis covering similar numbers showed that calcium supplementation significantly enhanced the effect of estrogen on bone. It is therefore logical to recommend sufficient additional calcium after menopause to cover at least the extra obligatory loss of calcium in the urine. The additional dietary calcium needed to meet an increased urinary loss of 30mg (0.75mmol) is 260mg/day (6.5mmol/day) (Figure 3), which raises the daily requirement from 840mg (21mmol) to 1100mg (27.5 mmol) and the recommended intake from 1000 to 1300mg/day (25 to 32.5mmol/day) (Table 2), which is a little higher than that recommended by Canada and the United States.

Ageing Adults

Not enough is known about bone and calcium metabolism during ageing to enable calculation of the calcium requirements of older men and women with any confidence. Calcium absorption tends to decrease with age in both sexes but whereas there is strong evidence that calcium requirement rises during menopause, corresponding evidence about ageing men is less convincing. Nonetheless, as a precaution an extra allowance of 300mg/day (7.5 mmol/day) for men over 65 years to raise their requirement to that of postmenopausal women was proposed (Table 2).

Pregnant women

The calcium content of the newborn infant is about 24 g (600mmol). Most of this calcium is laid down in the last trimester of pregnancy, during which the fetus retains about 240mg (6mmol) of calcium daily. There is some evidence that pregnancy is associated with an increase in calcium absorption (associated with a rise in the plasma 1,25-$(OH)_2$ D level). For a maternal urinary calcium of 120mg (3mmol) and a maternal skin loss of 60mg (1.5mmol), the absorbed calcium should be 420mg (10.5mmol) daily. To achieve this optimal calcium absorption, the corresponding calcium intake would need to be at least 940 mg (23.5 mmol) (Figure 6). The recommended nutrient intake was thus set at 1200mg (30mmol) (Table 2), which is similar to that proposed by Canada and the United States.

Lactating Women

The calcium content of human milk is about 36mg/100ml (9mmol/l). A lactating woman produces about 750 ml of milk daily, which represents about 280mg (7.0 mmol) of calcium. For a maternal urinary calcium of 100mg/day (2.5 mmol/day) and a maternal skin loss of 60mg/day (1.5mmol/day), the required absorption is 440mg/day (11mmol/day)—the same as at puberty. If calcium absorption efficiency is maximal (i.e. 2 SD above the normal adult mean)—possibly because of the effect of prolactin on the production of 1,25- $(OH)_2$ D —the requirement would be about 1040 mg (26.0mmol) and the recommended intake would be about 1300mg (32.5mmol). However, although it is known that bone is lost during lactation and restored after weaning, early reports that this bone loss could be prevented by calcium supplementation have not been confirmed in controlled studies.

The prevailing view now is that calcium absorption does not increase, and may even decrease, during lactation. It is increasingly thought that lactational bone loss is not a nutritional problem but may be due to the parathyroid hormone-related peptide secreted by the breast and is therefore beyond the control of dietary calcium. In view of this uncertainty, the present recommendations do not include any extra calcium allowance during lactation (Table 2); any risk to adolescent mothers is covered by the general recommendation of 1300 mg for adolescents.

Upper Limits

Because of the inverse relationship between fractional calcium absorption and calcium intake (Figure 4), a calcium supplement of 1000mg (25mmol) in conjunction with a Western-style diet only increases urinary calcium by about 60mg (1.5 mmol). Urinary calcium also rises very slowly with intake (slope of 5–10%) and the risk of kidney stones from dietary hypercalciuria must therefore be negligible. In fact, it has been suggested that dietary calcium may protect against renal calculi because it binds dietary oxalate and reduces oxalate excretion. Toxic effects of a high calcium intake have only been described when the calcium is given as the carbonate form in very high doses; this toxicity is caused as much by the alkali as by the calcium and is due to precipitation of calcium salts in renal tissue (milk-alkali syndrome). However, in practice an upper limit on calcium intake of 3g (75mmol) is recommended.

Nutritional Factors Affecting Calcium Requirement

The calcium requirements proposed in Table 2 are based on data from developed countries (notably Norway and the United States) and can only be applied with any confidence to countries and populations with similar dietary cultures. Other dietary cultures may entail different calcium requirements and call for different recommendations. In particular, the removal or addition of any nutrient that affects calcium absorption or excretion must have an effect on calcium requirement. Two such nutrients are sodium and animal protein, both of which increase urinary calcium and therefore must be presumed to increase calcium requirement. A third candidate is vitamin D because of its role in calcium homeostasis and calcium absorption.

Sodium

It has been known at least since 1961 that urinary calcium is related to urinary sodium and that sodium administration raises calcium excretion, pre-sumably because sodium competes with calcium for reabsorption in the renal tubules. Regarding the quantitative relationships between the renal handling of sodium and calcium, the filtered load of sodium is about 100 times that of calcium (in molar terms) but the clearance of these two elements is similar at about 1 ml/min, which yields about 99% reabsorption and 1% excretion for both. However, these are approximations which conceal the close dependence of urinary sodium on sodium intake and the weaker dependence of urinary calcium on calcium intake. It is an empirical fact that urinary sodium and calcium are significantly related in normal and hypercalciuric subjects on freely chosen diets. The slope of urinary calcium on sodium varies in published work from about 0.6% to 1.2% (in molar terms); a representative figure is about 1%, that is, 100mmol of sodium (2.3g) takes out about 1mmol (40mg) of calcium. The biological significance of this relationship is supported by the accelerated osteoporosis induced by feeding salt to rats on low-calcium diets and the effects of salt administration and salt restriction on markers of bone resorption in postmenopausal women.

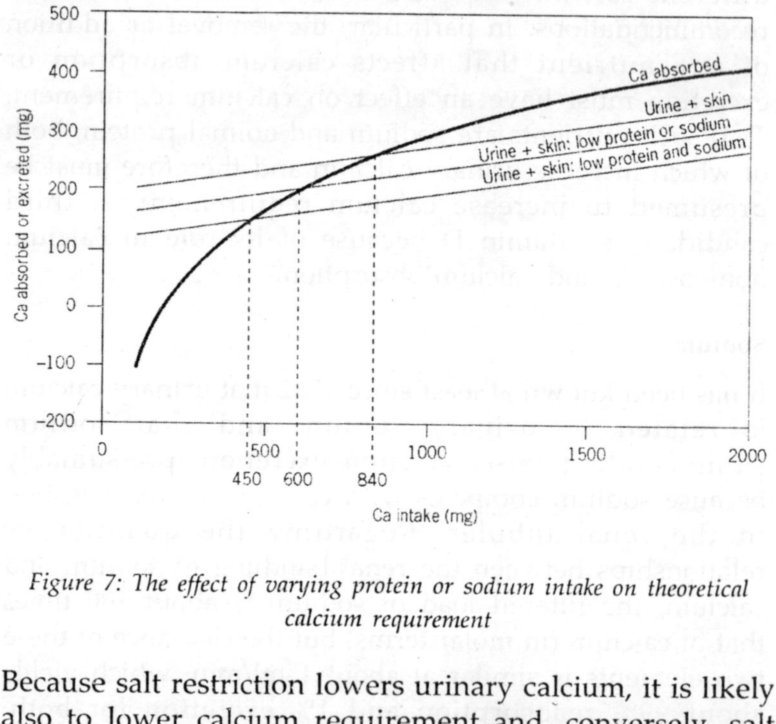

Figure 7: The effect of varying protein or sodium intake on theoretical calcium requirement

Because salt restriction lowers urinary calcium, it is likely also to lower calcium requirement and, conversely, salt feeding is likely to increase calcium requirement. This is illustrated in Figure 7, which shows that lowering sodium intake by 100mmol (2.3g) from, for example, 150 to 50mmol (3.45 to 1.15 g), reduces the theoretical calcium requirement from 840mg (21mmol) to 600mg (15mmol). However, the implications of this for global calcium requirements cannot be computed because information on sodium intake is available from only a very few countries.

Protein

The positive effect of dietary protein—particularly animal protein—on urinary calcium has also been known since at least the 1960s. One study found that 0.85 mg of calcium was lost for each gram of protein in the diet. A meta-analysis of 16 studies in 154 adult humans on protein intakes of up to 200 g found that 1.2 mg of calcium was lost in the urine for every 1-g rise in dietary protein. A small but more focused study showed a rise of 40 mg in urinary calcium when dietary animal protein was raised from 40 to 80 g (i.e. within the physiological range). This ratio of urinary calcium to dietary protein (1 mg to 1 g) was adopted by the Expert Consultation as a representative value. This means that a 40-g reduction in animal protein intake from 60 to 20 g (roughly the difference between the developed and developing regions shown in Table 1) would reduce calcium requirement by the same amount as a 2.3-g reduction in dietary sodium (i.e. from 840 to 600 mg) (Figure 7).

How animal protein exerts its effect on calcium excretion is not fully understood. A rise in glomerular filtration rate in response to protein has been suggested as one factor but this is unlikely to be important in the steady state. The major mechanisms are thought to be the effect of the acid load contained in animal proteins and the complexing of calcium in the renal tubules by sulphate and phosphate ions released by protein metabolism. Urinary calcium is significantly related to urinary phosphate (as well as to urinary sodium), particularly in subjects on restricted calcium intakes or in the fasting state, and most of the phosphorus in the urine of people on Western-style diets comes from animal protein in the diet. Thus, the empirical observation that an intake of 1g of protein results in 1 mg of calcium in the urine agrees very well with the phosphorus content of animal protein (about 1% by weight) and the observed relationship between calcium and phosphate in the urine. Similar considerations apply to urinary sulphate but it is probably less important than the phosphate ion because the associa- tion constant for calcium sulphate is lower than that for calcium phosphate.

Vitamin D

One of the first observations made on vitamin D after it had been identified in 1918 was that it promoted calcium absorption. It is now well established that vitamin D (synthesized in the skin under the influence of sunlight) is converted to 25-OH-D in the liver and then to 1,25-$(OH)_2$ D in the kidneys and that the latter metabolite controls calcium absorption. However, plasma 25-OH-D closely reflects vitamin D nutritional status and because it is the substrate for the renal enzyme which produces 1,25-$(OH)_2$ D, it could have an indirect effect on calcium absorption. The plasma level of 1,25-$(OH)_2$ D is principally regulated by gene expression of 1-a-hydroxylase (CYP1a) and not by the plasma concentration of 25-OH-D. This has been seen consistently in animal studies, and the high calcium absorption and high plasma concentrations of 1,25-$(OH)_2$ D observed in Gambian mothers are consistent with this type of adaptation. However, vitamin D synthesis may be compromised at high latitudes, to the degree that 25-OH-D levels may not be sufficient to sustain adequate 1,25-$(OH)_2$ D levels and efficient intestinal calcium absorption—although this theory remains unproved.

Regardless of the mechanism of compromised vitamin D homeostasis, the differences in calcium absorption efficiency have a major effect on theoretical calcium requirement, as illustrated in Figure 8, which shows that an increase in calcium absorption of as little as 10% reduces the intercept of excreted and absorbed calcium (and therefore calcium requirement) from 840 to 680 mg. The figure also shows the great increase in calcium intake that is required as a result of any impairment of calcium absorption.

Implications

In light of the major reduction in theoretical calcium requirement which follows animal protein restriction, an attempt has been made to show (in Table 3) how the calcium allowances recommended in Table 2 could be modi-fied to apply to countries where the animal protein intake per capita is around 20–40g rather than around the 60–80 g typical of developed countries.

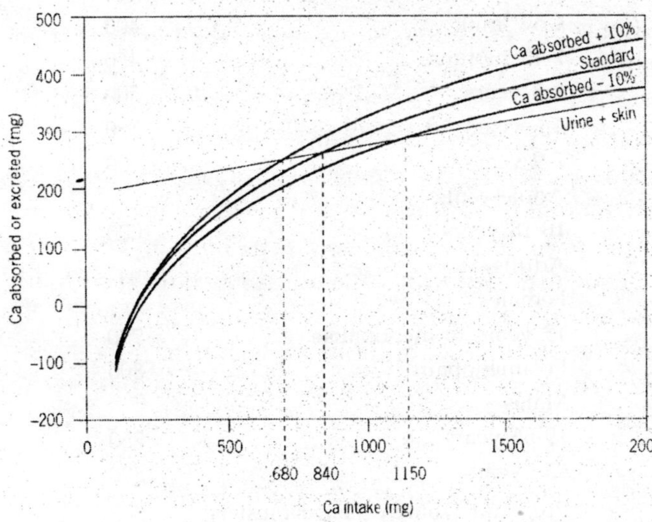

Figure 8: The effect of varying calcium absorptive efficiency on theoretical calcium requirement

These hypothetical allowances take into account the need to protect children, in whom skeletal needs are much more important determinants of calcium requirement than are urinary losses and in whom calcium supplementation is likely to have a beneficial effect, for example, as has been reported in the Gambia. However, adjustment for animal protein intake has a major effect on the recommended calcium allowances for adults as Table 3 shows. It also brings the allowances nearer to what the actual calcium intakes are in many parts of the world.

Table 3: Theoretical calcium allowances based on an animal protein *intake of 20-40g*

Group	Recommended intake (mg/day)
Infants and children	
0-6 months	
Human milk	300
Cow milk	400
7-12 months	450
1-3 years	500
4-6 years	550
7-9 years	700
Adolescents	
10-18 years	1000
Adults	
Females	
19 years to menopause	750
Postmenopause	800
Males	
19-65 years	750
65+ years	800
Pregnant women (last trimester)	800
Lactating women	750

If sodium intakes were also lower in developing than in developed countries or urinary sodium were reduced for other reasons, such as increased sweat losses, the calcium requirement might be even lower, for example, 450mg (Figure 7). This would be reduced still further by any increase in calcium absorption as illustrated in Figure 8, whether resulting from better vitamin D status because of increased sunlight exposure or for other reasons. Because the increase in calcium absorption in Gambian compared with British women is much more than 10%, this is likely to have a major—although not at present calculable—effect on calcium requirement there. However, the adjusted bone mineral density in Gambian women is reported to be some 20% lower in the spine (but not in the forearm) than in British women, a finding which emphasizes the need for more data from developing countries.

12

Vitamin B_{12}

Role of Vitamin B_{12} in Human Metabolic Processes

Although the nutritional literature still uses the term vitamin, a more specific name for vitamin is cobalamin. Vitamin $B_{12}$is the largest of the B complex vitamins, with a relative molecular mass of over 1000. It consists of a corrin ring made up of four pyrroles with cobalt at the centre of the ring.

There are several vitamin B_{12}-dependent enzymes in bacteria and algae, but no species of plants have the enzymes necessary for vitaminB_{12} synthesis. This fact has significant implications for the dietary sources and availability of vitamin B_{12}. In mammalian cells, there are only two vitamin B_{12}—dependent enzymes. One of these enzymes, methionine synthase, uses the chemical form of the vitamin which has a methyl group attached to the cobalt and is called methylcobalamin. The other enzyme, methylmalonyl coenzyme (CoA) mutase, uses a form of vitaminB_{12} that has a 5'-adeoxyadenosyl moiety attached to the cobalt and is called 5'-deoxyadenosylcobalamin, or coenzymeB_{12}. In nature, there are two other forms of vitamin B_{12}: hydroxycobalamin and aquacobalamin, where hydroxyl and water groups, respectively, are attached to the cobalt. The synthetic form of vitaminB_{12} found in supplements and fortified foods is cyanocobalamin, which has cyanide attached to the cobalt. These three forms of vitaminB_{12} are enzymatically activated to the methyl- or deoxyadenosylcobalamins in all mammalian cells.

Dietary Sources and Availability

Most microorganisms, including bacteria and algae, synthesize vitaminB_{12}, and they constitute the only source of the vitamin. The vitaminB_{12} synthesized in microorganisms enters the human food chain through incorporation into food of animal origin. In many animals, gastrointestinal fermentation supports the growth of these vitaminB_{12} synthesizing microorganisms, and subsequently the vitamin is absorbed and incorporated into the animal tissues. This is particularly true for the liver, where vitaminB_{12} is stored in large concentrations. Products from herbivorous animals, such as milk, meat, and eggs, thus constitute important dietary sources of the vitamin, unless the animal is subsisting in one of the many regions known to be geochemically deficient in cobalt. Milk from cows and humans contains binders with very high affinity for vitaminB_{12}, though whether they hinder or promote intestinal absorption is not entirely clear. Omnivores and carnivores, including humans, derive dietary vitaminB_{12} almost exclusively from animal tissues or products (i.e. milk, butter, cheese, eggs, meat, poultry). It appears that the vitaminB_{12} required by humans is not derived from microflora in any appreciable quantities, although vegetable fermentation preparations have been reported as being possible sources of vitaminB_{12}.

Absorption

The absorption of vitaminB_{12}in humans is complex. VitaminB_{12} in food is bound to proteins and is only released by the action of a high concentration of hydrochloric acid present in the stomach. This process results in the free form of the vitamin, which is immediately bound to a mixture of glycoproteins secreted by the stomach and salivary glands. These glycoproteins, called R-binders (or haptocorrins), protect vitaminB_{12} from chemical denaturation in the stomach. The stomach's parietal cells, which secrete hydrochloric acid, also secrete a glycoprotein called intrinsic factor. Intrinsic factor binds vitaminB_{12} and ultimately enables its active absorption. Although the formation of the vitaminB_{12}–intrinsic factor complex was initially thought to happen in the stomach, it is now clear that this is not the case. At an acidic pH, the affinity of the intrinsic factor for vitamin$B_{12}$is low whereas its affinity for the R-binders is high. When the contents of the stomach enter the duodenum, the R-binders become partly digested by the pancreatic proteases, which in turn causes them to release their vitaminB_{12}. Because the pH in the duodenum is more neutral than that in the stomach, the intrinsic factor has a high binding affinity to vitaminB_{12}, and it quickly binds the vitamin as it is released from the R-binders. The vitaminB_{12}–intrinsic factor complex then proceeds to the lower end of the small intestine, where it is absorbed by phagocytosis by specific ileal receptors.

Consequences of VitaminB_{12} Deficiency

Vegetarians

Because plants do not synthesize vitaminB_{12}, individuals who consume diets completely free of animal products (vegan diets) are at risk of vitaminB_{12} deficiency. This is not true of lacto-ovo vegetarians, who consume the vitamin in eggs, milk, and other dairy products.

Pernicious Anaemia

Malabsorption of vitamin B_{12} can occur at several points during digestion. By far the most important condition resulting in vitamin B_{12} malabsorption is the autoimmune disease called pernicious anaemia (PA). In most cases of PA, antibodies are produced against the parietal cells causing them to atrophy, and lose their ability to produce intrinsic factor and secrete hydrochloric acid. In some forms of PA, the parietal cells remain intact but autoantibodies are produced against the intrinsic factor itself and attach to it, thus preventing it from binding vitamin B_{12}. In another less common form of PA, the antibodies allow vitamin B_{12} to bind to the intrinsic factor but prevent the absorption of the intrinsic factor–vitamin B_{12} complex by the ileal receptors. As is the case with most autoimmune diseases, the incidence of PA increases markedly with age. In most ethnic groups, it is virtually unknown to occur before the age of 50, with a progressive rise in incidence thereafter. However, African American populations are known to have an earlier age of presentation. In addition to causing malabsorption of dietary vitamin B_{12}, PA also results in an inability to reabsorb the vitamin B_{12} which is secreted in the bile. Biliary secretion of vitamin B_{12} is estimated to be between 0.3 and 0.5mg/day. Interruption of this so-called enterohepatic circulation of vitamin B_{12} causes the body to go into a significant negative balance for the vitamin. Although the body typically has sufficient vitamin B_{12} stores to last 3–5 years, once PA has been established, the lack of absorption of new vitamin B_{12} is compounded by the loss of the vitamin because of negative balance. When the stores have been depleted, the final stages of deficiency are often quite rapid, resulting in death in a period of months if left untreated.

Atrophic Gastritis

Historically, PA was considered to be the major cause of vitamin B_{12} deficiency, but it was a fairly rare condition, perhaps affecting between one and a few per cent of elderly populations. More recently, it has been suggested that a far more common problem is that of hypochlorhydria associated with atrophic gastritis, where there is a progressive reduction with age of the ability of the parietal cells to secrete hydrochloric acid. It is claimed that perhaps up to one quarter of elderly subjects could have various degrees of hypochlorhydria as a result of atrophic gastritis. It has also been suggested that bacterial overgrowth in the stomach and intestine in individuals suffering from atrophic gastritis may also reduce vitamin B_{12} absorption. The absence of acid in the stomach is postulated to prevent the release of proteinbound vitamin B_{12} contained in food but not to interfere with the absorption of the free vitamin B_{12}found in fortified foods or supplements. Atrophic gastritis does not prevent the reabsorption of biliary vitamin B_{12} and therefore does not result in the negative balance seen in individuals with PA. Nonetheless, it is agreed that with time, a reduction in the amount of vitamin B_{12}absorbed from the diet will eventually deplete vitamin B_{12} stores, resulting in overt deficiency.

When considering recommended nutrient intakes (RNIs) for vitamin B_{12} for the elderly, it is important to take into account the absorption of vitamin B_{12} from sources such as fortified foods or supplements as compared with dietary vitamin B_{12}. In the latter instances, it is clear that absorption of intakes of less than 1.5–2.0mg/day is complete—that is, for daily intakes of less than 1.5–2.0mg of free vitamin B_{12}, the intrinsic factor-mediated system absorbs that entire amount. It is probable that this is also true of vitamin B_{12} in fortified foods, although this has not been specifically examined. However, absorption of food-bound vitamin B_{12} has been reported to vary from 9% to 60% depending on the study and the source of the vitamin, which is perhaps related to its incomplete release from food. This has led many to estimate absorption as being up to 50% to correct for the bioavailability of vitamin B_{12} from food.

Vitamin B_{12} Interaction with Folate or Folic Acid

One of the vitamin B_{12}-dependent enzymes, methionine synthase, functions in one of the two folate cycles, namely, the methylation cycle. This cycle is necessary to maintain availability of the methyl donor, *S*-adenosylmethionine. Interruption of the cycle reduces the level of *S*-adenosylmethionine. This occurs in PA and other causes of vitamin B_{12} deficiency, producing as a result demyelination of the peripheral nerves and the spinal column, giving rise to the clinical condition called subacute combined degeneration. This neuropathy is one of the main presenting conditions in PA. The other principal presenting condition in PA is a megaloblastic anaemia morphologically identical to that seen in folate deficiency. Disruption of the methylation cycle also causes a lack of DNA biosynthesis and anaemia.

The methyl trap hypothesis is based on the fact that once the cofactor 5,10-methylenetetrahydrofolate is reduced by its reductase to form 5-methyltetrahydrofolate, the reverse reaction cannot occur. This suggests that the only way for the 5-methyltetrahydrofolate to be recycled to tetrahydrofolate, and thus to participate in DNA biosynthesis and cell division, is through the vitamin B_{12}-dependent enzyme methionine synthase. When the activity of this synthase is compromised, as it would be in PA, the cellular folate will become progressively trapped as 5-methyltetrahydrofolate. This will result in a cellular pseudo-folate deficiency where, despite adequate amounts of folate, anaemia will develop, which is identical to that seen in true folate deficiency. Clinical symptoms of PA, therefore, include neuropathy, anaemia, or both. Treatment with vitamin B_{12}, if given intramuscularly, will reactivate methionine synthase, allowing myelination to restart. The trapped folate will be released and DNA synthesis and generation of red cells will cure the anaemia. Treatment with high concentrations of folic acid will treat the anaemia but not the neuropathy of PA. It should be stressed that the so-called "masking" of the anaemia of PA is generally agreed not to occur at concentrations of folate found in food or at intakes of the synthetic form of folic acid at usual RNI levels of 200 or 400mg/day. However, there is some evidence that amounts less than 400mg may cause a haematologic response and thus potentially treat the anaemia. The masking of the anaemia definitely occurs at high concentrations of folic acid (>1000mg/day). This becomes a concern when considering fortification with synthetic folic acid of a dietary staple such as flour.

In humans, the vitamin B_{12}-dependent enzyme methylmalonyl CoA mutase functions both in the metabolism of propionate and certain amino acids—converting them into succinyl CoA—and in the subsequent metabolism of these amino acids via the citric acid cycle. It is clear that in vitamin B_{12} deficiency the activity of the mutase is compromised, resulting in high plasma or urine concentrations of methylmalonic acid (MMA), a degradation product of methylmalonyl CoA mutase. In adults, this mutase does not appear to have any vital function, but it clearly has an important role during embryonic life and in early development. Children deficient in this enzyme, through rare genetic mutations, suffer from mental retardation and other developmental defects.

Assessing Vitamin B_{12} Status

Traditionally it was thought that low vitamin B_{12} status was accompanied by a low serum or plasma vitamin B_{12}

level. Recently, Lindenbaum et al. challenged this assumption, by suggesting that a proportion of people with normal serum and plasma vitamin B_{12} levels are in fact vitamin B_{12} deficient. They also suggested that elevation of plasma homocysteine and plasma MMA are more sensitive indicators of vitamin B_{12} status. Although plasma homocysteine can also be elevated because of folate or vitamin B_6 deficiency, elevation of MMA apparently always occurs with poor vitamin B_{12} status. However, there may be other reasons why MMA is elevated, such as renal insufficiency, so the elevation of MMA, in itself, is not diagnostic. Thus, low serum or plasma levels of vitamin B_{12} should be the first indication of poor status and this could be confirmed by an elevated MMA if this assay was available.

Vitamin B_{12} Intakes

The Food and Nutrition Board of the National Academy of Sciences (NAS) Institute of Medicine has recently conducted an exhaustive review of the evidence regarding vitamin B_{12} intake, status, and health implications for all age groups, including the periods of pregnancy and lactation. This review has lead to calculations of what they have called an estimated average requirement (EAR), which is defined by NAS as "the daily intake value that is estimated to meet the requirement, as defined by the specific indicator of adequacy, in half of the individuals in a life-stage or gender group". The NAS then estimated a recommended dietary allowance (RDA) for vitamin B_{12}, as this daily intake value plus 2 standard deviations (SDs).

Some members of the present FAO/WHO Consultation were involved in the preparation and review of the NAS recommendations and judge them to be the best estimates currently available.

Table 1: Estimated average requirements (EARs) and recommended nutrient intakes (RNIs) for vitamin B_{12}, by group

Group	EAR (mg/day)	RNI (mg/day)
Infants and children		
0-6 months	0.3	0.4
7-12 months	0.6	0.7
1-3 years	0.7	0.9
4-6 years	1.0	1.2
7-9 years	1.5	1.8
Adolescents		
10-18 years	2.0	2.4
Adults		
19-65 years	2.0	2.4
65+ years	2.0	2.4
Pregnant women	2.2	2.6
Lactating women	2.4	2.8

The FAO/WHO Consultation thus felt it appropriate to adopt the same approach used by the NAS in deriving the RNIs for vitamin B_{12}. Therefore, the EARs given in Table 1 are the same as those proposed by the NAS, and the RNIs (which are equivalent to the RDAs used by the NAS) calculated as the EAR plus 2 SD. Supporting evidence for the recommendations for each age group is summarized below.

Infants

As with other nutrients, the principal way to determine requirements of infants is to examine the levels in milk from mothers on adequate diets. There is a wide difference in the vitamin B_{12} values reported in human milk because of differences in methodology. The previous FAO/WHO Expert Consultation based their recommendations on milk vitamin B_{12} values of normal women of about 0.4mg/l. For an average milk production of 0.75 l/day, the vitamin B_{12} intake by infants would be

0.3mg/day. Other studies have reported concentrations of vitamin B_{12} in human milk in the range 0.4–0.8mg/l. Although daily intakes ranging from 0.02 to 0.05mg/day have been found to prevent deficiency, these intakes are totally inadequate for long-term health. Thus, based on the assumption that human milk contains enough vitamin B_{12} for optimum health, an EAR between 0.3 and 0.6mg/day seems reasonable giving an RNI of between 0.4 and 0.7mg/day. It would seem appropriate to use the lower RNI figure of 0.4mg/day for infants aged 0–6 months and the higher RNI figure of 0.7mg/day for infants aged 7–12 months (Table 1).

Children

The Food and Nutrition Board of the NAS Institute of Medicine suggested the same intakes for adolescents as those for adults with progressive reduction of intake for younger groups.

Adults

Several lines of evidence point to an adult average requirement of about 2.0mg/day. The amount of intramuscular vitamin B_{12} needed to maintain remission in people with PA suggests a requirement of about 1.5mg/day, but they would also be losing 0.3–0.5mg/day through interruption of their enterohepatic circulation. This might suggest a requirement of 0.7–1.0mg/day for those without PA. Because vitamin B_{12} is not completely absorbed from food, an adjustment of 50% has to be added, giving a range of 1.4–2.0mg/day. Therapeutic response to dietary vitamin B_{12} suggests a minimum requirement of something less than 1.0mg/day, which again suggests a requirement of 2.0mg/day, allowing for the conservative correction that only half of dietary vitamin B_{12} is absorbed. Diets containing 1.8mg/day seemed to maintain adequate status but intakes lower than this resulted in subjects showing some signs of deficiency. Furthermore, dietary intakes of less than 1.5mg/day were reported to be inadequate in some subjects.

In summary, the average requirement could be said to be 2mg/day. Assuming the variability of the requirements for vitamin B_{12} is accounted for by adding 2 SDs, the RNI for adults and the elderly becomes 2.4mg/ day.

Pregnant Women

FAO/WHO Expert Consultation estimated that 0.1–0.2mg/ day of vitamin B_{12} is transferred to the fetus during the last two trimesters of pregnancy. On the basis of fetal liver content from postmortem samples, there is further evidence that the fetus accumulates, on average, 0.1–0.2mg/day of vitamin B_{12} during pregnancies of women with diets which provide adequate levels of vitamin B_{12}. It has been reported that children born to vegetarians or other women with a low vitamin B_{12} intake subsequently develop signs of clinical vitamin B_{12} deficiency such as neuropathy. Therefore, in order to derive an EAR for pregnant women, 0.2mg/day of vitamin B_{12} was added to the EAR for adults, to give an EAR of 2.2mg/day and a RNI of 2.6mg/day during pregnancy.

Lactating Women

It is estimated that 0.4mg/day of vitamin B_{12} is found in the human milk of women with adequate vitamin B_{12} status. Therefore, an extra 0.4mg/day of vitamin B_{12} is needed during lactation in addition to the normal adult requirement of 2.0mg/day, giving a total EAR of 2.4mg/ day and a RNI of 2.8mg/day during lactation.

Upper Limits

The absorption of vitamin B_{12} mediated by the glycoprotein, intrinsic factor, is limited to 1.5–2.0mg per meal because of the limited capacity of the receptors. In addition, between 1% and 3% of any particular oral administration of vitamin B_{12} is absorbed by passive diffusion. Thus, if 1000mg vitamin B_{12} (sometimes used to treat those with PA) is taken orally, the amount absorbed would be 2.0mg by active absorption plus up to about 30 mg by passive diffusion. Intake of 1000mg vitamin B_{12} has never been reported to have any side-effects. Similar large amounts have been used in some preparations of nutritional supplements without apparent ill effects. However, there are no established benefits for such amounts. Such high intakes thus represent no benefit in those without malabsorption and should probably be avoided.

13

Protein Requirements in Human Nutrition

Addressing the energy and nutrient needs of populations has been a long-standing activity of FAO and WHO – perhaps the longest existing technical activity. The first FAO Expert Committee on requirements met in Washington, DC, in 1949, only four years after the establishment of the United Nations and its technical agencies, and the topic at that time was "Calories". The second FAO Expert Consultation was six years later and focused on protein requirements, followed a year later by the second Expert Consultation on Calorie Requirements. In 1963, protein was again reviewed; this marked the beginning of the collaborative work between FAO and WHO on protein requirements. The 1971 Joint FAO/WHO ad hoc Expert Committee on Energy and Protein Requirements was unique in that energy and protein were considered together for the first time. The United Nations University became part of this joint initiative in 1981.

Ideas on the assessment of protein requirements have progressed in a rather different way from considerations of energy, which is one reason why separate consultations have been held, despite aspects of overlap and synergy. It is, for example, largely accepted that nitrogen balance reflects both protein and energy intake from the diet. The FAO Committee on Protein Requirements, which met in 1955, placed particular emphasis on the pattern of human amino acid requirements and the definition of requirements in terms of a reference protein with an "ideal" amino acid composition. Quantitative estimates of protein requirements were based on information available at that time on the needs for indispensable amino acids. In 1963, a Joint FAO/WHO Expert Group on Protein Requirements introduced the new concept that the requirement for protein is determined by the rate of obligatory nitrogen loss from the body (principally in the urine, but also in faeces and through the skin) when the diet contains no protein. Measurement of these losses should provide an estimate of requirement, with correction for protein quality.

The 1971 Ad Hoc Expert Committee made advances in two directions. First, it recognized that, even with protein of high biological value, the minimum nitrogen intake needed to ensure balance, which has generally been used as the criterion for the maintenance requirement, is larger than the so-called obligatory nitrogen loss. An attempt was made, in the light of the information available at the time, to determine the magnitude of this difference. The second advance was the clear recognition that in estimating requirements for groups, the principles are not the same for energy as for protein. For energy, an individual's intake must match his or her output if that individual is to remain in a steady state, and it is accepted that physiological mechanisms exist by which this balance is normally maintained, albeit not on a day-byday basis or even over longer periods. For protein, in contrast, there is no evidence for a regulatory mechanism that matches intake to requirement. However, there is also no reason to suppose that an intake moderately larger than the individual's physiological need will be harmful, at least within fairly wide limits. Together, these considerations led to an approach that described on the one hand an *average* requirement for energy and, on the other hand, a *safe level of intake* for protein. The safe level for a population was defined as the average protein requirement of the individuals in the population, plus twice the standard deviation (SD). There was little information about the variability of individual requirements, and the 1971 Committee accepted an estimate of 15% for the coefficient of variation. These considerations were further developed in the 1985 report, and again during the 2002 consultation.

In 1975, WHO and FAO, unusually, convened an informal gathering of experts to consider problems that had arisen in the application of the report of the 1971 Committee. They considered a number of situations in which it was thought that the 1973 report had been misused or was incomplete. They also recognized that the emphasis placed by previous groups of experts on specifying nutrient requirements for healthy populations was an ideal. They began to tackle some of the problems that arise in reconciling this ideal with reality. Of particular importance are two questions relating to children: adjustment of requirements for deficits in growth and for the effects of frequent infections. One of the recurring themes in the 2002 meeting was the need to address again, and more directly, the requirements of children and adults for protein and amino acids in populations with a high disease burden. Another major area that continues to need attention is requirements and demands in catch-up growth.

In October 1977, a further informal meeting of experts continued the review process begun in 1975. This group identified five main areas of uncertainty relating to protein requirements. These areas were addressed, and recommendations were made in the 1985 report. With a view to reconsidering these matters, as well as incorporating new research results and national experience, the 2002 Consultation again discussed these same topics, among others (in particular, quality of protein and labelling). The following areas of uncertainty remain.

- It continues to be questioned whether the 1973 and subsequent higher recommendations on adult protein requirements, based largely on data from healthy, well-nourished individuals, are realistic for developing countries, especially as they might be extrapolated to apply to children.
- Since 1971, a number of studies have re-emphasized the important relationship between energy intake and nitrogen balance, and it has been suggested that protein requirements determined from balance measurements at high levels of energy intake may have been set erroneously low.
- The 2002 Consultation felt that the previously suggested requirements for amino acids were lower than they should be and, in the light of new evidence, duly revised the requirements upwards. The 2002 Consultation considered that previous reports had given too little attention to the requirements of women, adolescents, and older children, and that further review was needed of the requirements for pregnant and lactating women and for the elderly. It is somewhat disappointing that there seems to have been so little new research since 1981 on the amino acid requirements of infants and children. Such research is also important with regard to the elderly, in view of their increasing numbers in both industrialized and developing countries.

— More information continues to be needed on the ability of some local diets to meet protein needs, and on the extent to which amino acid scores and biological assays in rats give realistic estimates of the protein values of human diets. The 1985 Consultation concluded that few natural diets provide insufficient amounts of indispensable amino acids, except those of infants and preschool children. Nevertheless, it was apparent that more attention should be given to the digestibility of the proteins in a mixed diet, especially in the diets of people in developing countries. It is clear that the availability of dietary protein for all age groups can be significantly affected by digestibility, and that protein requirements should be appropriately adjusted for increased faecal and dermal losses of nitrogen.

— A preliminary attempt was made in the 1977 informal meeting to estimate the extra protein and energy requirements for compensatory growth in malnourished children and for recovery from frequent infections. The 2002 Consultation identified this as an area needing more attention.

— The question continued to be raised of whether or not adaptation to low protein intake involves any disadvantages, provided that the intake is sufficient to achieve balance and normal growth.

The 1981 Consultation concluded that a further full-scale expert consultation, along with further research, was essential. It identified key issues as needing to be addressed by an expert consultation, which the present report partially does. The mandate of the 2002 Consultation was to revise and update the conclusions and recommendations of the 1981 Consultation. In preparation for the 2002 Consultation, well-known scientists were asked to examine and review extant literature and their own experience, and write background papers on various topics that required revision. Several of the authors and other leading scientists met in Rome from 27 June to 05 July 2001 to discuss and analyse critically the contents of the background papers, which were subsequently modified as required. The modified papers, together with other documents and the conclusions of the discussion, were provided to all members of the Expert Consultation for analysis and consideration in their deliberations, and much of the present report is based on those background documents, many of which have been subsequently published.

Recommendations on protein and amino acid requirements are essential to support the following activities:

- determining food and nutrition adequacy of population food intakes;
- setting of national food and nutrition guidelines by countries worldwide;
- determining nutrient needs, and evaluating and ensuring the adequacy of ration quality and quantity for vulnerable groups such as refugees or displaced populations, in emergency situations, conflicts, time of food shortage and the like (of particular concern to the World Food Programme, the Office of the United Nations High Commissioner for Refugees, and nongovernmental organizations active in relief work);
- guidance to the Codex Alimentarius Commission, particularly with respect to labelling and in drawing up regulations on the protein and amino acid content of industrially processed foods;
- providing information to manufacturers of infant formula and processed complementary foods,

concerning protein and amino acid requirements of infants over six months of age or with special needs, and of young children;

- mapping and monitoring (potential and actual) food shortages and undernutrition in developing countries and globally, including early warning systems (e.g. Food Insecurity and Vulnerability Information and Mapping Systems);
- research on relationships between excessive or deficient protein intakes and long-term health outcomes or the occurrence of diseases.

Ideally, a group set up to advise on requirements would include representatives of a wide range of disciplines, but this was not feasible either in 1985 or in 2002. The multidisciplinary perspective could be appropriately incorporated when food-based guidelines are being designed at a national level. As the 1985 report shows, despite all the work that has been done, many difficult biological and statistical problems remain. The statistical and broader tasks identified by the 2002 Consultation are: estimation of the distribution of the requirements; and interpretation of the distribution of recommended requirements. As in previous reports, the primary task of this Consultation has been to provide the United Nations agencies with tools for addressing practical questions on such matters as the adequacy of food supplies, targets for food and nutrition policy, and labelling of protein quality, as well as for providing specific recommendations for infants, children and adults throughout the life-course. It is hoped that, like the guidance provided in past reports, the conclusions and recommendations in the present report will help guide the decisions of national committees in developing estimates of requirements appropriate to local conditions and applications.

International meetings of experts, conferences and other forums have been extremely productive in generating new ideas and stimulating new research. This is particularly apparent in relation to protein requirements; each successive meeting, building on the work of its predecessors, has identified gaps in current knowledge, which research workers in many countries have done their best to fill. There continues to be a need for more research results from developing countries. It is hoped that capacity-building activities of the United Nations agencies and others will help this. Identifying problems and stimulating further research continue to be extremely important functions of expert consultations.

The 2002 Joint WHO/FAO/UNU Expert Consultation on Protein and Amino Acid Requirements in Human Nutrition, the primary objectives were as follows:

— to review, revise and update protein and amino acid requirements for all age groups (infants, children, adolescents, adults, elderly), and for women during pregnancy and lactation;
— to review and develop recommendations on protein requirements in health and disease, including their implications for developing countries;
— to develop recommendations on protein quality and labelling, with respect to new requirement levels, for use worldwide and in the Codex Alimentarius.

Conceptual Framework for Estimating Protein and Amino Acid Requirements

Access to sufficient food of an adequate quality to maintain normal body composition and function throughout the life-cycle is fundamental to maintaining health. A source of protein is an essential element of a healthy diet, allowing both growth and maintenance of the 25 000 proteins encoded within the human genome, as well as other nitrogenous compounds, which together form the body's dynamic system of structural and functional elements that exchange nitrogen with the environment. The amount of protein that has to be consumed, as part of an otherwise nutritionally adequate diet, to achieve the desired structure and function is identified as the requirement.

Basic Concepts

- A generic model for the dietary protein requirement (as with any nutrient) defines the requirement in terms of the needs of the organism, i.e. *metabolic demands,* and the dietary amount which will satisfy those needs, i.e. *efficiency of utilization,* thus: dietary requirement = metabolic demand/efficiency of utilization.
- For planning and public health purposes and to minimize risk of deficiency, requirements are expressed as dietary allowances, which take into account variation between individuals. *Metabolic demand* is determined by the nature and extent of those metabolic pathways that consume amino acids and are conventionally identified in most factorial models of requirements as maintenance and special needs. Special needs include growth, pregnancy and lactation. Maintenance comprises all those processes that consume amino acids and give rise to urinary, faecal and other losses, which include a small component of net protein synthesis in skin, hair and secretions.
- *Dietary requirement* is the amount of protein or its constituent amino acids, or both, that must be supplied in the diet in order to satisfy the metabolic demand and achieve nitrogen equilibrium. The requirement will in most cases be greater than the metabolic demand because of those factors that

influence the efficiency of protein use, i.e. net protein utilization. These are factors associated with digestion and absorption, which influence the digestibility and consequent amount of dietary nitrogen lost in the faeces, and the cellular bioavailability of the absorbed amino acids in relation to needs, which influences the biological value.

— There is general agreement that when the dietary intake of nitrogen is zero, and energy and all other nutrients are consumed in adequate amounts, there is an ongoing loss of nitrogen from the body, identified as *obligatory nitrogen losses*. There is also general agreement that as the intake of protein, amino acids and nitrogen increases, there is a level of intake adequate to enable nitrogen balance to be achieved, which we can define as the *minimum protein requirement*. This is the lowest level of intake that has to be consumed in order to enable nitrogen equilibrium to be achieved in the short and long term, i.e. it will involve the highest efficiency of utilization. In practice, measurements of the minimum protein requirement have varied widely within and between individuals – and to a greater extent than observed with measurements of the obligatory nitrogen losses – for a variety of reasons, some of which are not entirely understood. For this reason, identification of the minimum protein requirement is inherently difficult. This is in sharp contrast with the basal metabolic rate, from which energy requirements can be calculated, after taking into account other components of energy expenditure, and which can be measured with relatively little variation, under carefully defined standardized conditions. What follows describes those factors that can influence the minimum protein requirement.

Metabolic Demand

- The metabolic demand for amino acids and protein is the flow of amino acids through those pathways that together maintain the structure and function of the body. This comprises conversion of some individual amino acids into important metabolites, which are further transformed into nitrogenous endproducts, mainly urea and other compounds in urine, faeces or sweat, as well as net synthesis of proteins lost from the body as skin, hair and any other secretions. This demand is inherently variable between individuals and in the same individual at different times during the day and at different stages in life. A complete description of the metabolic demand would include the rates at which each individual amino acid flows through all metabolic pathways under all likely circumstances, as well as the interconversions of the different forms of nitrogen available to provide for the appropriate amino acid proportions. Measurement of such a demand cannot be made with any certainty or precision, but can be exemplified or characterized for different situations.
- The basal demand for nitrogen is usually considered to equate to the obligatory nitrogen losses, the sum of all nitrogenous losses by all routes from the body after stabilization on a nitrogen-free but otherwise nutritionally adequate diet. It is, however, recognized that the obligatory nitrogen losses represent the special circumstances where the metabolic demands are met by protein mobilized from body tissues. If the pattern of amino acids in body protein is not an exact match of the pattern of the metabolic demands, and there are reasons to believe that it is not, then the obligatory nitrogen losses will include nitrogen from amino acids which

are surplus to demand, and to this extent will overestimate the magnitude of the metabolic demands, at least in terms of total amino acid equivalents.

— The extent and amino acid pattern of demand will vary according to genotype and those factors that determine phenotype, i.e. programmed metabolic capacity, age, sex, diet, body composition, physiological state, pathological or environmental stressors, and lifestyle, especially physical activity, with all factors potentially acting separately and together. Where necessary, adaptive factors may be brought into play to enable the demand to be met, and these factors may or may not be either fully effective or costless. Current knowledge extends to only a limited understanding of this range of variation in the demand, namely the effect of other factors of importance in "model" or "reference" situations.

— While it might reasonably be assumed that genotype, programmed metabolic capacity, sex, age, and body composition are all factors that might contribute to the variation in the basal demand, in practice the extent of such influences has yet to be quantified. Indeed it is not clear how far the observed variability in the basal protein requirement can be attributed to methodological considerations, or reflects inherent biological variability.

Growth

— During growth in infancy and childhood, there are increases in length, mass, development and maturation of function. For pregnant and lactating women, there are the demands for net tissue deposit or milk formation. In each of these cases, the needs are for a pattern of amino acids that matches the material being deposited, including extracellular proteins, DNA, RNA, cell membranes, creatine, haem, etc. There is good evidence that the pattern of amino acids that is needed to meet these demands is different from that in the basal state.

— During the rapid gain in weight associated with recovery from a pathological insult, there may be extensive deposit of lean tissue. This has been used as a suitable model with which to characterize the energy and nutrient needs for net tissue deposition. The information obtained from studies using this model is of value in extending our understanding, but the needs thus determined for tissue repletion of a deficit cannot be presumed to be the same as the needs during normal growth and development.

Dietary Influences on Demand

— Efficient dietary provision of protein, amino acids and nitrogen to meet basal demands in an individual will occur only when demands for energy and all other nutrients for normal cellular and tissue function are met. There are complex responses of protein and amino acid metabolism to alterations in dietary intakes of other nutrients.

Energy

— There are well-established responses to variation in dietary energy and protein intakes. At constant levels of energy expenditure, increased energy intake improves nitrogen balance independently of the nature of the excess energy (i.e. carbohydrate or fat). The basis for this is not entirely clear, although the hormonal responses to energy intake, especially insulin secretion, can reduce demands by minimizing net protein loss through the inhibition of both proteolysis and the oxidation of amino acids. In contrast to this, an excess of dietary energy also leads to the accumulation of excess adipose tissue, which results in an increase in lean body mass and an associated increase in demands over time.

— Overall food consumption is, for most situations, determined by the level of energy expenditure, and the greatest variability reflects differences in levels of activity. A more active person expends greater amounts of energy, consumes greater amounts of food, and hence has a higher absolute level of protein consumption. Since, with increasing activity, the demand for amino acids and nitrogen increases to a much lesser extent (if at all) than energy demands, it becomes easier to satisfy nitrogen demands, and the amino acid pattern of the diet becomes of lesser importance. In contrast, as activity levels fall, food consumption falls and hence absolute protein intake falls, so any relative imbalance between the pattern of amino acids provided by the diet and the pattern required by the body will become more evident. Thus, at lower levels of food consumption, a diet that might have been adequate for protein at high levels of activity, may no longer be adequate at lower levels of activity.

Micronutrients

— The pathways of amino acid metabolism and interchange are critically dependent upon an adequate micronutrient status, and hence upon the amount and quality of food consumed. Although to date this is a poorly understood area, inadequate amounts of B vitamins or zinc will influence dietary biological value. In addition, with either supplementation or food fortification, disposal of any excess consumption of micronutrients can impose a metabolic demand or stress on the body. For example, excessive dietary zinc induces the synthesis of metallothionein, which can increase demands for sulfur amino acids, whereas the synthesis of ferritin in response to excessive iron can divert amino acids from other functions such as growth.

Lifestyle and Environmental Influences

- The most important lifestyle influence that may modify demands for protein is the level of physical activity. Variation in levels of activity influences the patterns of food consumption, as well as influencing body composition and metabolic demands. Indeed, activity itself can play an important part in the integration of intermediary metabolism, influencing amino acid interchange and the availability to the rest of the body of compounds containing nitrogen, for example the flow of nitrogen from branched-chain amino acids through glutamine to arginine or other compounds. While activity can increase the demand for protein, the extent of this may be minimized by training and by adequate and appropriate energy intake. There is evidence that the high protein intakes consumed by some athletes may increase the oxidation of amino acids during exercise and thus increase apparent demands.
- Smoking and alcohol consumption can each influence both intake and demand. Also detoxification and excretion of those chemical agents and xenobiotics consumed as a normal part of the diet can place unbalanced demands upon amino acid metabolism. Medications that consume amino acids during their detoxification include paracetamol (acetaminophen), which can account for a considerable demand for sulfur amino acids.

— Exposure to environmental challenge imposes metabolic stress, which induces either nonspecific inflammatory responses, or more specific immune responses when infections occur. At their most severe, such exposures result in a complete re-ordering of metabolic priorities, unbalanced losses from the system, and a fundamental change in the requirements for protein, amino acids and nitrogen. Furthermore, recovery from such responses requires increased and altered metabolic demands to make good the specific losses.

Achieving Nitrogen Balance

— Adequate amounts of amino acids of a suitable pattern must be provided in the diet, either in a preformed state, or as appropriate precursors that can be used to generate a suitable mix of amino acids following endogenous transformations, in order to match the demand for protein synthesis and other metabolic pathways. Any demand that involves an irreversible net removal of part or all of indispensable amino acids from the system can only be satisfied from the diet.

— The most general model that characterizes this movement of amino acids is shown in Figure 1. The demand within the system is the flow of amino acids to protein synthesis and other metabolic pathways, with any amino acids in excess of this demand flowing through oxidative pathways.

This demand has to be satisfied with amino acids that derive from protein degradation, from the de novo synthesis of amino acids, or from dietary ingestion. To a substantial degree, the amino acids deriving from protein degradation will match the amount and pattern going to protein synthesis (apart from a minor fraction of amino acids which have undergone post-translational modifications such as methylations), so the demand will be dominated by the flow to other pathways.

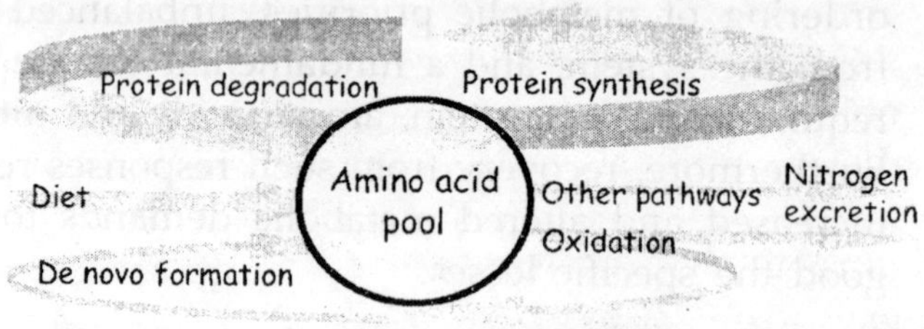

Figure 1

— One area of uncertainty relates to the usual assumption that dispensability and indispensability are absolute and mutually exclusive categorizations. This is almost certainly an oversimplification. For those amino acids identified as dispensable, there is in fact a variable extent to which endogenous formation might take place, with little reliable information about the upper limit of this capability, i.e. whether the endogenous capacity for their formation can always meet their demand. For the indispensable amino acids, this capacity is assumed to be zero, but in fact there is now evidence for some de novo synthesis of such amino acids following urea salvage in the lower gut. The extent of this and its nutritional significance remains uncertain, but has critical practical implications given the widespread use of stable isotope studies of amino acid oxidation as alternatives to nitrogen balance studies. Similarly, the extent to which de novo formation of dispensable amino acids might limit function in certain circumstances is important in terms of ensuring dietary adequacy during the formulation of special diets in clinical nutrition.

— By its nature the system is more complex than we can characterize effectively at present but there are elements which can be measured with variable degrees of reliability. Ultimately, the practical objective is to determine the extent and form of dietary nitrogen needed to enable a flow of amino acids sufficient to maintain health (body weight, nitrogen balance, and physiological, metabolic and psychological function).

Maintenance Amino Acid Catabolism and Obligatory Nitrogen Losses

— The obligatory nitrogen losses on a protein-free but otherwise adequate diet have been assumed to indicate the magnitude of the maintenance metabolic demand. The obligatory nitrogen losses are assumed to reflect a demand for amino acid precursors for any net protein synthesis (mainly epidermal losses, plus menstrual blood in premenopausal women), for all non-protein products derived from amino acids that give rise to urinary nitrogen end-products, and any nitrogen lost in the large bowel. In reviewing the nature of the obligatory nitrogen losses, Reeds emphasized that, with the exception of phenylalanine, tryptophan and methionine, current understanding indicates that the maintenance demand for amino acids is mainly for dispensable or conditionally dispensable amino acids. These obligatory nitrogen losses are assumed to be a fixed function of the lean body mass, although this is not known with any certainty. Factorial estimates of protein requirements calculate a dietary protein supply which provides for such losses, after adjustment for any inefficiency of utilization of dietary protein. This assumes that on a protein-free diet the extent of amino acid catabolism indicates the usual metabolic demand, which is met from net tissue protein catabolism.

— It is agreed that there is a demand for amino acid precursors for a range of non-protein products deriving from either amino acid carbon skeletons or amino nitrogen, such as nucleic acids, diverse smaller molecules such as creatine, taurine, glutathione, catecholamines, thyroxine, serotonin, dopamine or nitric oxide, and some irreducible amino acid catabolism (e.g. of the branched-chain amino acids) which has not been identified as purposeful. These various compounds are themselves catabolized, giving rise to various nitrogenous end-products. There is also catabolism during bacterial fermentation of carbon skeletons of amino acids that pass into the large bowel, with amino nitrogen reabsorbed as ammonia. In other words, the ileal digestibility of some indispensable amino acids is less than faecal digestibility. The overall pattern of these various pathways is unknown, but it has long been accepted that the amino acid pattern of the maintenance metabolic demand differs from that needed for tissue growth. Also, there is evidence that addition of individual amino acids (sulfur amino acids and threonine) to protein-free diets can lower the nitrogen excretion, in the same way that diets from which deletions of single amino acids have been made will induce negative nitrogen balances that are not proportional to the tissue content of the deleted amino acids.

— There is little evidence to suggest that the magnitude of the obligatory nitrogen losses varies much between comparable age groups from different parts of the world. There may be differences in the distribution of these losses between faecal and urinary nitrogen, with higher faecal losses in subjects from developing countries, who maintain a higher faecal biomass resulting in higher overall losses. Thus in Indian and Nigerian men, faecal nitrogen = 40% (urinary nitrogen + faecal nitrogen), compared with 20% for Massachusetts Institute of Technology students, although it is not clear whether this reflects the higher non-protein nitrogen content of the experimental diets. Nevertheless, this higher faecal nitrogen seems to have metabolic implications, since it is associated with an inverse correlation between urinary and faecal nitrogen excretion suggestive of a link between the size and nitrogen content of the faecal biomass and urea salvage, which might influence urinary urea excretion.

Digestibility of Dietary Proteins

— The concept of digestibility, usually defined in terms of the balance of amino acids across the small intestine (mouth to terminal ileum: ileal digestibility), or across the entire intestine (mouth to anus: faecal digestibility), is based on the principle that the difference between intake and losses provides a measure of the extent of digestion and absorption of food protein as amino acids by the gastrointestinal tract for use by the body. In fact, such net balance across the intestine involves considerable exchange of nitrogen in terms of protein, amino acids and urea between systemic pools and the gut lumen, as shown in Figure 2. Thus digestibility is more complex than usually assumed.

— The dietary supply of nitrogen-containing compounds into the system is predominantly protein, but also includes free amino acids, nucleotides and creatine, each of which may be important for health. The integrity of the gastrointestinal tract is maintained through net secretion of nitrogen-containing compounds such as mucins and antibodies, and the ongoing sloughing away of enterocytes. Further, there is significant secretion of proteins associated with the processes of digestion and absorption.

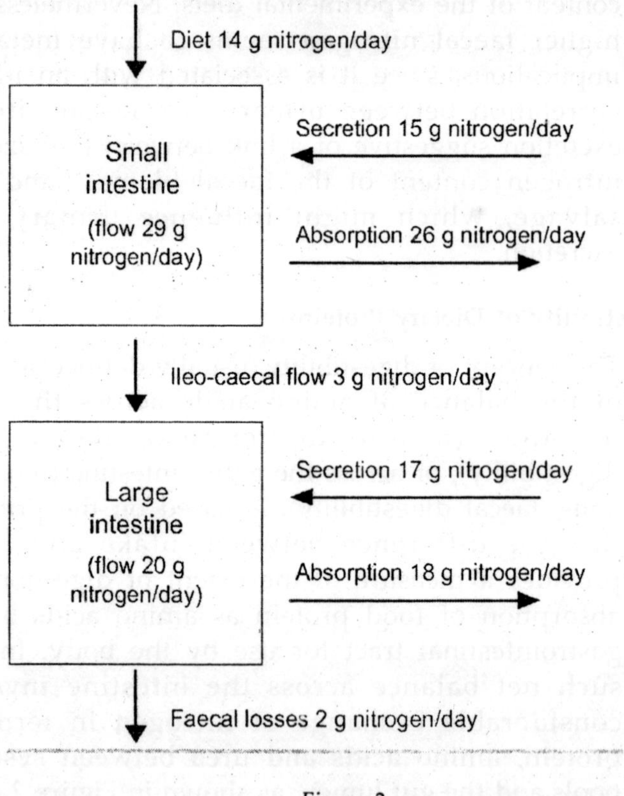

Figure 2

Most proteins are digested and the resulting amino acids or peptides absorbed. The overall flow of endogenous nitrogen-containing compounds into the lumen of the small intestine is not known with reliability, but is estimated to be around 70 to 100 g protein each day. This mixes with amino acids derived from dietary consumption and, regardless of dietary consumption, the luminal concentration of amino acids appears indistinguishable by the mid-jejunum. Dietary protein and endogenous secretion are substantially absorbed by the time they reach the terminal ileum.

14

Trends in Child Nutrition

Anthropometric Measurement

For children, anthropometric indicators are typically based on age, height and weight. Three standard indicators are "height for age", "weight for height", and "weight for age". Low heightfor-age is often referred to as "stunting", low weight-for-height as "wasting", and low weightfor-age as "underweight".

Stunting is a cumulative indicator of nutritional deprivation from birth (or rather, conception) onwards. It is relatively independent of immediate circumstances, since height does not change much in the short term. Wasting, by contrast, is usually taken to be an indicator of short-term nutritional status. From the measurement point of view, one advantage of wasting is that it does not require information on the age of the child, which is often hard to ascertain precisely. "Weight-for-age" can be seen as a more comprehensive indicator, which captures stunting as well as wasting: both stunted and wasted children are likely to fall in the "underweight" category. Thus, if a single "summary" indicator is to be used, weight-for-age would claim special attention.

The rationale of this approach is not that there is anything intrinsically "wrong" with being short or lean. While Amitabh Bachchan's height probably served him well, Sunil Gavaskar and Sachin Tendulkar are not doing too badly either. In many cases, being short or lean is not a serious impairment. However, there is evidence that pronounced stunting or wasting in childhood is associated with serious deprivations, such as ill health, diminished learning abilities, or even higher mortality. More precisely, there is a great deal of variation in the genetic potential of individuals to be small or large, but nutritional deprivation in early life, resulting in a failure to attain one's genetic potential, is likely to cause lasting harm, see for example the review article by Victora et al (2008) which focuses on low and middle-income countries. While genetics are important at the individual level, they are much less so—and arguably completely unimportant—at the population level, so that population with a high fraction of people who are stunted or underweight are population where there is evidence of nutritional deprivation.

Children's anthropometric status is usually evaluated on the basis of international standards, which reflect the anthropometric features of children in a well-nourished reference population. The distribution of heights and weights in the reference population is used to set "cut-offs" below which a child would be considered stunted, wasted or underweight. A standard cut-off is "median minus two standard deviations", based on the reference population so that, for example, a child of a given age who is shorter than this cut-off would be considered stunted.

This procedure is based on the assumption that the anthropometric achievements of children in the focus population (here, India) would be much the same as in the reference population, if these children were well nourished. In other words, anthropometric standards are similar in both population. Since this procedure tends to be applied all over the world, it amounts to saying that there are "universal" anthropometric standards for children. We shall return to this assumption, but accept it for now.

Nutrition Status of Indian Children

There are two major sources of anthropometric data for Indian children: the National Nutrition Monitoring Bureau (NNMB) at the National Institute of Nutrition, Hyderabad, and the National Family Health Survey (NFHS). Considering the former first, the NNMB surveys go back to the 1970s, but are available for nine states only: Andhra Pradesh, Gujarat, Karnataka, Kerala, Madhya Pradesh, Orissa, Maharashtra, Tamil Nadu and West Bengal (hereafter the "NNMB states"). In each state, the NNMB surveys cover 20 households per village in 120 villages. From 1991-2 onwards, the NNMB sample villages are sub-samples of National Sample Survey (NSS) samples. In the "repeat surveys" (1975-79, 1988-90 and 1996-97), the 120 sample villages consist of 90 villages from the previous survey and 30 "new" villages. The repeat surveys are meant to be fully comparable and provide perhaps the safest basis for assessing nutrition trends from NNMB data, at least if height selective out-migration is not important.

One difficulty with this exercise is that some states are "skipped" in some surveys: specifically, West Bengal in 1975-79 and 1988-90, and Madhya Pradesh in 1996-7. Further, it is not possible to construct a consistent series of aggregate figures for the remaining seven states from the NNMB reports, due to missing data. However, weight-for-age data are available statewise for each survey year from the NNMB reports, and close scrutiny of these data shows that omission of one of these two states makes little difference to the aggregates. Thus, the aggregate figures presented in the NNMB reports (for nine states, with Madhya Pradesh "missing" in one year and West Bengal missing in two years) are good enough for the purpose of assessing broad nutrition trends.

For instance, between 1975-9 and 2004-5, there have been reductions of around 50 per cent in the prevalence of severe undernutrition (measurement below 3 standard deviations of the median of the reference distribution), whether one looks at weight-for-age (37 percent of the child population to 18 percent) or height-for-age (53 percent to 25 percent). The retreat of severe undernourishment can also be seen from the sharp decline over the same period in the prevalence of clinical signs of nutritional deficiency, such as marasmus and oedema.

Having said this, the overall levels of child undernutrition in India (including not only severe but also "moderate" undernourishment) are still very high, both in absolute terms as well as relative to other countries. Even today, close to half of all Indian children are underweight, and about half suffer from anemia. These are appalling figures, which place India among the most "undernourished" countries in the world. According to the 2007 World Development Indicators, only two countries have higher proportions of underweight children (based on the *same* standards): Bangladesh and Nepal. While Pakistan and Sri Lanka have somewhat lower levels of child undernutrition, the whole South Asian region stands apart from the rest of the world in this respect. In particular, child undernutrition is much higher in South Asia (48.5 percent underweight in 1999) than in Sub-Saharan Africa (29.6 percent underweight in 2005), although the most undernourished countries in both regions fare much the same, as Table 1 indicates.

Table 1: Countries with the Highest Levels of Child Undernutrition, 1996-2005

Country	Proportion (%) of children with low "weight for age"
Nepal	48.3
Bangladesh	47.5
India	46.7
Timor-Leste	45.8
Yemen	45.6
Burundi	45.1
Madagascar	41.9
Sudan	40.7
Lao (People's Dem Rep)	40.4
Niger	40.1
Eritrea	39.6
Afghanistan	39.3

National Family Health Survey (NFHS) data corroborate these basic patterns, with some qualifications. Three rounds of the NFHS are available so far. They were conducted in 1992-3, 1998-9 and 2005-6. We shall refer to them as "NFHS-1", "NFHS-2" and "NFHS-3" respectively. As far as *levels* of undernutrition are concerned, NNMB and NFHS data are broadly consistent. For instance, both NNMB and NFHS place the proportion of underweight children at around half in the latest year for which data are available (2004-5 and 2005-6, respectively).

However, there are significant differences between these two sources as far as trends in child nutrition are concerned.

Recent Trends in Child Nutrition

Until recently, trends in anthropometric indicators presented a reasonably clear picture. Whether one looked at, say, the heights or weights of children, or the "Body

Mass Index" (BMI) of adults, the dominant pattern was one of sustained improvement. We have already noted some of these trends in the preceding section, as they emerge from NNMB data. The first two rounds of the National Family Health Survey (NFHS-1 and NFHS-2) appeared to be broadly consistent with the NNMB data in this respect. For instance, according to NFHS data, the proportion of underweight children declined from 52 per cent in 1992-3 to 47 per cent in 1998-9.NNMB data suggest a similar rate of decline—about one percentage point per year in the 1990s. As discussed below, BMI data for Indian adults also show a sustained improvement over time, albeit from levels of height and weight that were (and still are) among the lowest in the world.

However, the most recent data, from the third round of the National Family Health Survey, (NFHS-3), tell a different story. According to NFHS-3, the proportion of underweight children in 2005-6 (using the same standards as in NFHS-1 and NFHS-2) was 46 per cent—virtually the same as in 1998-9. This apparent "stalling" of nutritional improvement came as a rude shock when these numbers were published in late 2006, at a time of widespread euphoria about India's rapidly growing economy. If correct, this statistic raises serious questions about what is currently holding up the progress of child nutrition in India.

The NFHS-3 data on weight-for-age, however, are not quite conclusive in this respect, for several reasons. First, the evidence on weight-for-age needs to be read together with other indicators of child nutrition, such as height-for-age and weight-for-height. The stagnation of underweight indicators can be thought of as an averaging of the opposite movements of stunting and wasting but it is far from clear why wasting should increase while stunting goes down. Perhaps the decline of stunting in this period reflects continued improvements in maternal health, themselves related to nutritional improvements that occurred twenty or thirty years ago (when today's mothers were children). The increase in wasting, for its part, is quite puzzling, and it is difficult to come to any firm conclusion without a better understanding of these opposite trends.

Second, there are also contrasting indications from NFHS and NNMB data. Indeed, the latest NNMB survey, conducted in 2004–5, suggests a continuation of the earlier decline of undernutrition as reflected in weight-for-age data, in contrast with the "stalling" pattern in the NFHS data. Further, this decline is associated with a sharp *decline* in wasting, and some *increase* in stunting—almost the "reverse" of the NFHS trends on these indicators.

Third, there is a possible issue of comparability between NFHS-2 and NFHS-3 data. This is not immediately obvious from anthropometric data, but other indicators give reason for doubt in this respect. For instance, the NFHS surveys suggest that there has been a *decline* of school attendance between 1998-99 and 2005-06, even though there is much independent evidence of major *increases* in school attendance during that period, from the National Sample Survey and other sources.There are also inconsistencies between NFHS-2 and NFHS-3 in the measurement of adult height, which we discuss in the next subsection. In short, the "crisis" signals emerging from NFHS-3 data on weight-for-age are yet to be corroborated, and further research (and evidence) is required to make sense of thee contrasting indications on recent nutrition trends.

Having said this, even if we ignore the most recent crisis signals and take a somewhat longer view (for which there is evidence of sustained improvement, as mentioned earlier), the progress of nutrition indicators in

India seems to be undistinguished, given the country's high rates of economic growth from the early 1990s onwards. To illustrate the point, one recent study of international data concludes that the rate of decline of child undernutrition (based on weight-forage) tends to be around half of the rate of growth of per-capita GDP.If this rough benchmark can be applied to India, which grew at 4.2 percent a year from 1990 to 2005, we would have expected the proportion of underweight children to have declined by 2.1 percent a year, or by about 27 percent since 1990. But the actual decline was only about 20 per cent, according to NNMB data for nine states, and much less (barely 10 per cent) according to NFHS data. Over the longer period, from 1980 to 2005, which includes the earlier decade of somewhat slower growth, the predicted decline is 38 percent, and the actual improvement was 29 percent.

The contrast between India and China is also of some interest in this context. There is evidence of a steady growth in the heights of Chinese children in recent decades, not only during the period of fast economic growth that followed the "economic reforms" of the late 1970s, but also before that. For instance one recent study reports that, in a representative sample of Chinese children aged 2-5 years, the average increase in height between 1992 and 2002 was 3 cm in rural areas (for both boys and girls), and even higher in urban areas (3.6 cm and 3.8 cm for boys and girls, respectively); see Yang et al (2005). And, according to an earlier study, "the average heights of Chinese children between the ages of 7 and 14 years increased by approximately 8.04 cm between 1951-8 and 1979".

NNMB data suggest much slower growth rates and heights of Indian children. For instance, in the "NNMB states" the increase in children's heights between 1975-9 and 2004-5 was a little below 2 cm per decade at age 3, and barely 1 cm per decade at age 5. The NNMB data also suggest that the growth rates of heights and weights were particularly slow in the later part of this period, with, for instance, very little growth in the heights of children at age 5 between 1996-7 and 2004-5.

Here again, however, there are significant differences between NNMB and NFHS data. For instance, a comparison between NFHS-1 and NFHS-3 suggests that children's height at age 3 increased by about 2.5 cm per decade between 1992-3 and 2005-6, which looks much closer to the Chinese rates of increase. Further work is required to reconcile these different sources, and to assess the comparative progress of nutrition indicators in India and China.

Adult Weights and Heights

Recent nutrition trends can be further scrutinized from available data on adult weights and heights. A useful starting point is the "Body Mass Index" (BMI), defined as the ratio of weight (in kilos) to the square of height (in meters). The proportion of individuals with low BMI, like that of underweight children, declined steadily during the last 30 years or so. In spite of this, Indian adults today (like Indian children) have some of the highest levels of undernutrition in the world, with 36 per cent of adult women suffering from low BMI (rising to well over 40 per cent in several states). Among 23 countries of sub-Saharan Africa for which comparable data are available from the Demographic and Health Surveys, only one (Eritrea) is doing worse than India in this respect. In fact, the proportion of adult women with low BMI is above 20 per cent in only four of these 23 countries (Burkina Faso, Chad, Eritrea and Ethiopia), and the population-weighed average for all these countries together is 16 per cent, much less than half of the Indian figure.

Data on the height of Indian adults also shed further light on nutrition and nutritional trends in the past. Because people's heights do not change after they are fully grown—at least until age 50 after which there is some shrinkage—and because adult height is set in childhood and in adolescence, we can look at the history of nutrition and the disease environment by comparing the adult heights of contemporary Indians who were born at different dates in the past. This can be done using NFHS-2 which collected data on the heights of adult women, and NFHS-3 which collected data on both men and women. Figure 1 shows plots of average height by year of birth for women from both surveys, and for men and women from NFHS-3. In order to fit both men and women on the same graph, we have subtracted 10 centimeters from average men's heights. The scale for women is on the left, and the scale for men is on the right; note that apart from the 10 centimeter shift, the scales are the same.

Recall that NFHS-2 was collected in 1998–99 and NFHS-3 in 2005–06, so that adult height is attained only for those born prior to around 1978 in NFHS-2 and around 1985 in NFHS-3, and that the apparent declines of heights after those dates in the figure come from the fact that the relevant individuals are not fully grown. That adult height is attained so late in India—in the early or mid 20s, compared with age 18 in the West—is itself a mark of poor nutrition. And indeed, Indian women, along with Nepalese and Bangladeshi women—for whom data are also available from the DHS surveys—are today among the shortest in the world.

Figure 1 shows also that later-born men and women are taller, an indication that net nutrition has been improving, which is consistent with the NNMB data on child nutrition discussed above. The figure also shows that the rate of growth of men's heights, at 0.056 cm a year, is more than three times the rate of growth of women's heights which is 0.018 cm a year in NFHS-3 and 0.012 cm a year in NFHS-2. Since we do not see any such differential improvement in stunting or wasting in infants, the relatively favourable growth of boys must reflect discriminatory factors that operate in later childhood. We do not know what these factors might be—though differential access to healthcare is certainly a possibility—and the finding echoes the similar (largely unresolved) puzzles about the decline in female-male ratios in the Indian population in the 20th century.

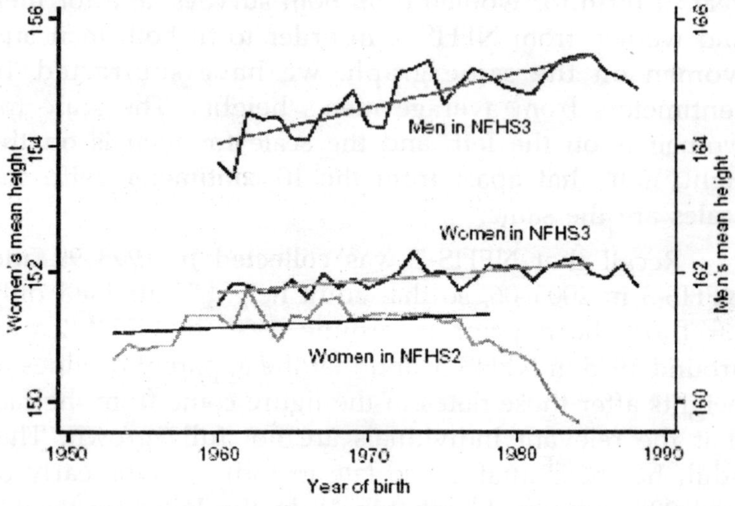

Figure 1: Average heights of Indian men and women by age

To set adult heights in India in context, it is of interest to compare their growth with other countries, as well as to look at differences between Indian states. Data from the China Health and Nutrition Survey between 1989 and 2004 show that Chinese adults, both men and women, have been gaining height at around one centimeter per decade. Not only have Chinese men grown taller at twice the rate of Indian men, but there is no evidence in China of the differential disfavoring of women that we see in India. In this respect, other neighbouring countries also appear to be doing better than India, although not as well as China. Women in Bangladesh have been growing at about 0.24 cm. a decade, and women in Nepal at 0.59 cm per decade; these data come from Demographic and Health Surveys which do not include data on mean's heights, at least as yet. That the Chinese growth rates are not impossible in India is clearly shown by the data for Kerala, where men and women are growing taller at 1.29 and 1.16 cm per decade respectively, even faster than in China. Indeed, decadal rates of height increase of around one centimeter have previously been reported for a range of European countries between 1870 and 1970, Floud, Wachter, and Gregory. For those born between 1950 and 1980, Scandinavians grew taller by a little less than one centimeter per decade, while southern European countries such as Spain, Portugal, and Italy, where people are shorter, were catching up with growth rates closer to 2 cm. a decade, Bozzoli et al. Taking all this together, the growth rates of heights in China and Kerala are in line with historical experience, while India as a whole is making much slower progress, especially but not exclusively for women.

The graphs in Figure 1 show that the data on women's heights are inconsistent between NFHS2 and NFHS3, with women of the same birth cohort apparently taller in the later survey. The difference between the two lines is only 0.16 cm, but this is quite large relative to the annual growth rate and, because it happens for all dates of birth, it is clearly not attributable to random sampling error in the estimation of mean heights. We noted earlier that other questions have arisen about the NFHS-3 so there was perhaps some sampling difference between the two surveys. With a taller sample of women in NFHS-3, we would expect to see taller children—so that the reduction in stunting between the two surveys may be overstated—as well as thinner children—the children of taller women tend to have lower weight for height—which would mean that the increase in wasting over the two surveys may be overstated. We can assess this using NFHS-2 by estimating the effects of mother's height on the probability of her child being wasted or stunted. But when we do so, the effects are tiny and make no difference to the trends discussed earlier; a sample of women that is 1.6 millimeters taller will have a fraction of children stunted that is 0.26 of a percent lower, and a fraction wasted that is 0.03 of a percent higher.

Interpretations

Calorie Decline

Food prices

Returning to the puzzle of falling calorie intake, the first possibility to consider is that the decline was driven by an increase in food or calorie prices relative to the prices of other things. In spite of the fact that people buy food, and not calories, we can think of price indexes of food as price indexes of calories.

To see this, suppose the price of food i is $i\ p$ per kilo, and its calorie content is $i\ k$ per kilo, then the price per calorie through good i is $/\ i\ i\ p\ k$, so that provided the calorie contents do not change over time—an issue to which we will return—calorie prices are just food prices in different units and any index of food prices can be reinterpreted as an index of calorie prices, at least for foods that have non-zero calorie content. In consequence, calories become relatively more expensive or cheaper according to whether food prices rise faster or slower than non-food prices. Figure 2 shows the monthly ratios of food to general price indexes for the rural (CPIAL) and urban (CPIIW) sectors. All four indexes, CPIAL food, CPIAL general, CPIIW food, and CPIIW general have been scaled to be 100 in 1993–94, and are shown as ratios of food to general within sectors. In rural India, food (and therefore calorie) prices moved along with general prices from 1983 until about 2000, and then fell by a little less than five percent relative to general prices.

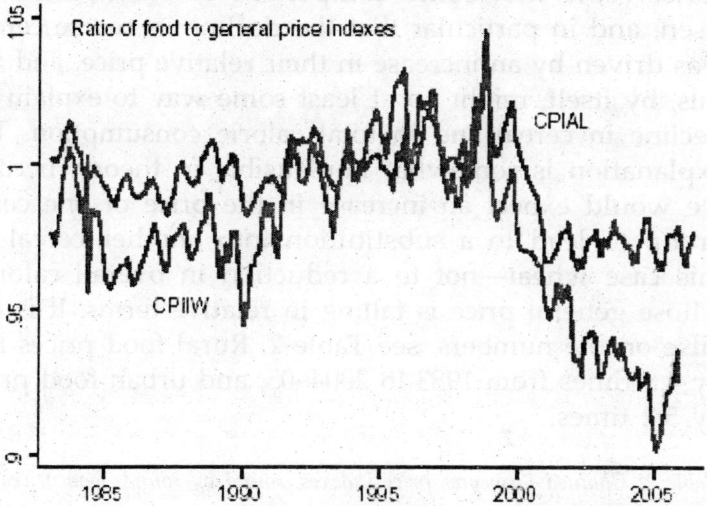

Figure 2: Ratio of food to non-food price, urban and rural

In urban India, there was a slow secular increase in the relative price of food, by less than five percent, from 1983 until the late 1990s, followed by a more pronounced decline, by more than ten percent, until the end of the period. In both sectors, the relative price of food was *lower* in 2004–05 than at the start of the period in 1983. The decline in calorie consumption cannot therefore be attributed to any increase in the relative price of food. In Deaton (2008) one of us has argued that the food component of the CPIAL, as well as the CPIAL itself, is understated after 2000 through the use of outdated weights in the official indexes. However, there is no question about the relative decline in food prices after 2000, or about the long term decline between 1983 and 2004–05.

Coarse cereal prices

Although food prices may not have risen in general, it is conceivable that some component of food prices has risen, and in particular that the decline in coarse cereals was driven by an increase in their relative price, and that this, by itself, might go at least some way to explain the decline in cereal and in total calorie consumption. This explanation is somewhat implausible in theory, because we would expect an increase in the price of one cereal group to lead to a substitution into another cereal—in this case wheat—not to a reduction in overall calories, whose general price is falling in relative terms. It is also false on the numbers, see Table 2. Rural food prices rose by 4.8 times from 1983 to 2004–05, and urban food prices by 5.2 times.

Table 2: Chained Laspeyres price indexes, round by round, food prices and coarse cereal prices

	RURAL	URBAN		
	Food	Coarse Cereals	Food	Coarse Cereals
38-43	1.353	1.139	1.399	1.150
43-50	1.780	1.598	1.796	1.762
50-55	1.804	2.075	1.785	2.253
55-61	1.118	0.940	1.168	1.000
38-61	4.857	3.550	5.238	4.565

The corresponding figures for coarse cereals are 3.6 times and 4.6 times, so that coarse cereals (and calories from coarse cereals) have become systematically cheaper than food (and calories from food) as a whole. Only in the period from 1993–94 to 1999–2000 did the price of coarse cereals rise more rapidly than other food prices.

Impoverishment

If it is not relative prices that are shifting the calorie Engel curves, what can be causing the calorie decline? One account, most prominently argued by Patnaik (2004, 2007), is that hunger and deprivation are increasing, especially in agriculture, and that people are purchasing fewer calories, particularly cereal calories, because they cannot afford to do otherwise. Some combination of falling incomes, rising prices, and rising agricultural unemployment has impoverished a substantial fraction of the rural population.

However, there is little direct evidence of sustained, widespread impoverishment of the rural population in the 1980s and 1990s. Further, the impoverishment argument jars with the fact that the decline of nutrient intakes has been proportionately larger—much larger—in the higher percapita expenditure groups. There is strong evidence that these groups have enjoyed sustained increases in living standards in the 1980s and 1990s. Clearly, something other than "impoverishment" (e.g. a reduction in nutrient requirements associated with reduced activity levels or better health) needs to be invoked to explain the decline of nutrient intakes among these groups. And it is quite possible that this hidden factor, whatever it was, also played a role in the stagnation of nutrient intakes among lower-income groups.

The impoverishment view also requires us to challenge some aspects of the data presented so far. In particular, it implies that the rise in real per capita expenditure in the NSS must somehow be incorrect, possibly because expenditures are overstated, price inflation understated, or some combination of the two. Or perhaps there has been a substantial widening of the income distribution, with the majority of people getting worse off, so that growth at the mean is driven only by progress at the top. But with a few minor exceptions to do with weighting, the inflation rate in the CPIAL is supported by the unit values observed in the NSS surveys. And while the NSS expenditure figures have been robustly challenged, the general complaint—and one that we endorse, at least to some extent—is that, in light of the national accounts, they appear to underestimate (rather than overestimate) the growth of per-capita expenditure over time.

Sen's argument

In an interesting paper (concerned mainly with the method of poverty measurement), takes up the question of why it is that people around the current poverty line are purchasing many fewer calories than the 2,400 (rural) and 2,100 (urban) recommended allowances that played a part in the original derivation of the lines. Since the purchasing power of the poverty line has been held constant, by construction, the recommended allowances are, in principle, no less (or more) affordable than when they were established. As Sen points out, however, it is possible that the food budget has been squeezed out because "the cost of meeting the minimum non-food requirements has increased". To illustrate, suppose that poor households have access to schooling facilities that were not available earlier. Schooling expenses (including, say, adequate clothes for children) would become a new item on the household budget, and food expenditure may be curtailed to make room for it.

In response to this argument, Sen notes that households around the poverty line could still achieve the recommended calorie intakes *within their current food budget* by spending their actual food budgets, not as they do, but on the foods that yield the same number of calories per rupee as are actually purchased by people below the poverty line on average. In other words, people at the line could meet the calorie norms within their current actual food budgets if they had the same food purchasing patterns as the typical poor person. This is a useful point to note, if food purchases below the poverty line are not of much lower quality than food purchases at the line. But it does not establish that there is no "squeeze' in the food budget.

What would be more useful to know is whether households around the poverty line can or cannot use their current expenditures on food to purchase their baseline food basket, which meets the calorie requirements, by definition. The answer to this is likely to be "no". Indeed, since the poverty line has constant purchasing power in real terms, and since the relative price of food (and thus of calories) did not change much from 1983 until 2004-5, purchasing that baseline food basket with its recommended calorie content would require these households to spend the same share of total per-capita expenditure on food as in the initial scenario. In fact, the food share has fallen at all levels of per-capita expenditure, including the poverty line. Thus, it is not possible for households around the poverty line to purchase their initial food basket *within their* current food budget

In short, there is no simple "revealed preference argument" that refutes the hypothesis of a squeeze in the food budget due to rising essential expenditure on non-food items. It is worth noting, however, that in the event of such a squeeze, one would expect poor households to switch towards *cheaper* calories. But the opposite is actually happening—poor rural households have made a modest switch towards more expensive calories, away from cereals and other sources of cheap energy. This does cast some doubt on the hypothesis of a squeeze in the food budget. It is also consistent with the possibility that people need fewer calories today than they used to, an alternative hypothesis we examine below.

Are the calorie Engel curves misleading?

Income is notoriously difficult to measure in rural India, especially for self-employed cultivators, and measurement error can easily cause the Engel curve to be spuriously flattened. However, measurement error will only turn a negative slope into a positive one if richer people systematically report lower incomes than poorer people, which is quite unlikely. One possible source of bias in the NSS Engel curves arises from the fact that, in the NSS surveys, both total expenditures and total calories are estimated by "adding up" expenditures and quantities applying to various goods (in the NNMB surveys, by contrast, there are independent questions on income and food intake). Thus, measurement errors in reported quantities of goods will find their way both into total expenditures and totals (or subtotals) of calories and this common measurement error biases the estimated slope of the calorie Engel curve towards unity, and could conceivably convert a true negative slope into an apparent positive one. It is difficult to deal with this problem in a convincing way. The standard treatment is to look for some variable that is correlated with total expenditure, but which is measured in a way that is not contaminated by the measurement errors that are common to calories and to expenditures. We have done some experiments along these lines, for example using the ownership levels of the various durable goods that are collected in the NSS surveys. Better-off people are more likely to own a bicycle or an electric fan, so we can follow Filmer and Prtichett and compute an index of durable ownership that can be thought of as a proxy for living standards.

These experiments yield suggestive but ultimately inconclusive results. The simple count of the number of durable goods owned is (a) strongly positively correlated with per capita total household expenditure, and (b) negatively correlated with per capita consumption of cereal calories, which is consistent with the view that per capita cereal calories are negatively correlated with income. One problem with this story is that it is possible that ownership of at least some of the durable goods is directly linked to the consumption of cereals, not just indirectly as a proxy for living standards. Consider, for instance, the fact that household ownership of a bicycle or motor cycle is a positive predictor of per capita expenditure and negative predictors of cereal consumption. This could simply reflect that people who own bicycles do not use as many calories in walking to work or to school, rather than the fact that ownership of a bicycle indicates higher income and, through higher income, lower cereal consumption. Indeed, the increased ownership of (human) energy-saving durable goods over the last decade or two is likely implicated in the calorie decline, at least to some extent. Another problem is that these results are not replicated if we run the regressions state by state, or even if we pool states but allow for state dummies. Yet if the common measurement error account is correct, it should hold within states as well as across them.

Changes in food habits and non-market entitlements

A simple explanation for the shift from cereals, albeit a not very informative one, is that there has been a change in "consumer tastes", and some econometric studies have taken this route, at least implicitly, by including unexplained time trends in the analysis. While invoking changes in tastes is not helpful in itself, the last few decades have seen important changes in food habits in rural India that are not easily explained by standard factors such as changes in income and prices. Consider for example the sharp decline in the consumption of "coarse cereals". In so far as coarse cereals are "inferior goods" (with a negative income elasticity of demand), this decline can be interpreted as an income effect. But there is obviously more to it, since the consumption of coarse cereals is also falling at any given level of per-capita expenditure.

There are various possible reasons for this decline: growing emulation of the consumption patterns of affluent groups, exposure to new food items, influence of advertisement, and changes in food habits (specifically, substitution towards wheat and rice) induced by the Public Distribution System. It is possible that some of these changes have nutritional consequences about which people are not fully informed, for example, for the consumption of important micronutrients. To illustrate, while "coarse cereals" are generally considered quite healthy and nutritious by nutritionists (some of them even argue for calling them "nutritious grain" rather than "coarse cereals"), they may or may not be perceived as such by the consumers. Conversely, the nutrition value—or lack of it—of "junk foods" (some of which are rapidly gaining popularity in India, and not just in urban areas) is not always adequately understood. Thus, it is conceivable that recent changes in food habits (in particular, the decline in coarse cereal consumption) have had nutritional consequences that are not fully appreciated or taken into account by consumers. A related issue concerns the decline of certain types of food entitlements, not necessarily well captured in NSS-type data. For instance, buttermilk used to be widely available, often free of cost, in many Indian villages, particularly in the north-western region. In those days, large quantities of buttermilk were available as a by-product of ghee, butter and other local milk products. In many villages there was no market for buttermilk—it was just consumed at home or given away to neighbours, friends and visitors. With the growing commercialization of milk, these local processing activities have declined, and so has the availability of buttermilk. It is unlikely that this steep decline in the consumption of buttermilk is adequately captured in standard NSS data. Similarly, as the role of home-grown consumption has lessened, the effective price of food is likely to have risen in a way that is not captured in the usual indexes and which may help explain some of the decline in cereal consumption among the poor; the size of this effect is hard to document with available data.

Some studies have also noted the decline of a range of traditional food entitlements in various parts of rural India, such as the growing scarcity of wild spinach (*saag*) due to recent changes in cropping patterns, the reduced availability of fish in rice fields due to pesticide use, and deprivation of forest products or common property resources due to environmental degradation. All this could have an adverse impact on food intake and nutritional status. However, it does not help to explain the decline in measured calorie consumption (if these items were not covered by household survey data in the first place), or for that matter in cereal consumption, especially among the better off sections of the population.

Declining needs for calories?

The declining consumption of calories needs to be examined relative to changes in the various factors that might affect the need for calories. For example, as mentioned earlier the decline of the total fertility rate—from 6.6 in 1960 to 5.0 in 1980 and 2.8 in 2005—is a source of reduction in requirements (since pregnant and lactating women need more calories), though if those requirements are not met, this may not have had much effect on actual calories consumed. For the same reason, but working in the opposite direction, households today have fewer children relative to adults, so that the decline in per capita calories has most likely understated the decline in calories per adult equivalent.

One possible source of falling calorie requirements is an improved epidemiological environment, with less exposure to disease and infections. For example, there has been a major improvement in access to safe drinking water during the last twenty-five years or so: the proportion of households with access to piped water has risen sharply across the country. While piped water is not necessarily safe, much of the increase came from the construction of hand-pumps and tube-wells, whose water is usually safe, and certainly safer than water obtained from rivers, tanks, or open wells. Better water reduces the prevalence of diseases, especially diarrhoeal disease, and removes a potentially major source of calorie wastage. Other improvements in the disease environment may also reduce calorific needs. For instance, child vaccination rates have risen, and child health improves with mother's education, which has also risen rapidly in recent years. To the extent that these and other improvements in the health environment reduce the susceptibility of children (and adults) to disease and infection, calorie requirements would be reduced.

Another possible source of reduction in calorie requirements is the reduction of activity levels (especially in rural areas), see for example Rao (2000, 2005). Aside from reducing exposure to disease, improved access to piped water is likely to reduce the energy requirements associated with fetching and carrying water, a strenuous task (typically assigned to women and children in rural India). Similarly, the extension of road coverage and transport facilities has enabled more people to use motorised transport, and to save some of the energy spent earlier on long walks (another strenuous activity, especially when it involves carrying heavy loads). The general mechanisation of domestic activities and agricultural work would also contribute to reduced calorie requirements. For instance, aside from fetching water, rural women used to spend much energy on grinding flour at home (using heavy stone mills known as *chakkis*), but today this is typically done outside the home with energised devices such as electric mills.

The NSS survey data show a large increase in the ownership of durable goods over the last two decades, and many of these goods are likely to reduce the expenditure of human energy. In rural and urban India in 2004–05, 56 and 50 percent of households reported owning a bicycle, compared with 17 and 19 percent in 1987–88. In 2004–05, 31 percent of urban households owned a motorcycle, and 6 percent owned a car. Although the rural figures are only a third as high, there has been an almost tenfold increase in ownership rates over 17 years. The most recent figures are confirmed by NFHS-3, which estimated that in 2005–06, 12 percent of rural households and 32 percent of urban households owned a means of motorized transportation. Television watching, a sedentary leisure activity, has also increased: 30 percent of rural and 74 percent of urban households now own a television, and these estimates are the same in both surveys. In 1987–88, less than one percent of Indian households possessed a television.

The importance of accounting for activity levels in any calorie-based assessment of nutritional status arises from the fact that calorie requirements increase quite sharply with the level of activity. According to the Indian Council of Medical Research (ICMR), the calorie requirements of an "average Indian man" (weighing 60 kgs) are almost 60 per cent higher if he is engaged in "heavy activity" rather than "sedentary activity"—3,800 calories and 2,425 calories, respectively. Clearly, looking at calorie intake independently of activity could be quite misleading when the former varies so much with the latter.

Table 3: Activity levels and calorie requirements (adult men)

Proportion of adult men engaged in "moderate activity"	Proportion of adult men engaged in "heavy activity"			
	10%	20%	40%	60%
10%	2608	2745	3020	3295
20%	2653	2790	3065	3340
40%	2743	2880	3155	3430
60%	2833	2970	3245	n/a

For further illustration, Table 3 shows how the average calorie requirements of adult men vary with activity patterns, according to ICMR data. In this table, the column title indicates the proportion of the population engaged in "heavy" activity, the row title indicates the proportion engaged in the "moderate" activity, and it is understood that the rest of the population is engaged in "sedentary" activity. The cell entries give the corresponding average requirements, e.g. 2,790 calories per day when the proportions of adult men engaged in moderate and heavy activity are 20 per cent each. As the table indicates, relatively moderate reductions in activity levels would lead to reductions of calorie requirements of the same order as those that have been actually observed during the last twenty-five years or so. For instance, a reduction in the proportion of adult men engaged in "heavy activity" from 40 to 20 per cent, with no change in the proportion engaged in "moderate activity", would lead to a decline in average calorie requirements of close to 10 per cent, similar to the actual decline in average calorie consumption in rural areas between 1983 and

2004. It is also reasonable to expect that the percentage activity reductions would be larger among the better-off households, especially if a substantial part of the calorie reduction reflects a substitution of mechanical for human power. This would help to explain why the reduction in calorie intake is itself larger at higher levels of per-capita expenditure.

This line of explanation also helps to interpret the rural-urban contrasts. The rural-urban contrast, with lower intake levels in urban areas, has been traditionally attributed to differences in activity patterns, including the more sedentary lifestyle of a large fraction of the urban population, the heavy energy demands of agricultural and domestic work in rural areas, and the lack of transportation in the rural sector. The fact that calorie intake is going down in both sectors, but with larger reductions in rural areas, fits the activity story. This interpretation of the calorie decline, in terms of reduced requirements associated with lower activity levels, is difficult to substantiate further in the absence of reliable data on activity patterns. Time-use studies would help to shed further light on this account. Meanwhile, the activity story does have some plausibility, and this also applies to the more general notion that calorie requirements have declined, due not only to reduced activity levels but also to better health.

Engel curves re-examined

The focus on activity can also help to understand some features of the NSS-based Engel curves for calories and cereal calories. The basic point to recognize is that food consumption has a "dual" role. On the one hand, food is like any other commodity, which is valued (a source of "utility") for various reasons such as the pleasure of eating, the pursuit of better health, and the role of food in social occasions. On the other hand, calories are required to meet one's immediate energy requirements, themselves contingent on activity patterns. In particular, energy expenditure is required to work and earn.

From this perspective, the distinguishing feature of cereals is that they provide a cheap (often the cheapest) source of calories. At low levels of income, energy requirements tend to be met mainly from cereals, because other foods are unforgettable. As income rises, people typically switch to other, more expensive sources of calories that are also valued from the point of view of taste, healthiness, status, and so on. The calorie requirements, for their part, depend partly on the amount of work people do.

To see the implications of cereals being valued mainly as a source of cheap calories, and in particular as a cheap "fuel" for work, suppose that this is their *only* purpose. Further, consider a population of rural workers who vary in terms of the amount of work they do, for reasons that might include differences in health, in physical fitness, in work opportunities, or in individual preferences. For instance, some may be able to find work, others not; some may be able to put in long hours of hard work while others have limited strength or suffer from illness; and some may simply chose to work hard and earn more while others prefer a more leisurely life. To keep things simple, assume (to start with) that these workers face the same wage rate, and that calorie requirements depend exclusively on work.

In this setting, which we think of as applying to agricultural workers, we would find a positive relationship (across households) between total expenditure and calorie intake, because both are driven by a third factor, which is the amount of work people do and the effort they put into it. At these low levels of income, this relationship would be much the same for calories and cereal calories, since calorie requirements are met mainly from cereals. At somewhat higher income levels, the Engel curve for cereal calories would flatten out (and possibly even have a negative slope) as other sources of calories substitute for cereals.

What happens over time is different. As the wage rises, and with less work being required to earn a given amount of income, there will be a downward shift in the calorie Engel curve. This may be accentuated by technological change of the sort we have discussed in the preceding section. In the process, calorie intake may decline as incomes rise, in contrast to calorie intake increasing with income in the cross-section at a given point of time. To look at it another way, and emphasizing once again that we are talking about the lower portion of the Engel curve, variations in income over time are driven (in this model) by wage variations, while those observed at a given point of time are driven by variations in work and effort. The corresponding segments of the Engel curves may have opposite slopes, positive in the cross-section but negative over time.

This is a simplified model that applies, at best, to people with low wages whose income depends mainly on physical labour. To bring it closer to reality, we also have to bring in the people at the top of the Engel curve, among whom variations in income at a moment in time are more likely to be due to variations in wages (or salaries) than to variations in work and effort. Among these better off workers, it is reasonable to expect a negative relationship between cereal intake and income, partly because people are less likely to be involved in strenuous activities as they become better off, and partly because they would substitute away from cereals towards other foods. Calorie intake may rise or decline with income: even if activity levels are lower at higher levels of income, there are likely to be positive income effects that cause people to consume more. When wages rise over time, the earlier reasoning would still apply to the extent that the Engel curve is driven by variations in effort and work opportunities across people at any given wage. In addition, at higher levels of income, there may be substantial scope for reducing activity levels over time by adopting labour-saving technology such as agricultural machinery, courtyard hand-pumps, domestic appliances, and so on, some of which are expensive and more affordable by the better off.

This reasoning is also relevant in interpreting contrasts in calorie consumption between different places, e.g., Indian states. Within states, the Engel curves would have the shapes discussed earlier, with a relatively steep positive slope at the bottom, and some flattening (and possibly even a negative slope, in the case of cereal calories) at the top. But across states, things would look different, because the interpersonal differences in ability and opportunity to work would largely average out. Thus, across states, there would be a *negative* correlation between per-capita expenditure and cereal calories, driven by differences in wage rates. The correlation between per-capita expenditure and total calories, for its part, may be positive or negative, depending on the strength of different income effects. In fact, the correlation between state averages of per-capita cereal calories and per-capita expenditure (in logs) is –0.44, see Figure 3, while for per-capita total calories, the correlation is 0.53. It is, of course, also possible that this negative correlation is coincidental, in the sense that it reflects regional variations in calorie requirements (related, for instance, to the climatological or epidemiological environment) or food habits that have little to do with the factors discussed in this section. Nevertheless, it is interesting that, here again, the observed features of NSS-based Engel curves are consistent with the recognition of activity levels as an important determinant of calorie requirements.

This completes our brief tour of alternative explanations for the recent decline of calorie intake in India.

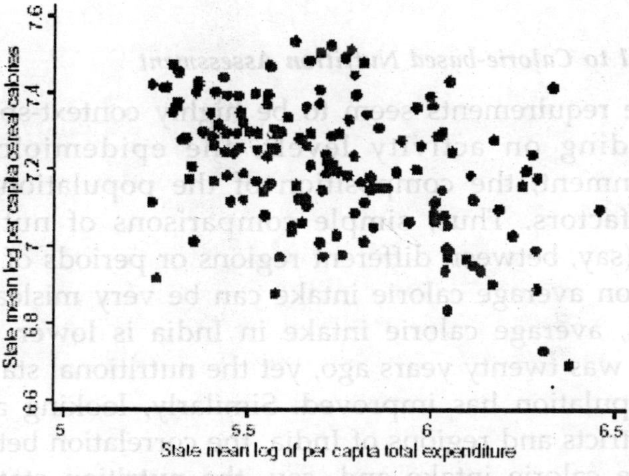

Figure 3: State averages of cereal calories and PCE, large rounds

If only by default, the hypothesis of declining calorie requirements commands serious attention as a possible clue to this puzzle. However, it would be premature to endorse it in the absence of adequate evidence on activity levels and other determinants of calorie requirements.

Because of the uncertainty as to what is going on, it is also difficult to assess the welfare implications of the decline in calorie intake. We have already noted that, had real wages and real incomes increased faster at the bottom of the distribution, it is likely that calorie consumption would have increased, at least for some sections of the population, and possibly even on average. On the other hand, to the extent that the calorie decline is driven by lower activity levels or a better health environment, it may be associated with improvements in some aspects of well-being (such as freedom from hard labour) that escape assessment in the standard poverty estimates and well-being indicators.

Nutritional Status

Farewell to Calorie-based Nutrition Assessment

Calorie requirements seem to be highly context-specific, depending on activity levels, the epidemiological environment, the composition of the population, and other factors. Thus, simple comparisons of nutrition levels (say, between different regions or periods of time) based on average calorie intake can be very misleading. Indeed, average calorie intake in India is lower today than it was twenty years ago, yet the nutritional status of the population has improved. Similarly, looking across the districts and regions of India, the correlation between average calorie intake and, say, the nutrition status of children is *negative,* child nutrition is worse in regions with higher levels of per-capita calorie intake. Even if there were a simple relationship between individual nutritional status and calorie consumption, there would be serious perils in making comparisons of nutrition based on NSS-type data on per capita calorie intake at the household level, with no idea of its distribution across people, let alone whether the distribution over individuals matches individual calorie needs.

It does mean, however, that approaches to nutrition assessment based on calorie intake data and "fixed" calorie norms (or on simple comparisons of average calorie intake) are both incomplete and misleading. There is a strong case not only for paying attention to other aspects of food intake (such as the consumption of essential vitamins and minerals) but also for shifting the focus away from food intake towards more "direct" indicators of the nutrition status of the population, such as the growth curves of children or other evidence of nutrition-related impairments.

Energy adequacy depends on *net* intake, which is calorie intake less the calories absorbed by a range of demands depending inter alia on the epidemiological environment as well as activity levels, and is influenced by variables such as age, birthweight, mother's education, breast-feeding practices, the composition of the diet, to cite a few. Adequate nutrition also requires a host of other inputs that are not adequately summarized by total calories, including a range of micronutrients and, at certain stages of life, especially childhood, a varied diet. Looking at calorie intake, or for that matter other specific nutrition *inputs*, independently of other relevant variables, is an exercise of limited value for assessing what matters, which is nutritional outcomes. These can be usefully measured by the various nutrition indicators such as anthropometric measurements, at least in so far as they capture the combined effects of various inputs (food and non-food) net of other demands.

Having said this, there are also possible difficulties with the use of anthropometric indicators based on currently available data. As noted earlier, for instance, different anthropometric indicators (e.g. weight-for-age and weight-for-height) do not always move in the same direction, and sometimes the same indicator moves in different directions according to different sources (e.g. NFHS and NNMB).

Multiple Deficiencies of Indian Diets

Before we proceed, two clarifications may help. First, nothing we have said justifies a downplaying of calorie deficiencies among poor households. Even if the recent decline of calorie intake is due to falling requirements, and has little to do with impoverishment, the fact remains that poor households have serious energy deficits. Had poverty decline been faster, it is quite likely that calorie intake would have risen among underprivileged households (and perhaps even on average). Reducing calorie deficits among poor households remains very important for the removal of nutritional deprivation in India, and this, in turn, would be hard to achieve without substantial income growth at the bottom of the distribution.

Second, by a similar reasoning, the findings we have presented do not detract from the crucial importance of improved diets in India, including not only reduced calorie deficits but also higher—possibly much higher—intakes of various nutrients for large sections of the population. While economic research on nutrition issues in India has tended to focus mainly on calorie intake, nutritionists have been deeply concerned for a long time about a range of nutritional deficiencies, including those of essential minerals and vitamins, animal protein, and fats. As Tara Gopaldas (2006) notes, for instance, "*all* members of low-income (and even middle-income) families are likely to be deficient in vitamins and minerals" (p. 3671). In fact, the deficiencies are large, in relation to current ICMR recommendations. For instance, in the age group of 4-6 years, the ratio of average intake to "recommended daily allowance" is only 16 per cent for Vitamin A, 35 per cent for iron and 45 per cent for calcium.While there is some debate as to how these deficiencies are best addressed, including lively controversies about the merits of various forms of "micronutrient supplementation", what is not in doubt is that large sections of the Indian population have diets that are missing much that they need.

Similar concerns apply to the intake of fats. In rich countries, and among affluent sections of the population in poor countries (including India), fat has acquired a bad name as a harbinger of diabetes, cardio-vascular diseases and other illnesses. Yet, fat intake among large sections of the Indian population is almost certainly too low, possibly much too low. This applies in particular to children in poor households. Fat is important for children not only because fat is a calorie-dense food and helps them to achieve adequate calorie intake despite small stomachs, and generally facilitates the absorption of various nutrients, but also because fat is useful in its own right, e.g. for the development of the brain.Current expert recommendations regarding optimal fat intake as a proportion of calorie intake for young children appear to be in the range of 30 to 45 per cent. In India, however, fat accounts for barely 15 per cent of average calorie intake, according to National Sample Survey data, with much lower figures among poor households. According to the National Nutrition Monitoring Bureau, fat intake among Indian children is only about 30 per cent of the "recommended daily allowance".

Overcoming these massive deficiencies would require a substantial shift from cereal-based diets to more diversified diets. Indeed, it is virtually impossible to meet these diverse requirements from a cereal-dominated diet. Even calorie requirements are difficult to meet from cereals alone, especially for children, due to absorption problems. Sometimes, cereal consumption even has an adverse effect on the consumption of essential nutrients. For instance, cereals, legumes, peas and nuts contain phosphorus compounds known as phytates which inhibit the absorption of iron (certain compounds found in tea have similar effects). This inhibition of iron absorption is one reason why iron-deficiency anaemia is so widespread in India, Baynes and Bothwell.

In this connection, there is also evidence from international data, suggesting that the diversification of diets is associated with better child nutrition.While the shift from cereal-based diets to more diversified diets is already happening to some extent in India, Indian diets remain very frugal. To illustrate, according to NFHS-2 data for 1998-99, only 55 per cent of adult women in India consume milk or curd at least once a week, only 33 per cent eat fruits at least once a week, and 28 per cent get an egg. Seven years later, the NFHS-3 survey yielded the same figure for "milk or curd" (55 per cent), and only slightly higher figures for fruits and eggs—40 and 32 per cent respectively.It is hard to see how mass undernourishment could be eliminated in India without a major improvement in the quantity, quality and diversity of food intake among poorer sections of the population.

Nutrition Status of Privileged Indian Children

The puzzlingly high levels of child undernutrition in India (and South Asia) point to the possible need to reexamine this assumption. Consider for instance Kerala. According to NFHS-3, 23 per cent of children below the age of 3 years in Kerala are underweight, 16 per cent are wasted and 25 per cent are stunted, International Institute for Population Sciences. However, other indicators of child health and well-being suggest that children in Kerala are doing quite well. For instance, the infant mortality rate is only 13 per 1,000—about the same as in, say, Kuwait, Costa Rica or Malaysia. Generally, child development indicators (other than anthropometric measurements) are much better in Kerala than in countries with similar proportions of underweight children. For instance, the proportion of underweight children in Kerala is not very different from the average for sub-Saharan Africa, but the infant mortality rate in sub-Saharan Africa (around 100 per 1,000) is nearly eight times as high as in Kerala. It is, of course, possible that children in Kerala would be doing even better in some respects if they were not "held up" by low weights and heights. But it is not clear, from available data, what these impairments actually are.

A related puzzle is that child undernutrition is also quite high (according to the anthropometric approach) among well-off households. Here, two different bodies of evidence need to be considered. On the one hand, some studies suggest that the anthropometric achievements of children in affluent Indian families are much the same as those of well-nourished children elsewhere, and indeed these Indian children are included in the international reference population that forms the basis of the most recent WHO "child growth standards".On the other hand, the NFHS data tell a different story, whereby a substantial proportion of Indian children are undernourished even among welloff households. To illustrate, Table 4 shows standard child nutrition indicators for different economic classes, defined in terms of the "wealth index" presented in the NFHS-3 report. As this table makes clear, child undernourishment declines sharply with increasing values of the index, as one might expect. However, even among the top 20 per cent of households, substantial proportions of children are undernourished: 20 per cent of children are underweight, 25 per cent are stunted, and 13 per cent are wasted (again, much the same figures as the sub-Saharan African averages).

Table 4: Child Nutrition and "Wealth"

"Wealth index"	Proportion (%) of undernourished childrena		
	Weight-for-age	Height-for-age	Weight-for-height
Lowest	57 (-2.2)	60 (-2.3)	25 (-1.2)
Second	49 (-2.0)	54 (-2.1)	22 (-1.1)
Third	41 (-1.8)	49 (-1.9)	19 (-1.0)
Fourth	34 (-1.5)	41 (-1.6)	17 (-0.9)
Highest	20 (-1.1)	25 (-1.1)	13 (-0.7)
All categories	42.5 (-1.8)	48.0 (-1.9)	19.8 (-1.0)

Also presented in this table are the "mean z-scores" of children in different economic classes. If children from wealthy households had the same "growth curves" as children from the international reference population, their mean z-scores would be zero. In fact, the mean z-scores are negative throughout the wealth scale.

It is perhaps not surprising that wealth alone provides inadequate protection against stunting or wasting. Following on this, Tarozzi used NFHS-2 data to investigate the nutrition status of highly privileged Indian children, where privilege is defined not only in terms of wealth but also involves urban residence, piped water, a flush toilet, and both parents having a high school degree. A little over 400 households in the NFHS-2 sample fall in this category (say "privileged households" for short). For this group of privileged households, an interesting pattern emerges: the mean z-score for "height-for-age" is still negative (–0.88), but the mean zscore for "weight-for-height" is very close to zero (0.105), Tarozzi. In other words, privileged Indian children are somewhat stunted, but they are not wasted.

The absence of any wasting among privileged Indian children is consistent with the plausible notion that these children have an adequate food intake. The question remains as to why they are stunted, in spite of the absence of any significant food deprivation, and presumably also of other basic deprivations (e.g. lack of sanitation), given the privileged environment in which these children live. Three possible (and not mutually exclusive) hypotheses are as follows.

— *"Social determinants" hypothesis*: Stunting among privileged children reflects social factors such as a poor epidemiological environment, inadequate social support, and inappropriate social norms relating (say) to breast-feeding or child feeding.

- *"Genetic potential" hypothesis*: Indian children do not have the same genetic potential as children in the international reference population—they are "naturally" shorter, even when they are well nourished.
- *"Gradual catch-up" hypothesis*: Indian children have the same genetic potential as children in the reference population, but it takes time for the heights of privileged children to catch up with the genetic potential, given the history of undernutrition.

The social determinants hypothesis is consistent with the claim that the international anthropometric standards are applicable in India. It implies that privileged children in India *are* often undernourished, though not due to lack of food. For instance, Bhandari et al found that, in a sample of well-off families in South Delhi, only 61 per cent of infants were breastfed within 12 hours of birth; only 25 per cent were exclusively breastfed up to the age of four months; almost two-thirds stopped breast-feeding before the age of one year; and only 2 per cent were fed non-vegetarian foods within a year (even though 58 per cent of the sample families were non-vegetarian). These observations indicate that, even in privileged families, breast-feeding and weaning practices are often at variance with current recommendations, such as breast-feeding within an hour of birth and exclusive breast-feeding for six months.It is quite possible that the same children would have benefited from more effective breast-feeding and weaning in a more conducive social environment, e.g. a society where there is better awareness of these matters and where breast-feeding counseling services (or, say, facilities for breast-feeding at the work place) are available. Having said this, if the social determinants hypothesis is correct, one would expect it to be reflected in wasting as well as in stunting, and not just in stunting. Yet, as we have seen, there is little wasting among privileged Indian children.

The genetic potential hypothesis, although certainly not disproved, is becoming less accepted in the scientific literature, if only because there is a long history of differences in population heights that were presumed to be genetic, and that vanished in the face of improved nutrition.

The "gradual catch-up" hypothesis has some plausibility, if only because (1) nutritional status is highly influenced by birthweight, and (2) birthweight, in turn, is highly correlated with mother's weight and height. This observation, which is at the root of the notion of intergenerational perpetuation of undernutrition, suggests that it would indeed take time for wellfed children to overcome the burden of undernutrition in the past. The catch-up hypothesis is also consistent with recent evidence about the secular increase in heights in Europe.

This hypothesis raises the further question whether well-nourished children suffer from any impairments during the catch-up period, due to being relatively short. The "small but healthy" debate suggests an affirmative answer to this question.A number of developed country studies also suggest that failure to reach one's genetic potential as a child is correlated with a range of negative outcomes throughout the life course. This applies whether this failure is due to low birthweight, or to poor nutrition after birth, and this suggests that stunted children do suffer from significant impairments even if they are well fed. The possibility remains that the impairments experienced by these short but well-fed children (e.g. those belonging to well-off families in Kerala) are less serious than those of children who suffer from inadequate nutrition as well as low birthweights (e.g. stunted children in Bihar).

The gradual catch-up hypothesis, if correct, would not invalidate the use of international reference standards to assess the nutritional status of Indian children. Indeed, it is appropriate for reference standards to be based on children who are not only well fed, but also have adequate birth-weights and healthy mothers (so that they are free from any burden of past undernutrition). However, this hypothesis might modify our interpretation of the data, depending on the nature of the impairments associated with stunting during the period when population height levels are rising towards the international norm. It would also make it a little easier to understand why anthropometric indicators appear to improve rather slowly at times (without necessarily implying that the consequences of slow improvement are any less serious), even when there is not only substantial poverty reduction but also major improvements in other determinants of child nutrition, such as maternal education and access to safe water. The gradual catch-up hypothesis may also be of some help in explaining why South Asians are so short: this is what one would expect if the region has a particularly long history of mass undernourishment, and if it takes time (perhaps many generations) to overcome this historical burden.

Having said this, the gradual catch-up hypothesis is of no help in explaining the recent "stalling" of weight improvement among Indian children, if such a stalling has actually taken place (as we saw, there is room for doubt on this). Indeed, if children's weights were improving steadily in the eighties and nineties, it is not clear why they should have stopped improving between NFHS-2 and NFHS-3. This is, as things stand, an unresolved puzzle.

15

Global Strategy on Diet, Physical Activity and Health

1. Recognizing the heavy and growing burden of noncommunicable diseases, Member States requested the Director-General to develop a global strategy on diet, physical activity and health through a broad consultation process. To establish the content of the draft global strategy, six regional consultations were held with Member States, and organizations of the United Nations system, other intergovernmental bodies, and representatives of civil society and the private sector were consulted. A reference group of independent international experts on diet and physical activity from WHO's six regions also provided advice.

2. The Strategy addresses two of the main risk factors for noncommunicable diseases, namely, diet and physical activity, while complementing the long-established and ongoing work carried out by WHO and nationally on other nutrition-related areas, including undernutrition, micronutrient deficiencies and infant- and young-child feeding.

The Challenge

3. A profound shift in the balance of the major causes

of death and disease has already occurred in developed countries and is under way in many developing countries. Globally, the burden of noncommunicable diseases has rapidly increased. In 2001 noncommunicable diseases accounted for almost 60% of the 56 million deaths annually and 47% of the global burden of disease. In view of these figures and the predicted future growth in this disease burden, the prevention of noncommunicable diseases presents a major challenge to global public health.

4. *The world health report 2002* describes in detail how, in most countries, a few major risk factors account for much of the morbidity and mortality. For noncommunicable diseases, the most important risks included high blood pressure, high concentrations of cholesterol in the blood, inadequate intake of fruit and vegetables, overweight or obesity, physical inactivity and tobacco use. Five of these risk factors are closely related to diet and physical activity.

5. Unhealthy diets and physical inactivity are thus among the leading causes of the major noncommunicable diseases, including cardiovascular disease, type 2 diabetes and certain types of cancer, and contribute substantially to the global burden of disease, death and disability. Other diseases related to diet and physical inactivity, such as dental caries and osteoporosis, are widespread causes of morbidity.

6. The burden of mortality, morbidity and disability attributable to noncommunicable diseases is currently greatest and continuing to grow in the developing countries, where those affected are on average younger than in developed countries, and where 66% of these deaths occur. Rapid changes in diets and patterns of physical activity are further

causing rates to rise. Smoking also increases the risk for these diseases, although largely through independent mechanisms.

7. In some developed countries where noncommunicable diseases have dominated the national burden of disease, age-specific death and disease rates have been slowly declining. Progress is being made in reducing premature death rates from coronary artery disease, cerebrovascular disease and some tobacco-related cancers. However, the overall burden and number of patients remain high, and the numbers of overweight and obese adults and children, and of cases, closely linked, of type 2 diabetes are growing in many developed countries.
8. Noncommunicable diseases and their risk factors are initially mostly limited to economically successful groups in low- and middle-income countries. However, recent evidence shows that, over time, patterns of unhealthy behaviour and the noncommunicable diseases associated with them cluster among poor communities and contribute to social and economic inequalities.
9. In the poorest countries, even though infectious diseases and undernutrition dominate their current disease burden, the major risk factors for chronic diseases are spreading. The prevalence of overweight and obesity is increasing in developing countries, and even in low-income groups in richer countries. An integrated approach to the causes of unhealthy diet and decreasing levels of physical activity would contribute to reducing the future burden of noncommunicable diseases.
10. For all countries for which data are available, the underlying determinants of noncommunicable diseases are largely the same. Factors that increase

the risks of noncommunicable disease include elevated consumption of energy-dense, nutrient-poor foods that are high in fat, sugar and salt; reduced levels of physical activity at home, at school, at work and for recreation and transport; and use of tobacco. Variations in risk levels and related health outcomes among the population are attributed, in part, to the variability in timing and intensity of economic, demographic and social changes at national and global levels. Of particular concern are unhealthy diets, inadequate physical activity and energy imbalances in children and adolescents.

11. Maternal health and nutrition before and during pregnancy, and early infant nutrition may be important in the prevention of noncommunicable diseases throughout the life course. Exclusive breast-feeding for six months and appropriate complementary feeding contribute to optimal physical growth and mental development. Infants who suffer prenatal, and possibly postnatal, growth restrictions appear to be at higher risk for noncommunicable diseases in adulthood.

12. Most elderly people live in developing countries, and the ageing of populations has a strong impact on morbidity and mortality patterns. Many developing countries will therefore be faced with an increased burden of noncommunicable diseases at the same time as a persisting burden of infectious diseases. In addition to the human dimension, maintaining the health and functional capacity of the increasing elderly population will be a crucial factor in reducing the demand for, and cost of, health services.

13. Diet and physical activity influence health both together and separately. Although the effects of diet

and physical activity on health often interact, particularly in relation to obesity, there are additional health benefits to be gained from physical activity that are independent of nutrition and diet, and there are significant nutritional risks that are unrelated to obesity. Physical activity is a fundamental means of improving the physical and mental health of individuals.

14. Governments have a central role, in cooperation with other stakeholders, to create an environment that empowers and encourages behaviour changes by individuals, families and communities, to make positive, life-enhancing decisions on healthy diets and patterns of physical activity.

15. Noncommunicable diseases impose a significant economic burden on already strained health systems, and inflict great costs on society. Health is a key determinant of development and a precursor of economic growth. The WHO Commission on Macroeconomics and Health has demonstrated the disruptive effect of disease on development, and the importance for economic development of investments in health. Programmes aimed at promoting healthy diets and physical activity for the prevention of diseases are key instruments in policies to achieve development goals.

The Opportunity

16. A unique opportunity exists to formulate and implement an effective strategy for substantially reducing deaths and disease worldwide by improving diet and promoting physical activity. Evidence for the links between these health behaviours and later disease and ill-health is strong. Effective interventions to enable people to live

longer and healthier lives, reduce inequalities, and enhance development can be designed and implemented. By mobilizing the full potential of the major stakeholders, this vision could become a reality for all populations in all countries.

Goal and Objectives

17. The overall goal of the Global Strategy on Diet, Physical Activity and Health is to promote and protect health by guiding the development of an enabling environment for sustainable actions at individual, community, national and global levels that, when taken together, will lead to reduced disease and death rates related to unhealthy diet and physical inactivity. These actions support the United Nations Millennium Development Goals and have immense potential for public health gains worldwide.
18. The Global Strategy has four main objectives:
    (1) to reduce the risk factors for noncommunicable diseases that stem from unhealthy diets and physical inactivity by means of essential public health action and health-promoting and disease-preventing measures;
    (2) to increase the overall awareness and understanding of the influences of diet and physical activity on health and of the positive impact of preventive interventions;
    (3) to encourage the development, strengthening and implementation of global, regional, national and community policies and action plans to improve diets and increase physical activity that are sustainable, comprehensive, and actively engage all sectors, including civil society, the private sector and the media;

(4) to monitor scientific data and key influences on diet and physical activity; to support research in a broad spectrum of relevant areas, including evaluation of interventions; and to strengthen the human resources needed in this domain to enhance and sustain health.

Evidence for Action

19. Evidence shows that, when other threats to health are addressed, people can remain healthy into their seventh, eighth and ninth decades, through a range of health-promoting behaviours, including healthy diets, regular and adequate physical activity, and avoidance of tobacco use. Recent research has contributed to understanding of the benefits of healthy diets, physical activity, individual action and population-based public health interventions. Although more research is needed, current knowledge warrants urgent public health action.

20. Risk factors for noncommunicable disease frequently coexist and interact. As the general level of risk factors rises, more people are put at risk. Preventive strategies should therefore aim at reducing risk throughout the population. Such risk reduction, even if modest, cumulatively yields sustainable benefits, which exceeds the impact of interventions restricted to high-risk individuals. Healthy diets and physical activity, together with tobacco control, constitute an effective strategy to contain the mounting threat of noncommunicable diseases.

21. Reports of international and national experts and reviews of the current scientific evidence recommend goals for nutrient intake and physical activity in order to prevent major noncommunicable diseases. These recommendations need to be

considered when preparing national policies and dietary guidelines, taking into account the local situation.

22. For diet, recommendations for populations and individuals should include the following:
    - achieve energy balance and a healthy weight
    - limit energy intake from total fats and shift fat consumption away from saturated fats to unsaturated fats and towards the elimination of *trans*-fatty acids
    - increase consumption of fruits and vegetables, and legumes, whole grains and nuts
    - limit the intake of free sugars
    - limit salt (sodium) consumption from all sources and ensure that salt is iodized.

23. Physical activity is a key determinant of energy expenditure, and thus is fundamental to energy balance and weight control. Physical activity reduces risk for cardiovascular diseases and diabetes and has substantial benefits for many conditions, not only those associated with obesity. The beneficial effects of physical activity on the metabolic syndrome are mediated by mechanisms beyond controlling excess body weight. For example, physical activity reduces blood pressure, improves the level of high density lipoprotein cholesterol, improves control of blood glucose in overweight people, even without significant weight loss, and reduces the risk for colon cancer and breast cancer among women.

24. For physical activity, it is recommended that individuals engage in adequate levels throughout their lives. Different types and amounts of physical activity are required for different health outcomes: at least 30 minutes of regular, moderate-intensity

physical activity on most days reduces the risk of cardiovascular disease and diabetes, colon cancer and breast cancer. Muscle strengthening and balance training can reduce falls and increase functional status among older adults. More activity may be required for weight control.

25. The realization of these recommendations, together with effective measures to prevent and control tobacco use, in the Global Strategy that leads to regional and national action plans, will require sustained political commitment and the collaboration of many stakeholders. The Strategy will contribute to the effective prevention of noncommunicable diseases.

Principal for Action

26. The world health report 2002 highlights the potential for improving public health through measures that reduce the prevalence of risk factors (most notably the combination of unhealthy diets and physical inactivity) of noncommunicable diseases. The principles set out below guided the drafting of WHO's Global Strategy and are recommended for the development of national and regional strategies and action plans.

27. Strategies need to be based on the best available scientific research and evidence; comprehensive, incorporating both policies and action and addressing all major causes of noncommunicable diseases together; multisectoral, taking a long-term perspective and involving all sectors of society; and multidisciplinary and participatory, consistent with the principles contained in the Ottawa Charter for Health Promotion and confirmed in subsequent conferences on health promotion, and recognizing

the complex interactions between personal choices, social norms and economic and environmental factors.

28. A life-course perspective is essential for the prevention and control of noncommunicable diseases. This approach starts with maternal health and prenatal nutrition, pregnancy outcomes, exclusive breast-feeding for six months, and child and adolescent health; reaches children at schools, adults at worksites and other settings, and the elderly; and encourages a healthy diet and regular physical activity from youth into old age.

29. Strategies to reduce noncommunicable diseases should be part of broader, comprehensive and coordinated public health efforts. All partners, especially governments, need to address simultaneously a number of issues. In relation to diet, these include all aspects of nutrition (for example, both overnutrition and undernutrition, micronutrient deficiency and excess consumption of certain nutrients); food security (accessibility, availability and affordability of healthy food); food safety; and support for and promotion of six months of exclusive breast-feeding. Regarding physical activity, issues include requirements for physical activity in working, home and school life, increasing urbanization, and various aspects of city planning, transportation, safety and access to physical activity during leisure.

30. Priority should be given to activities that have a positive impact on the poorest population groups and communities. Such activities will generally require community-based action with strong government intervention and oversight.

31. All partners need to be accountable for framing policies and implementing programmes that will

effectively reduce preventable risks to health. Evaluation, monitoring and surveillance are essential components of such actions.

32. The prevalence of noncommunicable diseases related to diet and physical activity may vary greatly between men and women. Patterns of physical activity and diets differ according to sex, culture and age. Decisions about food and nutrition are often made by women and are based on culture and traditional diets. National strategies and action plans should therefore be sensitive to such differences.

33. Dietary habits and patterns of physical activity are often rooted in local and regional traditions. National strategies should therefore be culturally appropriate and able to challenge cultural influences and to respond to changes over time.

Responsibilities for Action

34. Bringing about changes in dietary habits and patterns of physical activity will require the combined efforts of many stakeholders, public and private, over several decades. A combination of sound and effective actions is needed at global, regional, national and local levels, with close monitoring and evaluation of their impact. The following paragraphs describe the responsibilities of those involved and provide recommendations deriving from the consultation process.

Member States

35. The Global Strategy should foster the formulation and promotion of national policies, strategies and action plans to improve diet and encourage physical activity. National circumstances will determine

priorities in the development of such instruments. Because of the great variations in and between different countries, regional bodies should collaborate in formulating regional strategies, which can provide considerable support to countries in implementing their national plans. For maximum effectiveness, countries should adopt the most comprehensive action plans possible.

36. The role of government is crucial in achieving lasting change in public health. Governments have a primary steering and stewardship role in initiating and developing the Strategy, ensuring that it is implemented and monitoring its impact in the long term.

37. Governments are encouraged to build on existing structures and processes that already address aspects of diet, nutrition and physical activity. In many countries, existing national strategies and action plans can be used in implementing the Strategy; in others they can form the basis for advancing control of noncommunicable diseases. Governments are encouraged to set up a national coordinating mechanism that addresses diet and physical activity within the context of a comprehensive plan for noncommunicable-disease prevention and health promotion. Local authorities should be closely involved. Multisectoral and multidisciplinary expert advisory boards should also be established. They should include technical experts and representatives of government agencies, and have an independent chair to ensure that scientific evidence is interpreted without any conflict of interest.

38. Health ministries have an essential responsibility for coordinating and facilitating the contributions of other ministries and government agencies. Bodies

whose contributions should be coordinated include ministries and government institutions responsible for policies on food, agriculture, youth, recreation, sports, education, commerce and industry, finance, transportation, media and communication, social affairs and environmental and urban planning.

39. National strategies, policies and action plans need broad support. Support should be provided by effective legislation, appropriate infrastructure, implementation programmes, adequate funding, monitoring and evaluation, and continuing research.

    (1) National strategies on diet and physical activity. National strategies describe the measures to promote healthy diets and physical activity that are essential to prevent disease and promote health, including those that tackle all aspects of unbalanced diets, including undernutrition and overnutrition. National strategies should include specific goals, objectives, and actions, similar to those outlined in the Strategy. Of particular importance are the elements needed to implement the plan of action, including identification of necessary resources and national focal points (key national institutes); collaboration between the health sector and other key sectors such as agriculture, education, urban planning, transportation and communication; and monitoring and follow-up.

    (2) National dietary guidelines. Governments are encouraged to draw up national dietary guidelines, taking account of evidence from national and international sources. Such guidelines advise national nutrition policy, nutrition education, other public health interventions and intersectoral collaboration. They may be updated periodically in the light of

changes in dietary and disease patterns and evolving scientific knowledge.

(3) National physical activity guidelines. National guidelines for health-enhancing physical activity should be prepared in accordance with the goal and objectives of the Strategy and expert recommendations.

40. Governments should provide accurate and balanced information. Governments need to consider actions that will result in provision of balanced information for consumers to enable them easily to make healthy choices, and to ensure the availability of appropriate health promotion and education programmes. In particular, information for consumers should be sensitive to literacy levels, communication barriers and local culture, and understood by all segments of the population. In some countries, health-promoting programmes have been designed as a function of such considerations and should be used for disseminating information about diet and physical activity. Some governments already have a legal obligation to ensure that factual information available to consumers enables them to make fully informed choices on matters that may affect their health. In other cases, actions may be specific to government policies. Governments should select the optimal mix of actions in accordance with their national capabilities and epidemiological profile, which will vary from one country to another.

(1) Education, communication and public awareness. A sound basis for action is provided by public knowledge and understanding of the relationship between diet, physical activity and health, of energy intake and output, and healthy choice of food items. Consistent, coherent, simple and clear messages should be prepared

and conveyed by government experts, nongovernmental and grass-roots organizations, and the appropriate industries. They should be communicated through several channels and in forms appropriate to local culture, age and gender. Behaviour can be influenced especially in schools, workplaces, and educational and religious institutions, and by nongovernmental organizations, community leaders, and mass media. Member States should form alliances for the broad dissemination of appropriate and effective messages about healthy diet and physical activity. Nutrition and physical activity education and acquisition of media literacy, starting in primary school, are important to promote healthier diets, and to counter food fads and misleading dietary advice. Support should also be provided for action that improves the level of health literacy, while taking account of local cultural and socioeconomic circumstances. Communication campaigns should be regularly evaluated.

(2) Adult literacy and education programmes. Health literacy should be incorporated into adult education programmes. Such programmes provide an opportunity for health professionals and service providers to enhance knowledge about diet, physical activity and prevention of noncommunicable diseases and to reach marginalized populations.

(3) Marketing, advertising, sponsorship and promotion. Food advertising affects food choices and influences dietary habits. Food and beverage advertisements should not exploit children's inexperience or credulity. Messages that encourage unhealthy dietary practices or

physical inactivity should be discouraged, and positive, healthy messages encouraged. Governments should work with consumer groups and the private sector (including advertising) to develop appropriate multisectoral approaches to deal with the marketing of food to children, and to deal with such issues as sponsorship, promotion and advertising.

(4) Labelling. Consumers require accurate, standardized and comprehensible information on the content of food items in order to make healthy choices. Governments may require information to be provided on key nutritional aspects, as proposed in the Codex Guidelines on Nutrition Labelling.

(5) Health claims. As consumers' interest in health grows, and increasing attention is paid to the health aspects of food products, producers increasingly use health-related messages. Such messages must not mislead the public about nutritional benefits or risks.

41. National food and agricultural policies should be consistent with the protection and promotion of public health. Where needed, governments should consider policies that facilitate the adoption of healthy diet. Food and nutrition policy should also cover food safety and sustainable food security. Governments should be encouraged to examine food and agricultural policies for potential health effects on the food supply.

(1) Promotion of food products consistent with a healthy diet. As a result of consumers' increasing interest in health and governments' awareness of the benefits of healthy nutrition,

some governments have taken measures, including market incentives, to promote the development, production and marketing of food products that contribute to a healthy diet and are consistent with national or international dietary recommendations. Governments could consider additional measures to encourage the reduction of the salt content of processed foods, the use of hydrogenated oils, and the sugar content of beverages and snacks.

(2) Fiscal policies. Prices influence consumption choices. Public policies can influence prices through taxation, subsidies or direct pricing in ways that encourage healthy eating and lifelong physical activity. Several countries use fiscal measures, including taxes, to influence availability of, access to, and consumption of, various foods; and some use public funds and subsidies to promote access among poor communities to recreational and sporting facilities. Evaluation of such measures should include the risk of unintentional effects on vulnerable populations.

(3) Food programmes. Many countries have programmes to provide food to population groups with special needs or cash transfers to families for them to improve their food purchases. Such programmes often concern children, families with children, poor people, and people with HIV/AIDS and other diseases. Special attention should be given to the quality of the food items and to nutrition education as a main component of these programmes, so that food distributed to, or purchased by, the families not only provides energy, but also contributes to a healthy diet. Food and cash

distribution programmes should emphasize empowerment and development, local production and sustainability.

(4) Agricultural policies. Agricultural policy and production often have a great effect on national diets. Governments can influence agricultural production through many policy measures. As emphasis on health increases and consumption patterns change, Member States need to take healthy nutrition into account in their agricultural policies.

42. Multisectoral policies are needed to promote physical activity. National policies to promote physical activity should be framed, targeting change in a number of sectors. Governments should review existing policies to ensure that they are consistent with best practice in population-wide approaches to increasing physical activity.

(1) Framing and review of public policies. National and local governments should frame policies and provide incentives to ensure that walking, cycling and other forms of physical activity are accessible and safe; transport policies include nonmotorized modes of transportation; labour and workplace policies encourage physical activity; and sport and recreation facilities embody the concept of sports for all. Public policies and legislation have an impact on opportunities for physical activity, such as those concerning transport, urban planning, education, labour, social inclusion, and health-care funding related to physical activity.

(2) Community involvement and enabling environments. Strategies should be geared to changing social norms and improving

community understanding and acceptance of the need to integrate physical activity into everyday life. Environments should be promoted that facilitate physical activity, and supportive infrastructure should be set up to increase access to, and use of, suitable facilities.

(3) Partnerships. Ministries of health should take the lead in forming partnerships with key agencies, and public and private stakeholders in order to draw up jointly a common agenda and workplan aimed at promoting physical activity.

(4) Clear public messages. Simple, direct messages need to be communicated on the quantity and quality of physical activity sufficient to provide substantial health benefits.

43. School policies and programmes should support the adoption of healthy diets and physical activity. Schools influence the lives of most children in all countries. They should protect their health by providing health information, improving health literacy, and promoting healthy diets, physical activity, and other healthy behaviours. Schools are encouraged to provide students with daily physical education and should be equipped with appropriate facilities and equipment. Governments are encouraged to adopt policies that support healthy diets at school and limit the availability of products high in salt, sugar and fats. Schools should consider, together with parents and responsible authorities, issuing contracts for school lunches to local food growers in order to ensure a local market for healthy foods.

44. Governments are encouraged to consult with stakeholders on policy. Broad public discussion and involvement in the framing of policy can facilitate its

acceptance and effectiveness. Member States should establish mechanisms to promote participation of nongovernmental organizations, civil society, communities, the private sector and the media in activities related to diet, physical activity and health. Ministries of health should be responsible, in collaboration with other related ministries and agencies, for establishing these mechanisms, which should aim at strengthening intersectoral cooperation at the national, provincial and local levels. They should encourage community participation, and should be part of planning processes at community level.

45. Prevention is a critical element of health services. Routine contacts with health-service staff should include practical advice to patients and families on the benefits of healthy diets and increased levels of physical activity, combined with support to help patients initiate and maintain healthy behaviours. Governments should consider incentives to encourage such preventive services and identify opportunities for prevention within existing clinical services, including an improved financing structure to encourage and enable health professionals to dedicate more time to prevention.

(1) Health and other services. Health-care providers, especially for primary health care, but also other services (such as social services) can play an important part in prevention. Routine enquiries as to key dietary habits and physical activity, combined with simple information and skill-building to change behaviour, taking a life-course approach, can reach a large part of the population and be a cost-effective intervention. Attention should be given to WHO's growth standards for infants

and preschool children which expand the definition of health beyond the absence of overt disease, to include the adoption of healthy practices and behaviours. The measurement of key biological risk factors, such as blood pressure, serum cholesterol and body weight, combined with education of the population and support for patients, helps to promote the necessary changes. The identification of specific high-risk groups and measures to respond to their needs, including possible pharmacological interventions, are important components. Training of health personnel, dissemination of appropriate guidelines, and availability of incentives are key underlying factors in implementing these interventions.

(2) Involvement with health professional bodies and consumer groups. Enlisting the strong support of professionals, consumers and communities is a cost-effective way to raise public awareness of government policies, and enhance their effectiveness.

46. Governments should invest in surveillance, research and evaluation. Long-term and continuous monitoring of major risk factors is essential. Over time, such data also provide the basis for analyses of changes in risk factors, which could be attributable to changes in polices and strategies. Governments may be able to build on systems already in place, at either national or regional levels. Emphasis should initially be given to standard indicators recognized by the general scientific community as valid measures of physical activity, to selected dietary components, and to body weight in order to compile comparative data at global level. Data that provide insight into within-country patterns and variations

are useful in guiding community action. Where possible, other sources of data should be used, for example, from the education, transport, agriculture, and other sectors.

(1) Monitoring and surveillance. Monitoring and surveillance are essential tools in the implementation of national strategies for healthy diet and physical activity. Monitoring of dietary habits, patterns of physical activity and interactions between them; nutrition-related biological risk factors and contents of food products; and communication to the public of the information obtained, are important components of implementation. Of particular importance is the development of methods and procedures using standardized data-collection procedures and a common minimum set of valid, measurable and usable indicators.

(2) Research and evaluation. Applied research, especially in community-based demonstration projects and in evaluating different policies and interventions, should be promoted. Such research (e.g., into the reasons for physical inactivity and poor diet, and on key determinants of effective intervention programmes), combined with the increased involvement of behavioural scientists, will lead to better informed policies and ensure that a cadre of expertise is created at national and local levels. Equally important is the need to put in place effective mechanisms for evaluating the efficacy and cost-effectiveness of national diseaseprevention programmes, and the health impact of policies in other sectors. More information is needed, especially on the situation in developing countries, where

programmes to promote healthy diets and physical activity need to be evaluated and integrated into broader development and poverty-alleviation programmes.

47. Institutional capacity. Under the ministry of health, national institutions for public health, nutrition and physical activity play an important role in the implementation of national diet and physical activity programmes. They can provide the necessary expertise, monitor developments, help to coordinate activities, participate in collaboration at international level, and provide advice to decision-makers.

48. Financing national programmes. Various sources of funding, in addition to the national budget, should be identified to assist in implementation of the Strategy. The United Nations Millennium Declaration recognizes that economic growth is limited unless people are healthy. The most cost-effective interventions to contain the epidemic of noncommunicable diseases are prevention and a focus on the risk factors associated with these diseases. Programmes aimed at promoting healthy diets and physical activity should therefore be viewed as a developmental need and should draw policy and financial support from national development plans.

WHO

49. WHO, in cooperation with other organizations of the United Nations system, will provide the leadership, evidence-based recommendations and advocacy for international action to improve dietary practices and increase physical activity, in keeping with the guiding principles and specific recommendations contained in the Global Strategy.

50. It will hold discussions with the transnational food industry and other parts of the private sector in support of the aims of the Strategy, and of implementing the recommendations in countries.

51. WHO will provide support for implementation of programmes as requested by Member States, and will focus on the following broad, interrelated areas:

- facilitating the framing, strengthening and updating of regional and national policies on diet and physical activity for integrated noncommunicable disease prevention
- facilitating the drafting, updating and implementation of national food-based dietary and physical activity guidelines, in collaboration with national agencies and drawing upon global knowledge and experience
- providing guidance to Member States on the formulation of guidelines, norms, standards and other policy-related measures that are consistent with the objectives of the Global Strategy
- identifying and disseminating information on evidence-based interventions, policies and structures that are effective in promoting healthy diets and optimizing the level of physical activity in countries and communities
- providing appropriate technical support to build national capacity in planning and implementing a national strategy and in tailoring it to local circumstances
- providing models and methods so that interventions on diet and physical activity constitute an integral component of health care
- promoting and providing support for training of health professionals in healthy diets and an

active life, either within existing programmes or in special workshops, as an essential part of their curricula

— providing advice and support to Member States, using standardized surveillance methods and rapid assessment tools (such as WHO's STEPwise approach to surveillance of risk factors for noncommunicable diseases), in order to measure changes in distribution of risk – including patterns in diet, nutrition and physical activity – and to assess the current situation, trends, and the impact of interventions. WHO, in collaboration with FAO, will provide support to Member States in establishing national nutrition surveillance systems, linked with data on the content of food items

— advising Member States on ways of engaging constructively with appropriate industries.

52. WHO, in close collaboration with organizations of the United Nations system and other intergovernmental bodies (FAO, UNESCO, UNICEF, United Nations University and others), research institutes and other partners, will promote and support research in priority areas to facilitate programme implementation and evaluation. This could include commissioning scientific papers, conducting analyses, and holding technical meetings on practical research topics that are essential for effective country action. The decision-making process should be informed by better use of evidence, including health-impact assessment, cost-benefit analysis, national burden-of-disease studies, evidence-based intervention models, scientific advice and dissemination of good practices.

53. It will work with FAO and other organizations of the United Nations system, the World Bank, and research institutes on their evaluation of implications of the Strategy for other sectors.

54. The Organization will continue to work with WHO collaborating centres to establish networks for building up capacity in research and training, mobilizing contributions from nongovernmental organizations and civil society, and facilitating coordinated, collaborative research as it pertains to the needs of developing countries in the implementation of the Strategy.

International Partners

55. The role of international partners is of paramount importance in achieving the goal and objectives of the Global Strategy, particularly with regard to issues of a transnational nature, or where the actions of a single country are insufficient. Coordinated work is needed among the organizations of the United Nations system, intergovernmental bodies, nongovernmental organizations, professional associations, research institutions and private sector entities.

56. The process of preparing the Strategy has led to closer interaction with other organizations of the United Nations system, such as FAO and UNICEF, and other partners, including the World Bank. WHO will build on its long-standing collaboration with FAO in implementing the Strategy. The contribution of FAO in the framing of agricultural policies can play a crucial part in this regard. More research into appropriate agriculture policies, and the supply, availability, processing and consumption of food will be necessary.

57. Cooperation is also planned with bodies such as the United Nations Economic and Social Council, ILO, UNESCO, WTO, the regional development banks and the United Nations University. Consistent with the goal and objectives of the Strategy, WHO will develop and strengthen partnerships, including through the establishment and coordination of global and regional networks, in order to disseminate information, exchange experiences, and provide support to regional and national initiatives. WHO proposes to set up an ad hoc committee of partners within the United Nations system in order to ensure continuing policy coherence and to draw upon each organization's unique strengths. Partners can play an important role in a global network that targets such areas as advocacy, resource mobilization, capacity building and collaborative research.

58. International partners could be involved in implementing the Strategy by:
   - contributing to comprehensive intersectoral strategies to improve diet and physical activity, including, for instance, the promotion of healthy diets in poverty-alleviation programmes
   - drawing up guidelines for prevention of nutritional deficiencies in order to harmonize future dietary and policy recommendations designed to prevent and control noncommunicable diseases
   - facilitating the drafting of national guidelines on diet and physical activity, in collaboration with national agencies
   - cooperating in the development, testing and dissemination of models for community involvement, including local food production,

nutrition and physical activity education, and raising of consumer awareness

– promoting the inclusion of noncommunicable disease prevention and health promotion policies relating to diet and physical activity in development policies and programmes

– promoting incentive-based approaches to encourage prevention and control of chronic diseases.

59. International standards. Public health efforts may be strengthened by the use of international norms and standards, particularly those drawn up by the Codex Alimentarius Commission. Areas for further development could include: labelling to allow consumers to be better informed about the benefits and content of foods; measures to minimize the impact of marketing on unhealthy dietary patterns; fuller information about healthy consumption patterns, including steps to increase the consumption of fruit and vegetables; and production and processing standards regarding the nutritional quality and safety of products. Involvement of governments and nongovernmental organizations as provided for in the Codex should be encouraged.

Civil Society and Nongovernmental Organizations

60. Civil society and nongovernmental organizations have an important role to play in influencing individual behaviour and the organizations and institutions that are involved in healthy diet and physical activity. They can help to ensure that consumers ask governments to provide support for healthy lifestyles, and the food industry to provide healthy products. Nongovernmental organizations can support the Strategy effectively if they

collaborate with national and international partners. Civil society and nongovernmental organizations can particularly:

- lead grass-roots mobilization and advocate that healthy diets and physical activity should be placed on the public agenda
- support the wide dissemination of information on prevention of noncommunicable diseases through balanced, healthy diets and physical activity
- form networks and action groups to promote the availability of healthy foods and possibilities for physical activity, and advocate and support health-promoting programmes and health education campaigns
- organize campaigns and events that will stimulate action
- emphasize the role of governments in promoting public health, healthy diets and physical activity; monitor progress in achieving objectives; and monitor and work with other stakeholders such as private sector entities
- play an active role in fostering implementation of the Global Strategy
- contribute to putting knowledge and evidence into practice.

Private Sector

61. The private sector can be a significant player in promoting healthy diets and physical activity. The food industry, retailers, catering companies, sporting-goods manufacturers, advertising and recreation businesses, insurance and banking groups, pharmaceutical companies and the media all

have important parts to play as responsible employers and as advocates for healthy lifestyles. All could become partners with governments and nongovernmental organizations in implementing measures aimed at sending positive and consistent messages to facilitate and enable integrated efforts to encourage healthy eating and physical activity. Because many companies operate globally, international collaboration is crucial. Cooperative relationships with industry have already led to many favourable outcomes related to diet and physical activity. Initiatives by the food industry to reduce the fat, sugar and salt content of processed foods and portion sizes, to increase introduction of innovative, healthy, and nutritious choices; and review of current marketing practices, could accelerate health gains worldwide. Specific recommendations to the food industry and sporting-goods manufacturers include the following:

- promote healthy diets and physical activity in accordance with national guidelines and international standards and the overall aims of the Global Strategy
- limit the levels of saturated fats, *trans*-fatty acids, free sugars and salt in existing products
- continue to develop and provide affordable, healthy and nutritious choices to consumers
- consider introducing new products with better nutritional value
- provide consumers with adequate and understandable product and nutrition information
- practise responsible marketing that supports the Strategy, particularly with regard to the

promotion and marketing of foods high in saturated fats, *trans*-fatty acids, free sugars, or salt, especially to children

- issue simple, clear and consistent food labels and evidence-based health claims that will help consumers to make informed and healthy choices with respect to the nutritional value of foods
- provide information on food composition to national authorities
- assist in developing and implementing physical activity programmes.

62. Workplaces are important settings for health promotion and disease prevention. People need to be given the opportunity to make healthy choices in the workplace in order to reduce their exposure to risk. Further, the cost to employers of morbidity attributed to noncommunicable diseases is increasing rapidly. Workplaces should make possible healthy food choices and support and encourage physical activity.

Follow-up and Future Developments

63. WHO will report on progress made in implementing the Global Strategy and in implementing national strategies, including the following aspects:

- patterns and trends of dietary habits and physical activity and related risk factors for major noncommunicable diseases
- evaluation of the effectiveness of policies and programmes to improve diet and increase physical activity

- constraints or barriers encountered in implementation of the Strategy and the measures taken to overcome them
- legislative, executive, administrative, financial or other measures taken within the context of the Strategy.

64. WHO will work at global and regional levels to set up a monitoring system and to design indicators for dietary habits and patterns of physical activity.

Bibliography

Aaron J.E., et al. "Frequency of osteomalacia and osteoporosis in fractures of the proximal femur", *Lancet,* 1974.

Aaron J.E, Gallagher J.C, Nordin B.E.C., "Seasonal variation of histological osteomalacia in femoral neck fractures", *Lancet,* 1974.

Abe E et al., "1,25-dihydroxyvitamin D3 promotes fusion of mouse alveolar macrophages both by a direct mechanism and by a spleen cell-mediated indirect mechanism", *Proceedings of the ’ tional Academy of Sciences,* 1983.

Bar-Shavit Z et al., "Induction of monocytic differentiation and bone resorption by 1,25-dihydroxyvitamin D3", *Proceedings of the National Academy of Sciences,* 1983.

Baker M.R et al., "Plasma 25-hydroxy vitamin D concentrations in patients with fractures of the femoral neck", *British Medical Journal,* 1979.

DeLuca H.F., "The vitamin D story: a collaborative effort of basic science and clinical medicine", *FASEB Journal,* 1988.

Furr H.C et al., "Vitamin A concentrations in liver determined by isotope dilution assay with tetradeuterated vitamin A and by biopsy in generally healthy adult humans", *American Journal of Clinical Nutrition,* 1989.

Haskell M.J et al., "Plasma kinetics of an oral dose of $[2H_4]$ retinyl acetate in human subjects with estimated low or high total body stores of vitamin A", *American Journal of Clinical Nutrition,* 1998.

Haussler M.R., "Vitamin D receptors: nature and function", *Annual Review of Nutrition,* 1986.

Jones G, Strugnell S, DeLuca H.F., "Current understanding of the molecular actions of vitamin D", *Physiology Reviews,* 1998.

Nordin B.E.C., "Calcium in health and disease", *Food, Nutrition and Agriculture,* 1997.

Morris H.A et al., "Vitamin D and femoral neck fractures in elderly South Australian women", *Medical Journal of Australia,* 1984.

Pike J.W., "Vitamin D3 receptors: structure and function in transcription", *Annual Review of Nutrition,* 1991.

Tang G et al., "Green and yellow vegetables can maintain body stores of vitamin A in Chinese children", *American Journal of Clinical Nutrition,* 1999.

Van den Berg H, van Vliet T., "Effect of simultaneous, single oral doses of bcarotene with lutein or lycopene on the b-carotene and retinyl ester responses in the triacylglycerol-rich lipoprotein fraction of men", *American Journal of Clinical Nutrition,* 1998.

Von Knorring J et al., "Serum levels of 25-hydroxyvitamin D, 24,25-dihydroxyvitamin D and parathyroid hormone in patients with femoral neck fracture in southern Finland", *Clinical Endocrinology,* 1982.

Index

(e.g. bile salts and hydrolytic enzymes) are essential for the efficient solubilization of retinol and especially for solubilization of the very lipophilic carotenoids (e.g. α- and β-carotene, β-cryptoxanthin, and lycopene) in the aqueous intestinal milieu. Micellar solubilization is a prerequisite to their efficient passage into the lipid-rich membrane of intestinal mucosal cells (i.e. enterocytes). Diets critically low in dietary fat (under about 5–10 g daily) or disease conditions that interfere with normal digestion and absorption leading to steatorrhoea (e.g. pancreatic and liver diseases and frequent gastroenteritis) can therefore impede the efficient absorption of retinol and carotenoids. Retinol and some carotenoids enter the intestinal mucosal brush border by diffusion in accord with the concentration gradient between the micelle and plasma membrane of enterocytes. Some carotenoids pass into the enterocyte and are solubilized into chylomicrons without further change whereas some of the provitamin A carotenoids are converted to retinol by a cleavage enzyme in the brush border. Retinol is trapped intracellularly by re-esterification or binding to specific intracellular binding proteins. Retinyl esters and unconverted carotenoids together with other lipids are incorporated into chylomicrons, excreted into intestinal lymphatic channels, and delivered to the blood through the thoracic duct.

Tissues extract most lipids and some carotenoids from circulating chylomicrons, but most retinyl esters are stripped from the chylomicron remnant, hydrolysed, and taken up primarily by parenchymal liver cells. If not immediately needed, retinol is re-esterified and retained in the fat-storing cells of the liver (variously called adipocytes, stellate cells, or Ito cells). The liver parenchymal cells also take in substantial amounts of carotenoids. Whereas most of the body's vitamin A reserve remains in the liver, carotenoids are also